Why Read

Also by Will Self

NOVELS

Cock and Bull
My Idea of Fun
The Sweet Smell of Psychosis
Great Apes
How the Dead Live
Dorian, an Imitation
The Book of Dave
The Butt
Walking to Hollywood
Umbrella
Shark
Phone

STORY COLLECTIONS

The Quantity Theory of Insanity
Grey Area
Tough, Tough Toys for Tough, Tough Boys
Dr. Mukti and Other Tales of Woe
*Liver: A Fictional Organ with a Surface Anatomy
of Four Lobes*
The Undivided Self: Selected Stories

NONFICTION

Junk Mail
Perfidious Man
Sore Sites
Feeding Frenzy
Psychogeography
Psycho Too
The Unbearable Lightness of Being a Prawn Cracker
Will

Why Read

Selected Writings 2001–2021

Will Self

Grove Press UK

First published in the United States of America in 2022 by
Grove Atlantic
First published in Great Britain in 2022 by Grove Press UK,
an imprint of Grove Atlantic

1 3 5 7 9 8 6 4 2

A CIP record for this book is available from the British Library.

Grove Press UK
Ormond House
26–27 Boswell Street
London
WC1N 3JZ

www.atlantic-books.co.uk

Hardback ISBN 978 1 61185 661 3
Ebook ISBN 978 1 61185 868 6

Printed and bound by CPI Group (UK) Ltd, Croydon CR0 4YY

MIX
Paper from
responsible sources
FSC® C171272

For Ivan, who reads

Table of Contents

Why Read?   1

The Death of the Shelf   12

Absent Jews and Invisible Executioners:
  W. G. Sebald and the Holocaust   25

Chernobyl   52

Kafka's Wound   75

A Care Home for Novels: The Narrative Art Form
  in the Age of Its Technical Supersession   109

The Last Typewriter Engineer   129

Isenshard   141

How Should We Read?   162

Junky   170

Being a Character   189

Australia and I   195

The Rise of the Machines   218

Literary Time   227

The Printed Word in Peril   232

The Secret Agent   255

What to Read?   266

On Writing Memoir   275

Apocalypse Then   285

The Technology of Journalism   295

St George for the French   301

Will Self-Driving Cars Take My Job?   309

Reading for Writers   316

Why Read?

The future St Augustine's account of his mentor Bishop Ambrose's reading habits, written during the fourth century of the Christian era, still stands as the first definitive account of anyone doing this: 'When he read his eyes scanned the page and his heart sought out the meaning, but his voice was silent and his tongue was still. Anyone could approach him freely and guests were not commonly announced, so that often, when we came to visit him, we found him reading like this in silence, for he never read aloud.' Augustine's astonishment is so palpable – while other references to such a practice prior to this are so scant – we can only infer that reading was indeed principally undertaken aloud. Certainly, with literacy uncommon in the Roman world, there were fewer readers than those desirous of knowing texts; while, with the rise of a religion in which God's revelation took a written form, this sacred imperative joined these more mundane motivations. Suffice it to say, it isn't until the tenth century that we gain a general sense of reading becoming a solitary pursuit rather than a collective endeavour.

So why do it? Why bury your head in a book? Because let's face it, the experience of solitary reading is qualitatively different from being read to aloud in a group – the former entails a deeper absorption in the text, and a more direct engagement with the mind shaping its language: immersive private reading leads one into a virtual reality, while being told a story with others keeps you in a social one. The analogy might be on the one hand with the individual liberty of conscience implicit in the Protestant confession, and on the other with collectively uttered Catholic credo. However, I suspect if you've even got this far you're a reader anyway – and have now further self-selected by showing an interest not just in the text, but also – if you like – in the meta-text: what lies beyond the text that shapes our apprehension of it. In which case, you almost certainly know why you yourself read: it's self-evidently to do with your enjoyment, experienced as the free play of your imagination, the stimulation of your intellect, and the engagement of your sympathy. But as to why it *should* be reading specifically that enables this – and what other values we project onto this ability – these are different questions, the answers to which may provide us with some insight into the vexed further one: whither reading?

In *Understanding Media* (1964), that revelatory and prophetic work of cultural philosophy, Marshall McLuhan speaks of the form of human consciousness engendered by the practice of solitary reading as 'the Gutenberg mind', and calls – implicitly – for a recognition of its potential limits. Indeed, to follow his most celebrated maxim is to recognise that the message of the codex, as a medium, is that acquiring knowledge and its understanding are undertakings separated from the social realm, whether by the bone of our skulls or the boards of our book covers.

In the current era the dispute between those who view the technological assemblage of the internet and the web as some sort of panacea for our ills, and those who worry it might herald the end of everything from independent thought (whatever *that* might be), to literacy itself, has a slightly muted feel. I suspect the reason for this is also to be found in *Understanding Media*: as McLuhan pointed out, the supplanting of one medium by another can take a long time – and just as the practice of copying manuscripts by hand continued for centuries after the invention of printing, so solitary reading – conceived of importantly as an individual and private absorption in a unitary text of some length – persists, and will continue to endure long after the vast majority of copy being ingested is in the form of tiny digitised gobbets.

2020 was an exceptional year, and the evidence is certainly not conclusive, but nonetheless the pandemic almost certainly resulted in renewed interest in long-form prose and the reading of it. There's a nice sort of asynchrony here, with the reviving of the Gutenberg mind being occasioned by the sort of plague with which he would've been all too familiar. But when we ask why should we read? The answer surely cannot be that it's the substrate best suited for cultivating a certain type of human persona – one that sees itself as unitary, maintaining identity through space and time, and capable of accounting for itself in a linear fashion conformable to external correlates – a persona, in other words, like a book. Yet just as the pandemic has got some of us scuttling back within its covers, so the longer-term decline in what we might call purposive reading has been inversely – arguably *per*versely – correlated with what the philosopher Galen Strawson terms 'strong narrativity': that belief not only in the book-like human persona, but in a categorical imperative to convey its contents to others.

The shibboleth 'everyone has a book in them' has mutated into the rather more hectoring: 'everyone has a tale to tell, and they must be able to recount it in order to be accorded full moral status.' It might be churlish of me – an autodidact, who believes the true writer to be necessarily so – to observe that this 'philosophy' has itself developed in lockstep with creative writing programmes, but there it is: having paid cash-on-the-nail to become proficient tale-tellers, creative-writing alumni and their instructors. alike (many of whom are themselves also alumni), move to enact a closure that cannot – given the underlying economic metric – be anything but for the most part ethical. From this righteousness proceeds the proposition: I read (and am read), therefore I am, and I am good.

But shorn of a progressive worldview based on Enlightenment values that equate technological with moral advance, and figure human being itself as a meta-narrative whereby the West writes itself into supremacy, it's impossible to argue for mandatory reading: 'To get up in the morning, in the fullness of youth, and open a book! Now, that's what I call vicious' is Nietzsche's admonition in *Ecce Homo* – and it's one I'm fond of retailing to my own students, withal that I'd like them to read a great deal more than they do. Why? Because, yes, I too have never seen anything lovelier than a tree, while some of the unloveliest things I've ever witnessed have been metaphors, arboreal and floral. Moreover, if the bi-directional digital medium is rendering us illiterate, it's as much because we can no longer read a map – which necessitates basic orientation – as a text. Put bluntly, we're becoming strangers in a strange land, moving dazedly through it, our faces wan in the up-light from our screens, as we all follow the little-blue-dot-that's-us. Under such circumstances, nostalgia for our Gutenberg minds, while understandable, is a bit like nostalgia for hand-tooled leather satchels: a move to accessorise rather than civilise.

Besides, what about those who can neither read nor write? You don't have to be Jacques Derrida or Paul de Man – as we've seen – to assert the primacy of text over speech; nor do we have to be Socrates in order to advance the case for cultural forms that stand outside of *ecriture*. One of the most tedious aspects of our literary culture is this reductio ad nauseam: the vast number of novels (and indeed non-fiction works) almost exclusively concerned with the complex thoughts, tortuous feelings and subtle velleities of people – or characters – who themselves spend far too much time reading books. In another of the pieces collected here I muse as to whether an MRI scan of someone reading about someone reading in an MRI scanner might teach us about *how* we should read – and I summon this alternative mise en abyme, of novels about people reading novels about people reading novels, to banish once and for all this bogus teleology.

By contrast, there's nothing I like reading about more than illiterate people and non-literate cultures. One of the books I read this year during my own protracted lockdown *à cause de la crise* was a taut little adventure tale by Jonathan Franklin, entitled *438 Days: An Extraordinary True Story of Survival at Sea*. Like all the best books, its title is synecdochical: in 2012 José Salvador Alvarenga, an El Salvadoran fisherman, was blown away from the Mexican coast aboard a 23-foot-long skiff. In short order he lost his engine, most of his supplies – and then his only companion. Subsequent to this, he did indeed drift across the Pacific Ocean for 438 days, eventually coming ashore in the Marshall Islands after travelling some 10,000 miles. Look, I can admit it – I get a cheap little thrill reading about people caught up in terrible natural disasters the way others do reading genre fiction of one kind or another. Indeed, I call this sub-genre 'schadenfic', since my pleasure is so closely related to their, um, pain.

But that being said, whereas the likes of E L James couldn't type their way out of the proverbial wet paper bag, Franklin is a skilled and even poetic writer, not least of whose skills is an ability to make vividly present to his readers scenes he himself has not witnessed. Arguably this is necessary for any competent narrative non-fiction writer – yet many fail spectacularly, often by their recourse to inventing reams of dialogue they never heard, and that almost certainly were never spoken. This is not a stratagem Franklin relies on; on the contrary, there's a scrupulous quality to his reportage I can't help but feel derives equally from his meticulous interviewing of his subjects, and from the fact that his principal one – Alvarenga himself – is illiterate.

The extraordinary capacity of non-literate people to remember things is a truth universally acknowledged, while the methods they adopt to do this demonstrate that there are semiotic systems that bridge the life-worlds of different species, while not necessarily conforming to received (human) notions of the symbolic. Alvarenga's exceptional skill as a fisherman and a sailor constituted just such a system; such that – as Franklin tells it – he was able to create for himself an imaginative world that kept him sane and functioning through almost a year and a half of the most extreme isolation imaginable. Some of the El Salvadorian's strategies may seem barbaric to our Gutenberg minds: such as catching seafowl who landed on his skiff, expertly crippling them by breaking their wings, and then keeping them – in substantial numbers – as at once larder, pets, and – when he felt the need for some entertainment – participants in bizarre football games, refereed by himself, and played with a dried puffer fish as a 'ball'. But needs must – and there's a nice symmetry here, because it's difficult to see how anyone who'd been relying on book learning to survive such a perilous predicament, could have deployed the necessary skills to invent such a sport.

In a way, Alvarenga was simply confirming the truth of Montaigne's observation in his seminal essay on cultural relativity, 'Of the Cannibals': 'They are savages at the same rate that we say fruits are wild, which nature produces of herself and by her own ordinary progress; whereas, in truth, we ought rather to call those wild whose natures we have changed by our artifice and diverted from the common order.' Not only did the fisherman find a mode of being that entertained and sustained him – he also undertook a complex theological and spiritual journey, interrogating – and ultimately confirming – his own faith as he struggled to cope with his guilt at surviving, while Ezequiel Cordoba, his younger companion, had died.

I've no wish to romanticise savagery – how could I, when I don't believe it exists as a state contrary to civilisation; and nor, of course, do I see literacy and illiteracy as opposites. But here's the paradox: while I, as a Gutenberg mind with no knowledge of the winds and the tides, the birds and the fish beyond the books I have read, would have undoubtedly gone the way of Cordoba in double-quick time, nonetheless, I'm privileged to be able to enter the mind of Alvarenga through the world summoned by Franklin's words. And of course, there's no going back anyway – unless we were to undergo some pinpoint-accurate laser-guided neuro-surgery to remove the pesky cells responsible for literacy from our mind/brains. Harsh critics of the web–internet technological assemblage, such as Nicholas Carr, see in our surfing of the imagistic zeit-geist it affords us, a dangerous brain-state emerging; one in which we no longer possess the intuitive capability to form those schemas necessary for the comprehension of new data sets – whether these be the figures on a spreadsheet or the lines on a storied page.

Even in the ten years I've been teaching university stu-dents, I've noticed a decline in their reading – both fewer works attempted, and these less deeply engaged with. But given I want them to read more books purely in order that they should, um, read more books, I can't claim to be either devoid of a desire for professional closure myself, or free of a Gutenberg mind's inherent biases: I just can't look outside of what it might be like to have an intellect and sensibility formed by interaction with texts. Or can I? After all, I sympathised heavily with Alvarenga – so perhaps, after all, this is the answer to the vexed question of why we should read: so as to anticipate, understand and so connect with the non-literate realms that surround us – whether we be separated from them by reason of space or time or technology. Carr may believe the denizens of the web are flopping about, breathless, on the verge of anoesis in these soi-disant 'shallows' – our duty as good readers, surely, is to extend our imaginative sympathy to them, just as we do to Anna Karenina.

But I stress: this isn't because I believe it makes us any better than these others in any other way; it's simply that to be able to read and not try to at least read *well*, strikes me as a profligate waste of a skill that it's difficult to acquire, and one which if mastered delivers such extraordinary delights. So, why read? Read because short of meeting and communing with them (and perhaps, because of this, writing about them), reading about diverse modes of being and consciousness is the best way we have of entering into them and abiding. To enter the flow-state of reading is to swim into other psyches with great ease, whatever their age, sex, sexual orientation, nationality, class or ethnicity. There's this – and, for the more intellectually minded of us, there's this conundrum: since the linguistic turn taken by Western philosophy in the early twentieth century, almost all the turf wars over belief – in its broadest, most encompassing sense – have been waged on the territory afforded by language itself. So, put simply: you cannot argue for this understanding of the Logos or that – for structuralism or deconstruction, *langue* or *parole*, the Imaginary or the Real – without being a reader, and a skilled one.

Of course, it could be that all these philosophical questions about language and its component parts – including reading – are simply the arcana of an age – and its scribal class – about to choke on its own lead-particulate-spewing tailpipe. In which case, we need to read in order to face with equanimity what's to come. You don't have to be the Unabomber to note that there's one medium that operates entirely efficiently not just off, but way off the grid – so: why read? Read because since the onset of bi-directional digital media, codices, predictably, have become pretty much free – while it remains entirely free and freeing to be able to experience them whenever and wherever; a phenomenon the Kindle reader program celebrates with its homepage illustration of a winsome-looking child, in profile, reading in silence beneath an equally winsome tree.

22 April 2021
Literary Hub

The Death of the Shelf

You might think that rumours of the death of the shelf are greatly exaggerated – at least if you visit my household, where shelves are a hot topic and a source of contention. I arrived home last week after a few days working on a book (one which will, I hope, eventually be printed, published, and require shelving), to discover that two new shelves had appeared in the kitchen. One of these was fairly utilitarian: a simple additional narrow shelf in the pantry to hold those troublesome pickle jars; but the other was positively baroque – a mosaic-encrusted ledge, high up above the work surface, supported by two ornate brackets, featuring dancing boys teased out of their wrought iron. I was informed that the brackets used to hold up a Victorian lavatory cistern, and I can assure you, had I expressed anything but wholehearted approval of the new shelf and its bog boys (as I immediately termed them), there would've been a domestic domestic.

My wife and I are of a generation – late baby-boomers, now in our early fifties – who revere the shelf. The shelf is, for us, the repository of culture-in-view; ranged along our shelves are all the artefacts we possess that indicate to ourselves, and to those we admit to the house, what we know, what we like, and what we consider to be of importance either for its use value, or its aesthetics. The application of shelving to our rooms makes of them individual chambers within a memory palace to which we and our invitees have open and continuous access. If you like, the shelves are the joinery knitting together the past and the present, the public and the private, the practical and the decorative. Far more than paintings, or other furniture, the shelves – whose raison d'être is to both contain and display – are, I would argue, the very lynchpins of a form of bourgeois domesticity dating from at least the early modern period.

At Skara Brae, the Neolithic village in Orkney that remained intact beneath a sand dune until being spectacularly and providentially revealed by a storm in the early 1900s, you can see Stone Age houses with fireplaces, beds and shelving systems that have endured for rising 5,000 years. On these petrified brick-and-board units (so suggestive of the neo-functionalism of the 1970s) are grouped small pots, domestic implements and other tools; and while it's the merest speculation as to whether the inhabitants viewed their arrangement and display in the same way my wife does the new kitchen shelf, with its assemblage of different-sized coffee percolators and cafetieres, I think it reasonable to imagine they did. Certainly there are plenty of depictions of shelves in pre-modern contexts which indicate exactly this dual-purposing of the presentational and the practical; and by the time the Renaissance arrives the shelf is fully integrated into pictorial space as a representational trope: a painted figuration of three-dimensional stone, that along with pediments, niches, entablatures and other architectural detailing serves to impose the manmade on the natural and even the heavenly: the pietà and the Madonna Lactans are both often to be seen shelved.

But arguably it is only in the nineteenth century that the domestic shelf becomes fully ideologically articulated. Somewhere in the functionalist-decorative fault lines between the Biedermeier, the belle époque and the Arts and Crafts, a different, distinctively modern and emphatically middle-class shelf is put up. The capitulation and recapitulation of the craftsman-like as the decorative exists in a paradoxical relation to the onset of the mass production of a whole range of objects: lest we forget, William Morris funded his socialist-aesthetical dreaming off the back of a hugely successful wallpaper business. I would argue that so long as books and bibelots remain highly expensive and crafted, the shelf is an insecure place to house them – after all, they may be knocked off; but between the 1860s and the 1880s these artefacts become cheaper and widely available, so shelves are put up for them. Culture ceases to be an aristocratic matter of congenital acquisition, but instead an attribute it's possible to acquire off the peg – from W.H. Smith or Whiteleys and show off on shelves supplied by Maple & Co or Heal's.

Writing half a century later, Walter Benjamin notes of this era: 'The middle-class interior of the 1860s with its giant sideboards heavy with woodcarving, the sunless corners where the palm stands, the bay window with its shielding balustrade, and those long corridors with the singing gas flame proves fit only to house the corpse.' Benjamin's idea was that the great writers anticipate the environments within which their narratives will take place; and that the golden age of logical-deductive detective fiction began with Edgar Allan Poe's proto-Sherlock, Auguste Dupin, at a time when these interiors had yet to crystallise. Dupin's solution of the case in 'The Purloined Letter' hinges crucially on concealment – in escritoires, behind books on shelves – and what Benjamin points us towards is the integration into the domestic space of information: the detective's method is to tell us, via an analysis of objects, about the homeowners' taste.

Again, this is not to suggest that the book in particular wasn't viewed as a decorative object prior to the late nineteenth century; however, just as the size, weight and cost of early codices demanded dedicated furniture – such as flat reading tables and storage shelving – so the library itself remained a specialised room. By the time Virginia Woolf writes *A Room of One's Own*, the invention of offset printing has made it possible for the lowliest Pooter to have a shelf of books in his living room (or drawing room as he'd probably style it); and while Woolf was just as afflicted by the snobberies of the era as others of her class, her ready assumption that all her readers will have a mental picture of a book-lined domestic interior readily to hand is suggestive of all the egalitarian, DIY shelves that are to come.

Woolf uses the recurrent image of retrieving books from shelves (or returning them) nine times in her essay; she not only pictures herself fetching down volumes, but

also imagines her female literary subjects doing the same
– these are, if you like, shelvings-within-shelving. It's not
only books that are so treated – jars are as well, and in proposing the necessary liberties for the nurturance of female
literary talent, I believe Woolf is unconsciously integrating
the female workplace of the time – the kitchen – with the
locus of literary production. The omnipresence of the shelf
for Woolf may also be a suppressed echo of the taunt commonly flung at bluestockings such as her at a time when
marriage was still considered the apotheosis of women's
lives: You'll be left on the shelf.

The arrival of the Victrola with its heavy 10-inch shellac
discs requiring storage; the inception, shortly afterwards,
of the radiogram as a distinct item of furniture; the spread
of full-colour printing and the long-playing record after
the Second World War – by the mid-twentieth century the
full integration of the decorative and the informational
within the home, and the fullest expression of this symbiosis is the multi-platform shelving unit, a combination
of flat open surfaces, racks, containers and niches that can
hold everything from pot plants to television sets, with a
few books – possibly a set of leather-bound encyclopaedias
– providing a weighty, traditional ballast. It is these shelving units that dominated the reception rooms of homes for
the next four decades; sometimes they were denser, more
modular and glass-fronted, pressed into the corners and
pinioned to the walls – as carpets are to floors – so as to
provide a total coverage. At other times the units became
airily insubstantial, seemingly positioning their contents in

mid-air, so creating a sort of net, from either side of which the guests at Abigail's party could volley the shuttlecock of their pretensions. And when the shelf first, as it were, began to ail, it was these shelving units that started to appear on the pavements outside the houses and blocks of flats in my neighbourhood: pathetic outcasts, like objectified old Inuit, thrust from the tribe of chattels so its other members may move on into the future unencumbered.

This would've been, I think, in the late 1990s or early 2000s, but I was finding it difficult to let go of the shelf. My father, having emigrated to Australia twenty years previously, died in 1998, and although he left his books to the university where he taught, I went to the trouble of shipping a selection of his shelving all the way back to London: two enormous freestanding oaken bookshelves, and an equally vast rotating library shelf. It was at around this time that my wife cried: *Ça suffit!* My own principle when it came to acquisition of books was, bring 'em on: Give me your tattered old Pelicans, your dog-eared copies of Rosemary Conley's *Hip and Thigh Diet*, your bound back numbers of *Popular Mechanics* – for me there was no volume too lowly or unreadable to be unworthy of shelving. Her view, by contrast, was robustly practical: There isn't any more space in the house to put up more shelves.

I understand where my own passionate involvement with the shelf originates – and it isn't altogether in a love of literature. In our three-bedroom semi-detached family home, mine was the back bedroom that had once been my much older half-brother's, and when he went to university (and my other brother and I still shared a room), my father's study. It had ended up as a repository of books and all sorts of other impedimenta, spread over a series of mismatched shelving units. I spent my time between the ages of eight and seventeen either staring at these shelves or rearranging them: interspersing books with things and things with books. When I was little I set up complicated string pulley systems linking one shelf with another, so my toys could zip-wire from Herbert Marcuse's *One-Dimensional Man* to John Updike's *Couples*. I also lay on my bed and read and reread *Alice's Adventures in Wonderland*, particularly taken by her long, safe fall down the shelf-lined well: 'First, she tried to look down and make out what she was coming to, but it was too dark to see anything; then she looked at the sides of the well, and noticed that they were filled with cupboards and book-shelves; here and there she saw maps and pictures hung upon pegs. She took down a jar from one of the shelves as she passed; it was labelled 'ORANGE MARMALADE', but to her great disappointment it was empty: she did not like to drop the jar for fear of killing somebody, so managed to put it into one of the cupboards as she fell past it.'

In a very important sense I think I'm still falling down that well; the shelves in the room where I'm writing this piece conform – at least in my imagination – to the ones Alice fell past: a higgledy-piggledy assemblage of objects, pictures and books overflowing from a series of wooden compartments and surfaces. It helps, I think, that the measurements I gave to the joiner who built the desk-cum-shelving unit were woefully inadequate: the actual bookshelves are too low for hardbacks and too deep for paperbacks, so they tend to be stacked horizontally two piles deep, or pushed to the back leaving plenty of room for clutter to accumulate at the front. The very idea that I should be able to put up a shelf myself is of course preposterous; and when I look back to the shelving of my youth, the intersection between bourgeois bricolage and bien-pensant revolutionary dreaming is probably best exemplified by the pseudo-artisanal functionalism of brick-and-board shelving. By the same token, the Ikea flat-pack is the three-dimensional analogue of a planned social democracy. But anyway, I digress – back to the clutter! There are mobile phone chargers and bottles of mouthwash, tobacco pouches and azimuth compasses, reading glasses and plastic bags of tea; old photographs and postcards are propped up here and there, while glass paperweights, little metal skeletons and a small Tinguelyesque machine given me by my children (featuring a severed arm that hammers a bit of tin when you crank a handle) all have their place. I could go on – and on. To realistically inventory the shelves would take days, and one time a celebrated mnemonist visited me here, and helped me learn the then forty-three US presidents using as an aide-memoire the objects ranged on a single shelf.

There has never really been any justification for the small clay bust of an ape, or the plaster one of Robert Schumann with a speech bubble attached to it reading 'Take me to the bridge!' But now I'm beginning to realise there's less and less requirement for the shelves at all. It may well be that the shelf is alive and well chez Self, but the new kitchen one is the shape of shelves to come: in the future they may support either objets d'art, those that have use value, or those that mix the two categories together, but what they won't do is integrate these modes with the third and most crucial one: the informational. The old shelving units in the road were followed in the early 2000s by still more pathetic cast-offs: CD towers and the occasional forlorn magazine rack. Neither the cassette nor the VHS tape ever really aspired to its own specialised shelving (except, it has to be said, in our shelf-mad domain, where we had a whole wall of VHS shelves built that were later repurposed for DVDs and are now moribund); but the CD was adopted with sufficient zeal, and was of a significantly different format to require a whole range of alternative housings. Now they're in the gutter, leaning lopsidedly, pathetic stained-wood menhirs marking the sites of the old religion of recorded sound, while overhead scuds the great crackling, emphatically digital cloud.

By rights there should be a fair number of bookshelves out there on the pavement as well, but while we do see these being discarded there doesn't appear to be the same mortality rate. In part this must be because of the sheer social and cultural embedding of the codex: half a millennium as against the CD's mere twenty years. In part it's due to architectural considerations: the bookcases are often inbuilt – they're bulkier, and will require more in the way of killing off. But there are also the haptic, tactile and other sensory aspects of the codex: for people who read, the book is something they have held on to for a very large portion of their lives; letting go of it will be a wrench. It's been a wrench for me, but perhaps five years ago when my wife deemed that total shelf coverage had been reached in our fairly large house, she began a book pogrom. At first only duplicate titles and obvious clunkers were got rid of, but soon enough perfectly good books were being consigned to the oblivion of the local Mind charity shop.

Having fought hard against the purges, once they were underway I became if not a willing accomplice, at any rate a functional one. I suspect I'm like quite a few people reading this piece: the onset of digital reading coincided with my own very analogue intimations of mortality. On the one hand there was the superabundance of books available via the web, on the other there was the chilly apprehension I had – looking about me at volumes I'd shelved a decade or more before, and promised myself annually that I'd read one day – that I already owned more than enough physical books to last me out three, four, even five score and ten. As for the delusion of legacy that had caused me to drag around aged copies of Herbert Marcuse's *One-Dimensional Man* and John Updike's *Couples* from habitation to habitation for a lifetime, as if they were my own meagre version of a presidential library, well, my four children are all very lovely in their ways, but none of them is what I would call a voracious reader.

I remain a voracious reader, but again, like many of us, with the advent of bi-directional digital media, I've become more of a snacker than someone on a hearty literary diet. I still read codices, but a tendency to read multiple texts concurrently that was well advanced before e-books, has now become near-pathological: I really am reading about a hundred books at the same time. Of the two digital reading apps I have on my phone (yes, phone – it really doesn't bother me), I favour the Kindle – I now realise – because it doesn't feature a skeuomorphic representation of a bookshelf. When you click on a book in the iBooks application, the 'volume' shoots towards you from this 'shelf', seemingly 'opening' in mid-air to reveal the text. Every time it does this I give a little shudder – it's as if I can feel angry out-of-work librarians walking over my grave; and I also shudder when I look about me at the overflowing shelves of my writing room, sensing that I have fully metamorphosed into an Alice who's falling past them slowly enough to pluck something from one, but that there's really very little point, because after all: I'm falling.

I'm dying and the shelf is dying with me. As I say, I don't doubt that shelves of the mosaic-encrusted bog-boy variety will continue to be put up: an exhibition this year at the Serpentine Gallery in London featured shelves of just this decorative kind. But the shelf as an omni-potential cultural platform is a thing of the past: the digital library is upon us, and whatever the nostalgic, the conservative and the downright reactionary Luddite may say, there's no turning back a clock that doesn't even have hands. I do mourn the passing of the shelf, because I think that the spatial and aestheticised arrangement of the informational is a physical analogue of the canon itself. To reach up and get a volume down from a shelf is to see, smell and touch the form of collective understanding, an apprehension that has no equivalent in the virtual realm. The great Argentinean fabulist Jorge Luis Borges anticipated the digitisation of all knowledge in his story 'The Library of Babel', which hypothesises a universe that is itself an illimitable library. Borges is quite particular about the physicality of the library, the infinite range of hexagonal galleries are comprised of: 'Twenty shelves, five long shelves per side, cover all the sides except two; their height, which is the distance from floor to ceiling, scarcely exceeds that of a normal bookcase.' As to the shelves themselves: 'There are five for each of the hexagon's walls; each shelf contains thirty-five books of uniform format; each book is of four hundred and ten pages; each page, of forty lines, each line, of some eighty letters which are black in colour. There are also letters on the spine of each book; these letters do not indicate or prefigure what the pages will say.'

This is information decoupled from anything but the most functionalist aesthetic, and ordered by no architectonic save that of the silicon chip. Needless to say, the contents of the infinite volumes are randomised: a few make sense, but the great majority are gobbledegook. And of course, there's nothing on this heaving multiplicity of shelves but information – no tobacco pouches, no little metal skeletons, and no propped-up postcards. There is this consolation for those of us who are dying in tandem with the shelf: we will meet our fitting apotheosis when the urn containing our ashes is carefully inserted into one of the columbarium's shelves.

22 May 2014
Prospect Magazine

Absent Jews and Invisible Executioners:
W. G. Sebald and the Holocaust

'I have been asked if I was aware of the moral implications of what I was doing. As I told the tribunal at Nuremberg, I did not know that Hitler was a Nazi. The truth was that for years I thought he worked for the phone company. When I did finally find out what a monster he was, it was too late to do anything as I had already made a down payment on some furniture. Once, towards the end of the war I did contemplate loosening the Führer's neck napkin and allowing a few tiny hairs to get down his back, but at the last minute my nerve failed me.'

Following Freud – himself an exile, driven out by the Nazis – there are some things too serious *not* to joke about; and this applies to Hitler, to the vile regime he initiated, and even to the murders – through aggressive war, through mass shootings, extermination camps and forced marches – that this regime enacted. Mass murders the true extent of which will never now be established with complete accuracy – twenty million, thirty? What can such figures tell us, how can they convey the sentience of a single individual crushed beneath the Nazis' juggernaut, let alone a myriad of such lived nightmares.

I should qualify the above: some things are too serious for some people *not* to joke about them. I cannot decide whether or not the late W. G. Sebald, in whose memory this lecture was inaugurated, would permit himself even the wryest of smiles in response to Woody Allen's parody of Albert Speer's *Inside the Third Reich*. After all, it isn't the Holocaust that 'The Schmeed Memoirs' seeks to extract humour from; rather, Allen is savagely mocking Speer's claim that at the time they were taking place, he personally knew nothing of the murder of the Jews. By transforming Hitler's erstwhile architect – who subsequently became his minister for war production – into a self-deluding barber, Allen performs the essential task of the satirist: to expose the lie of power for what it was, is, and always will be, and to strip away the protective clothing – of idealism, of denial, of retrospective justification – from the perpetrators of genocide.

Ours is an era intoxicated by its capacity to technologically reproduce history, in an instantaneous digitisation of all that has happened. This lays down layer upon layer of decadences. Far from tempering our ability to politicise history, the very existence of this dense stratigraphy seems to spur both individuals and regimes on to still greater tendentiousness. Among modern philosophers Baudrillard understood this development the best, and foresaw the deployment of symbolic events alongside the more conventional weaponry of international conflict.

W. G. Sebald understood it as well; in *The Rings of Saturn*, his fictive alter ego observes the Waterloo Panorama, a 360-degree representation of the battle warped round 'an immense domed rotunda', and muses: 'This then [. . .] is the representation of history. It requires a falsification of perspective. We, the survivors, see everything from above, see everything at once, and still we do not know how it was.' To counter this synoptic view – which, again and again throughout his work, Sebald links to dangerous idealisms and utopian fantasies – the writer offered us subjective experience. This was not, however, reportage that relies for its authority on the mere fact of witness; Sebald, as he wrote with reference to the Allied bombing of Hamburg in his essay 'Air War and Literature', mistrusted seeming clarity in the retelling of events that had violently disarranged the senses. Rather, his was a forensic phenomenology that took into account the very lacunae, the repressions and the partial amnesias that are the reality of lived life.

Sebald, perhaps better than anyone, would understand the threshold we are now upon. Last year Harry Patch, the final remaining British combatant in the First World War died, and with the extinguishing of his sentience another stratum of history was sealed shut. In the next two or three decades the same will happen in respect of the Second World War and the Holocaust. Last November John Demjanjuk was wheeled into a Munich courtroom to stand trial on charges of being an accessory to 27,900 murders in the Sobibor extermination camp, and despite the statement by the Zentralrat der Juden in Deutschland that 'All NS criminals still living should know that there won't be mercy for them, regardless of their age', it is generally understood that this will be the last Holocaust crimes trial of any significance.

The previous month convicted Holocaust denier Nick Griffin, in his guise as leader of a legitimate British political party, appeared on BBC One's *Question Time*, where he was subjected to carefully orchestrated liberal barracking. And throughout the Christmas period Mirosław Bałka's disturbing installation *How It Is* lowered in the turbine hall of Tate Modern a steely-black hole in the space–time fabric, beckoning the comfortable London gallery-goers into a psychic identification with those who were forced at gunpoint to entrain for an apocalypse.

And in a fortnight's time, on 27th of January – the 65th anniversary of the Soviet liberation of Auschwitz – we will have Holocaust Memorial Day, a national commemoration of the victims of German National Socialism, inaugurated by Tony Blair in 2001. W. G. Sebald died in December of that year, but had he lived I doubt he would have made any public comment about this. Nevertheless, while I don't wish to contribute to the world's stock of tendentiousness – of which we already have a superfluity – the message I take from Sebald's works and his scrupulous posture in relation to the remembrance of the Holocaust's victims, is that such events, far from ensuring a 'Legacy of Hope' (the theme of this year's Memorial Day), shore up a conception of history, of humanity, and of civilisation that depends on the Holocaust as an exceptional and unprecedented mass murder. It is not just in terms of the Zionist eschatology that the Holocaust is deployed as a symbolic event, but we also require it as a confirmation of our own righteousness in the democratic and industrialised West.

Albert Speer was, of course, the very personification of an industrialisation run amok; a Promethean orgy that saw fire stolen from the gods and brimstone wrested from the earth. The Nazis, for all the queered atavism of their ideology, were nothing if not modernisers. So, Speer could be significant for Sebald for many reasons – the grotesque giganticism of his designs for the new capital of Hitler's thousand-year Reich would seem the epitome of that bowdlerisation of Burke's 'objects great and terrible' which was the Nazis' vision of art as the servant of social control. In Sebald's *Austerlitz*, the eponymous protagonist, an architectural historian, circles the truth of his origins as he circles the terra incognita of Germany itself. Through his study of such buildings as factories, docks and fortifications hypertrophied by nineteenth-century industrialisation, Austerlitz is unconsciously zoning in on the most monstrous disjunction of human scale: the exterminatory assembly lines of the Holocaust.

Encrypted in Antwerp's Centraal Station, Austerlitz finds a programme of social control, and remarks to the novel's narrator: 'The clock is placed some twenty metres above the only baroque element in the entire ensemble, the cruciform stairway which leads from the foyer to the platforms, just where the image of the emperor stood in the Pantheon in a line directly prolonged from the portal; as governor of a new omnipotence it was set even above the royal coat of arms and the motto *Eendracht maakt macht.*' In English, 'Union is strength', but in Flemish it echoes *Arbeit macht frei*, just as Austerlitz is a near homophone for Auschwitz.

Then, there is Speer's awkward status as not only the preeminent German denier of Holocaust knowledge, but also its foremost passive resister, who, charged with Hitler's scorched earth policy saved as much of its industrial infrastructure as he could. Just as Speer refused the evidence of his own senses when he visited the slave labourers at the notorious Mittelbau-Dora missile factory, so we can imagine that Sebald's own father refused – at least in retrospect – to acknowledge the reality of what he witnessed as a career soldier in the Wehrmacht.

Sebald said of his own parents that they were typical of German petit bourgeoisie who 'went into the war not just blindly, but with a degree of enthusiasm . . . they all felt they were going to be lords of the world'. Sebald's father was in the Polish campaign, and in the family photo album there were pictures that initially had a 'boy scout atmosphere', but: 'Then the order came and they moved in. And now the photographs are of Polish villages instead, razed to the ground and with only the chimneys left standing. These photos seemed quite normal to me as a child [. . .] I look at them now, and I think, "Good Lord, what *is* all this?"'

It's easy to see this as Sebald's paradigmatic experience of the power of photography to both document and dissemble historical reality – power he himself would make great use of. In *Vertigo*, Sebald's alter ego says of an album that his father bought his mother in 1939 as a present for the first *Kriegsweihnacht* – or Nazi-sanctioned 'War Christmas': 'Some of these photographs show gypsies who had been rounded up and put in detention. They are looking out smiling from behind the barbed wire, somewhere in a far corner of Slovakia where my father and his vehicle repairs unit had been stationed for several weeks before the outbreak of war.' And there, below the text, is the photograph in question, which was, Sebald said in an interview: 'an indication that these things were accepted as part of the operation right from the beginning'.

Named 'Winfried' from a Nazi list of approved names, and 'Georg' after his father, Sebald preferred to be known as Max. Born in the Bavarian Alps in May 1944 as the Reich was collapsing beneath the Allied onslaught, his own literary achievement stands in almost diametric opposition to that of Speer. While Speer occupied himself exclusively with variations on the theme of what the psychoanalytic thinker Alexander Mitscherlich termed his *Lebenslüge*, or 'Great Lie', Sebald devoted his energies to exposing all the smaller lies of his parents' generation. He remained steadfast in his excoriation; when asked, in the course of an interview with the *Jewish Quarterly* after the publication of *The Emigrants*, whether he could talk to his parents about the so-called 'Hitler time', Sebald replied:

'Not really. Though my father is still alive, at eighty-five
. . . it's the ones who have a conscience who die early,
it grinds you down. The fascist supporters live forever.
Or the passive resisters. That's what they all are now in
their own minds. I always try to explain to my parents
that there is no difference between passive resistance and
passive collaboration – it's the same thing. But they cannot
understand this.'

There is, as yet, no direct access to Georg Sebald's war
record, but sifting through the clues in Sebald's texts and
cross-referencing these with his statements in interviews,
it seems likely to me that his father ended up serving with
the 1st Gebirgsjäger – or 'mountain huntsmen' – who were
indeed stationed in Slovakia before the invasion of Poland,
and whose war record includes a sorry tapestry of war
crimes, including the rounding up and shooting of Jews in
Lvov. Sebald, inevitably, was not close to his father, who
had been taken prisoner by the Americans in 1945 and only
returned home when the writer was three. But while it's
almost a cliché to say of a male writer's books that they are
acts of parricide, Sebald's great achievement lay in not succumbing to Oedipal rage so as to forestall tragic sadness.

In the eight years since Max Sebald's untimely death his
status – already high – has increased. In 2007 Horace
Engdahl, former secretary of the Swedish Academy, cited
Sebald as one of the writers who would have been a worthy
Nobel laureate. I don't take issue with this; however I am
interested in saving Sebald from the ossification of this kind

of critical regard which is the preserve of arts functionaries and their selective lists. As I've had cause to remark before: it's pets that win prizes, and I don't believe that Sebald was anyone's pet. Rather, let us resurrect him as a disciple of the writer and Holocaust survivor Jean Améry, of whom Sebald wrote, '(His) existentialist philosophical position . . . makes no concessions to history but exemplifies the necessity of continuing to protest, a dimension so strikingly lacking from German postwar literature.'

Sebald is rightly seen as the non-Jewish German writer who through his works did most to mourn the murder of the Jews. He said that he felt no guilt himself – and indeed why should he? He wasn't responsible – but that there was an irremediable 'sense of shame'. Subjected at school, as all Germans of his generation were, to a film of the concentration camps without explanation or contextualisation, Sebald was jolted out of what had been an isolated bucolic childhood; it impinged on him from then on that, 'While I was sitting in my pushchair and being wheeled through the flowering meadows by my mother, the Jews of Corfu were being deported on a four-week trek to Poland. It is the simultaneity of a blissful childhood and those horrific events that now strikes me as incomprehensible. I know now that these things cast a very long shadow over my life.'

The shadow lengthened through his university career where, in Freiburg, Sebald found himself being taught German literature by academics he later described as 'dissembling old fascists'. Only the returned exile Theodor Adorno offered any insight, and no doubt his remarks on the possibility of a post-Holocaust literature must have been something the young Sebald took to heart: 'To write poetry after Auschwitz,' Adorno wrote, 'is barbaric.' A statement he later amplified thus: 'The so-called artistic rendering of the naked physical pain of those who were beaten down with rifle butts contains, however distantly, the possibility that pleasure can be squeezed from it.'

Such 'action writing', and any possible voyeurism were modes that subsequently Sebald carefully avoided – just as he himself never visited a concentration camp. This was a pilgrimage that Sebald believed was 'not the answer', especially since such sites had become only way-stations on the profaning tourist trail. I wish I had the time here to plot carefully the journey that Sebald did undertake, from Freiburg to Francophone Switzerland where he completed his degree, and from there, in 1966, to Manchester where he became a teaching assistant and finished his master's. He returned briefly to Switzerland for an unsatisfactory Wittgensteinian experiment in school teaching, before going back to Manchester and then on to the University of East Anglia, where, apart from a spell in Munich at the Goethe Institute in 1975–6, he remained for the rest of his life.

I wish I also had the time to exhaustively map his intellectual and literary development, but for the purposes of my thesis a couple of significant episodes will have to suffice. First, there was Sebald's exposure to the Auschwitz-Birkenau trials of 1963–5 in Munich, which he followed assiduously in the newspapers. Sebald said of the trials: 'it was the first *public* acknowledgement that there was such a thing as an unresolved German past.' And, further, that, 'I realised there were things of much greater urgency than the writings of the German Romantics.' Sebald was struck both by the utter familiarity of the defendants – 'the kind of people I'd known as neighbours' – but still more by how the Jewish witnesses, initially strange and foreign, were in the course of the proceedings revealed to have been residents of Nuremberg and Stuttgart. For Sebald, awakening to the realisation that he had been living among tacit accomplices to the elimination of these people's relatives made him feel himself to be a tacit accomplice as well, and so he 'had to know what had happened in detail, and try to understand why it should have been so'.

We will return to that 'why', which I believe to be crucial, because with a less nakedly philosophic writer it would undoubtedly have been replaced by the 'how' of historicist instrumentality. But in the meantime let us consider Sebald's move to Britain, and in particular to Manchester, which in 1966 – as today – had a thriving Jewish community. In postwar Germany it was, of course, only too possible never to encounter a Jew, but now Sebald had a German-Jewish landlord whose own parents had been deported to Riga where they were murdered. This man subsequently became one of the models for Max Ferber, the painter in Sebald's *The Emigrants*, and the encounter hammered home the template for his subsequent modus operandi: 'To my mind,' Sebald later said, 'there is an acute difference between historiography and history as experienced history.'

The experience of real, live Jews was definitely important – and possibly equally significant was that these were English Jews; after all, if, as the old Jewish saying has it, the Jews are like everyone else but more so, then it can be inferred that English Jews are like the English – but more so. The uncanny portrayal of Dr Henry Selwyn in *The Emigrants* is a function of his almost perfect assimilation to English diffidence, and since Sebald based him on a real-life model who the writer did not even realise was of Polish-Jewish extraction until told so, he stands as a sign pointing towards that earlier age when German Jews, with names such as Hamburger and Berlin – evidence Sebald once remarked, of just how tragically close their identification with the Fatherland was – were quite as well camouflaged.

This is not to say that Sebald's Jews are anything but individuals. For a counterexample to his own meticulousness you can look no further than Bernhard Schlink's *The Reader*, a novel widely feted for its moving portrayal of the impact of the Holocaust – but on whom, exactly? Schlink's novel may present a schema of evolving Holocaust consciousness in the successor generation of Germans, but its effects depend on exactly the kind of 'action writing' that Sebald rejected. In Schlink's case this 'action' consists in the frisson of the protagonist's underage sex with a beautiful concentration camp guard. No wonder Schlink's novel became that tiresome cliché 'a major motion picture', complete with a titanic English actress indulging in artistic nudity. It is perhaps to Schlink's credit that he doesn't try and pretend sufficient familiarity with the sole Jewish character in the novel to actually provide her with a name; but, as some critics have done, to credit this as a sensitive allegory – one individual in lieu of the exterminated six million – seems special pleading to me.

Of course, in his writings and interviews Sebald never pretended that his artistic development was entirely sui generis; it's more that the lamentable insularity of the English-speaking world – if we can speak of something so mondial as an island – has made us generally impervious to foreign cultural influences that depend vitally on language. This cannot have been far from Sebald's own mind, not only when he rigorously collaborated on the translations of his own prose fictions from German into English, but also in his work as a pedagogue and as the founder, in 1989, of the British Centre for Literary Translation at UEA.

Be that as it may, the influence of Alexander Kluge – to name but one exemplar of the documentary literature of postwar Germany – on Sebald's methodology and concerns is difficult to assess for a non-German speaker, since none of Kluge's key texts are available in translation. We can identify, to some extent, Sebald's affinities with Jean Améry, or with Alfred Döblin, the subject of his own doctoral thesis, but the point needs to be stressed that these are *Jewish* German writers, the former a Holocaust survivor, the latter a Modernist whose sensibility was shaped during Weimar. What we cannot do is to place Sebald within the German literary context where he might be said to belong.

*

In cosmology there is what's known as 'the strong anthropic argument', which extrapolates from the coincidence of the physical laws of the universe and our ability to observe those laws, to the proposition that this is no coincidence but a necessity: the universe has evolved precisely to produce beings of our kind, QED, God. I suspect in our view of W. G. Sebald as the preeminent – or at least most widely and obviously revered – German-language writer in the English-speaking world, we are falling victim to a strong anthropic argument, when a weaker one will suffice.

Undoubtedly, it was precisely Sebald's own exile from Germany and his exposure to living Jewish communities that made it possible for him to transform the inchoate mistrust of his 'passive collaborator' background into an active literature of atonement. I suspect there is a degree of wishful thinking in the critiques of postwar German literature published in English, and the title of the most comprehensive of these – Ernestine Schlant's worthy if over-determined *The Language of Silence* – says it all. The literature of Holocaust survivors can tell us *how* it was, but it can do little to explain *why* it was, for that we have impotently required a fully self-actualised literature of the perpetrators; in other words: an impossibility. Hannah Arendt's much-quoted coinage from the subtitle to her study of the Eichmann trial – 'the banality of evil' – has become a shibboleth to be lisped in the nightmarish face of the Holocaust. In fact, Arendt avoided the term in the text, while stressing in her private letters from Jerusalem during the trial, that, after ploughing through the 3,000-page transcript of Eichmann's interrogation by the Israeli police, what impressed her most was his 'brainlessness'.

We cannot interrogate the brainless for their or our own self-actualisation, we cannot look to those who have capitulated to a regime which made evil just a civil norm for a moral re-evaluation. Instead, we have their sons and daughters, and we have Sebald; whose elegant, elegiac and haunting prose narratives reinstate the prelapsarian German-speaking world. His careful use of documentary sources places before the contemporary reader the *actualité* of a culture in which Jews played an integral part, while his style is at once discursive – looping in historic anecdote and literary reference – and incisive: cutting away at the surface of reality to expose the mysterious interconnections of things-in-themselves. To read Sebald is to be confronted with European history not as an ideologically determined diachronic – as proposed by Hegelians and Spenglerians alike – nor as a synchronic phenomenon to be subjected to Baudrillard's postmodern analysis. Rather, for Sebald, history is a palimpsest – and the reification implied is significant – the meaning of which can only be divined by rubbing away a little bit here, adding on some over there, and then – most importantly – stepping back to allow for a synoptic view that remains inherently suspect.

I think it's this beguiling overview – which Sebald calls our attention to again and again in his writings by describing the works of Dutch landscape painters and English watercolourists – that explains in part our willingness to ascribe to him some specifically *moral* ascendancy, and by implication a historiography he explicitly denies. For the English-speaking world – and the English in particular – Sebald is the longed for 'Good German'; he's everything Speer wanted to become but never could. Sebald has recognised the taint and moved to erase it by a systematic bearing of witness. But if he had remained behind in Germany, might he not have succumbed to the same pressures as many of his generation, and been carried along on the tide of Marxian posturing to a fallacious equivalence of the Federal Republic with the Third Reich? It's hard to imagine Sebald subsuming the emotional reality of the Holocaust to an intellectual abstraction, just as it's difficult to see him falling for the victimology of many German writers of the successor generation, who, in their torturous investigations of Oedipal hatred revealed only that it was all about *them*.

But then, recall that Sebald was no great believer in free will. 'This notion,' he said, 'of the autonomous individual who is in charge of his or her fate is one that I couldn't really subscribe to.' So presumably nor could he have subscribed to any view of his literary work as originating from a desire to do the right thing – that was then done. Indeed he never did: he disavowed any particular philo-Semitism, explaining his resurrection of German Jewry as a form of social history as much as anything else – which does indeed make Sebald sound more English than the English. But the urge to project holy motives onto writers in this godless age is quite as strong as our desire to damn them to a hell no one believes in.

In England, Sebald's onetime presence among us – even if we would never be so crass as to think this, let alone articulate it – is registered as further confirmation that we *won*, and won because of our righteousness, our liberality, our inclusiveness and our tolerance. Where else would the Good German have sprouted so readily, if not from our brown and nutritious soil? If he had remained at home might he not have become – at the very least – a German version of Thomas Bernhard: a refusenik, an internal exile, his solipsism not modulated by melancholy but intensified until it became a cachinnating cynicism? Instead, the writing is anecdotal in feel, and furnished with plenty of English quotidiana – Teasmades and coal fires, battered cod and dotty prep school masters, branch-line rail journeys and model-making enthusiasts; enough, at any rate, to submerge any disquieting philosophising.

I might be doing the *mittel*-English readership of Sebald – if indeed such people exist at all – a disservice, were it not that I'm prepared to take the rap myself: I find Sebald's path into the charnel house of the twentieth century quite reassuring – especially when it takes the form of a hearty English walk. To read exclusively *German* postwar German literature is to find myself in the position of the unnamed narrator of Walter Abish's *How German Is It*, who, on returning to his hometown after the war, becomes transfixed by the way Germanness inheres in everything he sets his eyes on – even the rivets that secure the map of the town to the station wall.

*

In too-German Germany Sebald is, of course, not quite German enough. In the past eight years there has been some upgrading of his reputation, but Sebald would've needed to be alive in order to have benefited from Günter Grass's own downgrading following the revelation of his SS membership. As for Martin Walser, paradoxically it is his insistence that Germans have done enough atoning which – or so German friends of mine assure me – people find 'boring'.

Sebald did enter the lists of the great controversies surrounding the history of the Hitler-time when in 1997 he delivered his series of Zurich lectures, posthumously published in English in an edited form, under the title *On the Natural History of Destruction*. When these writings appeared in Germany, Sebald's contention that the wholesale destruction of the German cities by Allied bombing, resulting in 600,000 civilian deaths and five million homeless, was singularly under-represented in postwar German literature, became a stick in the hands of both right and left, intent on beating each other with it. Sebald's reputation predictably suffered collateral damage. I suspect Sebald was not so much ingenuous as out of touch with contemporary opinion: to him the continuing and plangent shame Germans should feel for the murder of the Jews remained a given; it did not need to be restated in a thesis concerning a different mass killing. Besides, he did state explicitly in the text that it ill behoved Germans to castigate the wartime Allies – whatever their motivation – for prosecuting the war in this fashion.

You don't have to be an exile to be perceived as a *Nestbeschmutzer* (one who dirties his own nest) in the German-speaking world – but it helps; while exactly those Bakelite touches English critics find reassuring – even as they shade in the utter blackness – German ones are dismissive of. Reviewing *Austerlitz* for *Die Zeit*, Iris Radisch described its lapidary style as 'Holocaust and staghorn buttons' while averring that, 'Something's wrong here . . . Is it really possible to use the same model of archives to describe the search for your deported parents as the search for shells . . . in a school friend's house? . . . Is it persuasive to plaster the journey back to the places of expulsion, death and destruction with antique curiosities?'

Then again, given that if you hail a cab outside Frankfurt's rail station its driver is very likely to be writing a doctoral thesis *on* the Frankfurt School, Sebald's metaphysical bent – worrying to English empiricists – is viewed straightforwardly by this compatriot: 'Sebald is the same as those philosophers, of whom Kierkegaard said, all that they write about reality is just as confusing as reading a sign at a flea market stall that says "Washing done here". You come back with your things, hoping to have them washed, but instead you stand there like an idiot because the sign is merely there to be sold.'

None of which is to suggest that you cannot also find plenty of praise for Sebald's works among German critics, it's just that what's missing is the peculiar reverence that attaches to writings that – so long as they aren't read too closely – seem to confirm us English in some of our most comforting prejudices. Context, as Sebald himself knew, remains only too important, and before I reach the kernel of my thesis concerning W. G. Sebald and the Holocaust, I think it only fair to shade in my own. How English is that?

I began with a quote from a Woody Allen parody that I first read in his anthology *Getting Even* soon after its publication in 1971. I found 'The Schmeed Memoirs' uproariously funny, although aged eleven I had no idea who Albert Speer was. I did however have an awareness of the Holocaust – not least because my mother had told me for as long as I could remember that the Polish woman who lived alone in the detached house at the end of our block was a camp survivor. And moreover, that the reason why this woman's privet hedge was so spectacularly neglected was that she feared the return of the Nazis, and believed that they would – like the Angel of Death – pass by if they thought no one lived there.

I've no idea if any of this was true – my mother had a flair for dramatics – but it seemed credible, given that whenever I saw the Polish woman, her tightly belted grey gabardine raincoat and short, lank, dyed-black hair gave her a curiously anachronistic appearance, as if she were a black-and-white photograph pasted onto the verdant Ektachrome of the Hampstead Garden Suburb. I also knew about the 'passive collaborators' with the Holocaust from an early age – because my mother regularly accused my father of having been one.

In retrospect, and in the full light of the knowledge I now possess concerning the political consciousness of upper-middle-class English ex-public schoolboys in the late 1930s, this notion of my mother's is not just preposterous – but hateful. My father was twenty in 1939 when his call-up papers arrived. He just gone up for his first term at Oxford, and had for some time been a member of Dick Sheppard's Peace Pledge Union. He told me before he died that during the week after his call-up arrived he was wracked by doubts about what he should do, but in the end he decided to register as a conscientious objector. Intermittently, but with greater intensity as the years had passed, he had regretted this.

For my mother, an American Jew of Russian extraction, ignorance was no defence when it came to the Nazis' genocidal intentions towards Jewry, and therefore my father was exactly like those Germans who claimed to have been unaware of the mass murders even after they had occurred. While accepting that she, growing up in the New York borough of Queens in the 1930s, may well have been aware of the Nazis' persecutory zeal, because – as she told me – of letters our relatives in Europe were forced to send requesting money that was then stolen from them, I realised when I came to study the Holocaust in detail that neither she – nor indeed anyone, save possibly Hitler himself – could have known in 1939 that the Nazis' Final Solution would necessarily be an exterminatory one. This being noted, my father's further claim that he knew nothing at all of the Holocaust until Richard Dimbleby's famous broadcasts from Belsen in 1945, does suggest a certain willed ignorance on his part, which, if not exactly Speer-like, was far from uncommon among the British.

I don't wish to make too much of this; looked at one way there is something merely sad about such implausible culpability becoming domestic mud slung in a miserable marriage, but looked at differently it taught me early on to mistrust arguments founded on spuriously synoptic historical schemas, and to have my doubts when it came to the idea that the Germans' murdering of the Jews possessed any absolute exceptionality. Not that my mother – wilfully deracinated as she was – cleaved to any Jewish eschatology, Zionist or otherwise. Nor can I say that she ever articulated the conventional formulation of Holocaust remembrance: these things must never be forgotten, lest they occur again.

In *The Rings of Saturn*, W. G. Sebald cryptically alludes to Jorge Luis Borges's story 'Tlön, Uqbar, Orbis Tertius', which, in a typically Borgesian fashion, plays with the idea of an idealist world created by eighteenth-century encyclopaedists to bedevil their empiricist heirs. The passage Sebald had in mind was this: 'Things became duplicated in Tlön; they also tend to become effaced and lose their details when they are forgotten. A classic example is the doorway which survived so long it was visited by a beggar and disappeared at his death. At times some birds, a horse, have saved the ruins of an amphitheatre.'

In the preamble to this same strange tale, Borges's narrator recalls a dinner with a friend at which 'we became

lengthily engaged in a vast polemic concerning the composition of a novel in the first person, whose narrator would
omit or disfigure the facts and indulge in various contradictions which would permit a few readers – very few
readers – to perceive an atrocious or banal reality.' This is
of course W. G. Sebald's own fictive methodology, and I
believe only a very few readers have grasped the atrocious
and banal reality that he wishes us to perceive, despite the
myriad clues that are scattered throughout his texts.

Consider this, from *Austerlitz*, where the eponymous
survivor of the *Kindertransport* remarks, 'It does not seem
to me . . . that we understand the laws governing the return
of the past, but I feel more and more as if time did not exist
at all, only various spaces interlocking according to the
rules of a higher form of stereometry, between which the
living and the dead can move back and forth as they like,
and the longer I think about it the more it seems to me that
we who are still alive are unreal in the eyes of the dead.'

Again and again Sebald makes statements of a
transcendental idealism, again and again he points to
coincidence and déjà vu as evidence of the *unheimlich*
quality of subjectivity. This is Sebald's alter ego in *The
Rings of Saturn*: 'my rational mind is . . . unable to lay
the ghosts of repetition that haunt me with ever greater
frequency. Scarcely am I in company but it seems as if I
had already heard the same opinions expressed by the
same people somewhere or other, in the same way, with
the same words, turns of phrase and gestures.' If instead
of conventional linear narratives Sebald's prose fictions

are word-filigrees spun out of such atemporal coincidences, then they are also haunted by the congruence
of the things-in-themselves that constitute the material
world: in *The Emigrants*, Max Ferber returns to smoky
industrial Manchester, understanding intuitively that
while he may have escaped the Holocaust, it remains his
destiny to 'serve under the chimney'.

The echo of the Buna at Auschwitz is certainly inten-
tional, and just as willed by Sebald are the references
throughout his books to Theresienstadt, the 'model' concentration camp established by Reinhardt Heydrich in the
Bohemian hinterland. I speak not just of the extended passages concerning the camp in *Austerlitz*, but of tens and
scores of other references to it – far more than to any
of the other, more notorious nodes of the Holocaust. I
believe that in Theresienstadt, where tens of thousands of
'privileged' Jews were crammed into an eighteenth-century
fortified town a kilometre square, Sebald saw the very
synecdoche of the Holocaust.

With its theatre company and orchestra, its workshops
and its newspaper, Theresienstadt was given a grotesque makeover by the Germans so that it could serve
as a Potemkin village for a Red Cross inspection in 1944
designed to allay international suspicions. At the same
time a film was made depicting the idyllic existence of
those who shortly after the shooting stopped were transported to the gas chambers of Auschwitz, or else forced
east on the death marches that claimed 1.5 million more
Jewish lives in the Nazis' Götterdämmerung.

Theresienstadt is for Sebald only an extreme and specialised form of a holocaust he sees being perpetrated everywhere and at all times as civilisation marches on. If there is any exceptional character to the German Holocaust it is only that it is German, just as Belgian holocausts are Belgian, Rwandan ones Rwandan, and Croatian ones – albeit under German tutelage – are Croatian. Describing Joseph Conrad's arrival in Brussels to take up the commission which would gain him the material for *Heart of Darkness*, Sebald wrote: '(Conrad) now saw the capital of the Kingdom of Belgium, with its ever more bombastic buildings, as a sepulchral monument erected over a hecatomb of black bodies, and all the passers-by in the streets seemed to him to bear that dark Congolese secret within them.'

While historians such as Daniel Jonah Goldhagen might wish to arrogate a unique exterminatory impulse to the Germans, Sebald resists this facile view at every juncture. In his doctoral thesis on Alfred Döblin, Sebald was inclined to see aspects of *Berlin Alexanderplatz* as a shadow cast forwards, a kind of reverse memory. Commenting on Döblin's description of an abattoir, Sebald avers that 'Far more horrifying than the chaotic destruction of the Apocalypse is the well-ordered destruction contrived by man himself.'

Implicit in Sebald's work is the idea that human mass murder is only a suicidal form of the holocaust we are perpetrating on the natural world. It is there in *The Rings of Saturn* where the description of the destruction of the

European fisheries is juxtaposed with a double-page photograph of the naked bodies of the Nazis' victims lying among trees. It is there in *The Emigrants* where Manchester is described as a 'necropolis or mausoleum'; in *Vertigo* also when the vehicles crawling along the gleaming black roads out of Innsbruck are imagined as 'the last of an amphibian species close to extinction'. Encrypted in almost every line of *After Nature* we find the same message: 'Cities phosphorescent / on the riverbank, industry's / glowing piles waiting / beneath the smoke trails / like ocean giants for the siren's / blare, the twitching lights / of rail- and motorways, the murmur / of the millionfold proliferating molluscs, / woodlice and leeches, the cold putrefaction'.

In conclusion then, W. G. Sebald had no need of a Holocaust Memorial Day – and I believe that if we read him rightly nor have we English. In Germany, a Memorial Day for the Victims of National Socialism is indeed an appropriate response – if not an atonement – for crimes committed, but here Tony Blair might have done better to inaugurate a Refusal to Grant Refugee Jews Asylum Memorial Day, or an Incendiary Bombing of German Cities Memorial Day, or even – casting the shadow forward – an Iraqi Civilians Killed Due to Pusillanimous Atlanticist Foreign Policy Memorial Day, for these are deaths that more properly belong at our door.

For Sebald and for those of us who hearken to his metaphysic, there is no need to remember because the Nazis' Holocaust is still happening in an interlocking space, while right beside us are the poisoned seas, the glowing piles and the cold putrefaction of an environmental one. 'More and more,' the narrator of *The Emigrants* tells us concerning Dr Selwyn, 'he sensed that Nature itself was collapsing beneath the burden we placed upon it.' And as Gerhard Richter's fusion of slow oils and photographic quicksilver so perfectly expresses, upon that denuded foreground, Onkel Rudi is always posing for the camera, smiling, in front of the slave labourers' hecatomb.

11 January 2010

Chernobyl

Standing in a dank stairwell of Kindergarten No.7 in the abandoned Ukrainian city of Pripyat three miles from Chernobyl's Reactor No.4, I eyed the billboard-sized painting that had detached itself from the wall and now lay wedged across the banisters. It had probably been a garish affair when it was executed, but twenty-five subzero winters and twenty-four parched summers had distempered its colours, blurred its cartoon-like forms. I breathed in and out slowly, conscious of the ultrasonic whistling of my lungs, the synchronous wisps of vapour. I shifted slightly, and beneath my soles broken glass shattered a bit more; *the sands of time*, I thought idly. This is a story about time – but then aren't they all? This is a story about things – like the painting in the nursery school, or the rotten wallpaper that everywhere I went in Pripyat seemed to be flowing down the walls of the abandoned apartments in a series of slow-motion waves.

And, of course, it's also a story about people: the Ukrainian people, who, for the past quarter-century have lived with the consequences of the worst nuclear accident in history, lived with it irradiating their bodies and their minds. Yet it's about the rest of us, too – anyone born in time to witness the Chernobyl accident saw it crystallise a global anxiety about nuclear energy that, in the West at least, had already been stoked up by the 1979 accident at the Three Mile Island nuclear power plant in Pennsylvania. Twelve days before the Unit 2 reactor at Three Mile Island melted down, a movie called *The China Syndrome* was released, starring the time-would-not-wither-her beauty Jane Fonda. The movie was an eco-thriller about the cover-up of potentially lethal faults at a nuclear plant, and some wags suggested that the Three Mile Island accident must be a publicity scam organised by its producers.

I remember seeing *The China Syndrome*, and I can still picture news footage of Three Mile Island without recourse to that great repository of the collective con-sciousness, YouTube. Chernobyl I'm less sure about – in 1986 I was on a prolonged binge that put me in rehab, and personal meltdown eclipsed even this unearthly radiance: the release of 400 times as much radioactive material as the Hiroshima bomb. But the following spring I was out in the world – in North Wales, specifically, the part of the British Isles that received the highest levels of fallout from Chernobyl, and I can still recall a sheep farmer quipping to me that that season's lambs were going to be born with two heads.

So, this story is all about time – and it's all about timing. The day before I found myself standing in the ruined nursery school, I was sitting forty-odd miles to the southwest in the gloomy office of Dr Yuri Saienko at the charmingly named Center of Social Expertizes (that's what it said in English on his card), in central Kiev. Saienko, a tall, silver-haired and rather romantically cadaverous man in his sixties, had been telling me about his longitudinal studies of Chernobyl victims – the evacuees from the area surrounding the stricken plant, and those who, over the decades since, had crept back to their homes in the 'Zone of Alienation' – when, in typically Slavic fashion, he segued straight into poetry. Gesturing at the engraving of a bearded type on the wall above his head, he explained that this was Taras Shevchenko, the Ukrainian national bard '. . . some kind of saintly man, I think,' before quoting the line: 'On your righteous land we've installed some hell within the paradise.'

Dr Saienko's somewhat stilted diction can be accounted for by the fact that Irina Zaytseva, a young littérateur and all-round Miss Fix-it was simultaneously translating from the Russian for me. Saienko/Zaysteva continued: 'Shevchenko was born and died in spring – and all these catastrophes happen in spring: Three Mile Island, Chernobyl . . . and now Fukushima. This is not haphazard.' I bridled a little at such overt mysticism, although I knew what he meant: once we surface from the nightmare of history it's difficult not to impose an interpretation on such strange dream states. Looked at from the vantage point of May 2011 there did seem to be some kind of discernible rhythm to it all. In Ukraine, they had been gearing up for the twenty-fifth anniversary of the Chernobyl disaster on 26 April, when, on 12 March a devastating tsunami hit the northwest coast of Japan, followed three days later by an explosion at the Fukushima Daiichi nuclear plant. If Three Mile Island had been a trailer for the main feature, in the quarter-century since Chernobyl the tide of public support for nuclear power had first ebbed away, then began to trickle back in as anxieties about global warming started to seriously impact.

When the seer-like James Lovelock – whose Gaia theory set the agenda for environmental consciousness – began to strenuously advocate a new and intensive nuclear power programme, the tide had definitely turned. Writing in his book *The Revenge of Gaia*, Lovelock was forthright: 'Renewable energy sounds good, but so far it is inefficient and expensive. It has a future, but we have no time now to experiment with visionary energy sources: civilisation is in imminent danger and has to use nuclear energy now.' As if the gods – specifically Pluto – were mocking Lovelock, Fukushima waited in the wings; proof, if any were needed, that there were no easy solutions to the burgeoning energy requirements of 6.5 billion mortals.

As for my own timing, my editor at *Playboy* had asked me if I'd consider going to Chernobyl before the tsunami hit – and I said yes for three reasons. Yes because I'd heard that the Zone of Alienation had become a kind of wildlife refuge, with – despite the contamination – a resurgent flora and fauna now that the top predator, humankind, was largely gone. Yes because ruins – in particular Modernist ruins – have always intrigued me, and Chernobyl had to be a perfect exemplar of civilisation's increasingly ravenous auto-cannibalism; and yes, finally, because while I'm by no means a card-carrying Green, I have no doubts at all about the anthropic element in global warming – I had also hearkened to Lovelock's call to pile on more piles, although like so many others of the environmentally concerned, the time factor still bothered me, specifically the 704-million-year half-life of the uranium-235 used in nuclear reactors.

Then came the big wave, and while in the first shocked days after it hit it was clear than many thousands of dead Japanese were rotting in this awful tidal wrack, the world's attention became fixated on what was happening at Fukushima. Certainly, there was no percentage in underestimating the possible fallout from the explosions at these reactors, which were timed at intervals seemingly designed for dramatic effect. Then there was the spectacle of the plant's workers who struggled to get the meltdowns under control while withstanding almost certainly lethal doses of radioactivity – for the world's media they were like a hundred-odd aces in the hole, and so much easier to identify with than the thousands of strewn dead, and the hundreds of thousands displaced.

It was all about time. At the beginning of May the Fukushima plant's operator, Tokyo Electric Power, promised to stabilise radiation levels and achieve a safe 'cold shutdown' of the damaged reactors in six to nine months – meanwhile the first cohort of the 80,000 evacuated from the purlieus were allowed back for a scant two hours, masked, goggled, radiation-suited, to collect some personal effects. It was 5 May, around midday, and as I stood in the stairwell of Pripyat's Kindergarten No.7 I felt as if I could see not just the paint peeling from the distempered walls, nor only the slim birch saplings pushing inexorably through the cracked concrete steps – but time itself, time in its essence. From a room some way off I could hear the automatic shutter of Lesya Malskaya's camera whirring away. My Ukrainian photographer had already told me that she was nervous in anticipation of this moment: the inevitable confrontation with her own past in the abandoned city of Pripyat.

'I was thirteen when Chernobyl happened, and my parents – like so many others – managed to get me out of Kiev. They sent me to an aunt and uncle who lived in a town about an hour outside Moscow called Vladimir. As soon as I arrived my relatives took me straight to the hospital, and when the staff realised where I'd come from they made me strip and then burnt my clothes right in front of me. I remember this so well – because the hospital was very crowded, with many patients lying on gurneys in the corridors, yet they put me in a ward for maybe eight people, alone, just me. I was there for three weeks, and every day they fed me handfuls of vitamins, then, three times each day I was given a hu-uge glass of red wine, called Bear's Blood. Also, they would scrub me down each day with some kind of soap that smelled terrible – like a horse's coat.'

No, this you don't forget: that as a 13-year-old you were stripped naked and then dosed with red wine; nor do you forget the climate of fear – fear of an enemy at once omnipresent and yet invisible. Lesya had continued: 'I remember one time I was standing at the glass partition between the ward and the corridor, drawing on a pad they'd given me and all these nurses came and pointed at me, saying, ooh, look at her amazing drawing – it was like they thought I was drawing so well because of the radiation!'

The 38-year-old photographer comes to join me in the stairwell – and I can see she's spooked; like me, she's *seeing* time – but this is her time: her childhood, her adolescence, her young womanhood is spooling before her eyes. 'What's with the bearded dentist?' I ask her, indicating the collapsed painting which does, indeed, depict a white-robed and white-bearded dentist, sitting incongruously in a small Viking-style sailboat, examining a hippo's swollen chops. 'Oh, that,' Lesya says absently, 'he is called . . . how would you say it in English? Doctor Ouch . . . Hurts. Yes, Doctor Ouch-Hurts, he was a character in a famous kids' book – we all read it. He is like this dentist who goes around helping all the animals.'

'But what's with the tiny longboat?' I press her. 'Is it something to do with the Norsemen who came down the Dnieper to found Kiev?' But Lesya has moved on and is levering herself over the banisters. Her boots crunch on broken glass and soon I hear her camera's shutter whirring away in an upstairs room, slicing up photons and chopping time into thousandths of a second. I can understand her preoccupation – to say that Kindergarten No.7 is eerie would be a feeble understatement; I recall a line from Wagner's last opera, the mystique-drenched *Parsifal*: 'In this realm time becomes space . . .' In the gutted classrooms of the nursery school rusting iron bedsteads jostle, damp-bloated cloth dolls lie legs akimbo, a wooden clock once used to teach the infant comrades to tell the time sits on a rotten desk – a symbol beyond symbolism itself.

It's the same throughout Pripyat: in the trashed public buildings – the cultural centre, the gymnasium, the supermarkets and smaller shops – and especially in the cavernous apartment blocks, and indeed everywhere we crunch, the dank, glass-bedizened ruins are time-saturated. Dennis, our terminally grumpy and chain-smoking official guide, has already explained that every single building has been comprehensively looted – that the inhabitants crept back in the late 1980s and took what they could of their own effects, and that their actions were augmented by those of serious looters, who spirited away everything else, even tearing radioactive rebars from concrete walls, such was the poverty of the immediate post-Soviet years. But far from nullifying the uncanny atmosphere of the abandoned city, the ruptured elevator doors and dented post boxes only intensify it. Besides, what do remain are the shreds of the former regime: picture books scattered around the nursery school show heroic Lenin, his overcoat flapping in the wind as he strides towards a bright future, and paternal Stalin, his arms encompassing a typically happy Soviet family. A silver birch lances through the floor of a basketball court, a placard on its wall bellows in Russian: 'Strong, Fast, Agile', while nearby it on the rotten boards lies a book entitled: *The Foreign Anti-Fascist Novel*; everywhere in Pripyat there is this counterpointing of vegetable and political time, as if the entire city – which once housed 50,000 people, people who worked in the nearby nuclear plant, who held May Day parades, and who drove their Moskovich cars with pride – was a tableau, intended to convey a stark message: all things, all people, all civilisations . . . must pass.

I have seen modern ruins before; indeed, one of the formative epiphanies of my own life occurred in 1976, when, aged fifteen, during a long hot summer in North Wales, we camped beside the Llyn Trawsfynydd reservoir which had been created in the 1920s. I remember the sense of awe I had swimming alongside the dry-stone walls as they subsided into the warm peaty water. In the mid-distance a church spire lanced from wavelets; beneath my taut belly I could sense the abandoned houses, the currents coursing through their rooms – that these waters were now used to cool the nuclear pile of a power station looming on the far shore only heightened my sense of transcendence: what was I, with all my adolescent fevers and yearnings, only such stuff as dreams are made of. The ghost towns of the old West, the gutted projects of the South Bronx, the weedy downtown of Detroit . . . the soused *quartiers* of New Orleans – our era seems to specialise in the creation of ruins, they are the dark side of our ebullient urge to monumentalise and our astonishing reproductive success.

But their gestation seems to be getting shorter and shorter – as I stood in the ruins of the Communist dream, a new ghost town was being born on the other side of the world, seventeen miles downwind of the Fukushima plant, where the agricultural village of Namie stood denuded of its inhabitants, while cows lowed pitiably in its fields, fields blanched with 30,000 becquerels of radionuclides.

I had seen Modernist ruins before – and yet nothing was comparable to Pripyat, this was the coruscating jewel of Chernobyl's Zone of Alienation. True, the radiation levels here were now a fraction of what they had been in the days and weeks following the accident; however, on the drive from Chernobyl town – where at the government bureau our documentation had been finalised by a female dragon in bifocals straight out of some Lubyanka of the mind – we had stopped, briefly, within three hundred yards of the so-called Sarcophagus, the humungous concrete container that 300,000 workers had laboured to erect over Reactor No.4 in the months after 26 April 1986, when the pile within was still belching out alpha, beta and gamma particles. Standing on a neatly clipped verge, beside a ham-fisted monument – a miniature power station held in the palm of a giant hand – Dennis had chatted in a desultory way about his work: shifts of sixteen days on and then off to avoid contamination. In his late twenties, he too was a child of Chernobyl – his mother had been a guide before him, his father had worked at the power plant after the disaster, and they had lived in the town of Slavutych, which was built thirty miles away to replace Pripyat.

I might have found Dennis's *dégagé* manner more difficult to understand, had I not dined the previous evening, in Kiev, with the writer and academic Oksana Zabuzhko, who's the nearest thing Ukraine has to a literary superstar. Zabuzhko, whose novel *Fieldwork in Ukrainian Sex* was a bestseller in her native country – and has been translated into eight languages – has a formidable reputation as the doyenne of what was, effectively, Ukraine's first feminist wave, and the cynosure of its 'Post-Chernobyl' generation of writers. A fierce patriot, she had arranged to meet in a Ukrainian-themed restaurant near to my hotel – which in turn was a short distance from St Sofia Cathedral with its signature golden onion domes. Arriving with photographer Lesya Malskaya; translator Irina Zaytseva; and a third young woman – the writer, Julia Kadenko, who had brokered our summit – Zabuzhko eyed me sceptically, and when I told her I was writing for *Playboy* her gaze narrowed, as if she was thinking: Ha! With his entourage of young native women he is Western male chauvinist *Playboy* incarnate.

However, as we were served with honey mead and baked river perch by waitresses in cod-Cossack dress, Zabuzhko unbent enough to set me straight in her steely accented but exact English. It was said, I remarked, that the Chernobyl disaster marked the beginning of the end for the Soviet Union. 'In psychological terms,' she told me, 'the experience was unique and insurmountable . . . it *was* the real collapse of the Soviet Union, the remaining five years were just a technical matter . . . The essence of the

Soviet power was that the country was living in lethargy, and the reason for the lethargy was fear – Chernobyl killed the fear, because here was another fear much stronger than any provided by the KGB. And for the first time people saw the authorities – these people who were all-knowing and behaving like gods – for the first time they saw them as miserable, helpless, extremely ignorant and arrogant people not giving a damn about human lives.'

Zabuzhko recalled one such all-knowing authority, a physicist from the Soviet Academy, being interviewed on TV once the disaster had been partially admitted to. 'He said, "Science calls for victims – it demands sacrifice."' It had been an unnaturally warm spring in Kiev, and as May came the air was dense with blossom – everywhere the city's celebrated chestnut trees were in flower. The May Day parades were allowed to go ahead – science was offered its victims. The young Zabuzhko, who was teaching while studying for her doctorate, saw bizarre drifts of bees lying dead on the windowsills of her apartment block – then there was an apocalyptic cloud that split the sky in two, next an unseasonable snow shower. She assumes, now, these were side-effects of the seeding of clouds by the Soviet air force, in order that contaminated rain would fall away from urban centres. All that month she and her friends stayed shut up inside: 'We were trying to move in the streets as little as possible.' They drank red wine – like Lesya in Vladimir – because someone had said this would act as a prophylactic against the radiation, but even so: 'For 29 days *exactly* we spoke like the old miners, with these rasping voices – because of the iodine.'

Zabuzhko was referring to radioactive iodine-131, absorbed by the human thyroid gland. The Soviet authorities were blamed for not providing the affected population with ordinary iodine, which would've prevented the absorption of the radioactive isotope, and to date, the only cancers proven to have been caused by the disaster – among those not directly involved in the Chernobyl clear-up – have been of the thyroid, and readily treatable. This being noted, there is nothing more contentious than these epidemiological statistics, with a wild disparity between the highest estimates of Chernobyl-caused fatalities – in the hundreds of thousands – and the lowest, which put the human cost, to date, at less than 150 lives.

As I spoke with Oksana Zabuzhko it started to impinge on me that my ideas about how Ukraine had reacted psychically to Chernobyl were well wide of the mark – my very Western notions of a fizzing anxiety that haloes nuclear power, hadn't been operative here. 'This was never a concern with us,' Zabuzhko said. 'It's the primary concern for people who grew up in the atmosphere of public discussion . . . there was no public discussion in the Soviet Union, it was a Byzantine empire.' To be so preoccupied had been – and remained even now – a luxury that couldn't be afforded. After all, nuclear power had continued to be generated at Chernobyl until 2000 when the last reactor on the site was shut down. And just as the reaction to Chernobyl was a political rather than an environmental one, so my desire to visit the scene of this tragedy was dismissed by Oksana as 'some kind of voyeurism'; she herself had never felt the need to go.

But this remains a story about time – and timing. And while I may still be sitting in the themed Ukrainian restaurant, watching its *patron* flick his Taras Bulba-style forelock back and forth over his shaved pate while Oksana Zabuzhko straightens me out, I'm also still standing in that stairwell at Kindergarten No.7. Standing there watching time as it grows fungus-like in the dank atmosphere . . . From some corner of my mind floats the fact that mushrooms – whose rhizomes can spread in thin filaments through miles of earth – have some of the highest concentrations of contamination found in the Zone of Alienation, a bitter irony for the Ukrainians who, like their Russian cousins, love mushrooming above all other country pursuits. As for the rampant wildlife of the Zone – the wolves, the wild boar, the lynxes and reintroduced Przewalski horses – well, in an area twice as big as Rhode Island it would take more than a couple of days to run them to ground. Instead there was birdsong of a strength and intensity only heard – one imagines – before the Industrial Revolution.

Leaving the Sarcophagus behind, Dennis had stopped the car on an inconspicuous bridge over a railway and explained that this was known as 'the Bridge of Death', partly because when the rescue workers arrived during the night of 26 April 1986, it was across this that the maimed and the wounded were being carried – but also because it remained one of the most contaminated areas of the Zone. Donning cheap sneakers provided by Dennis so that we wouldn't have our own shoes impounded on leaving the Zone, Lesya and I scrambled down the embankment to the tracks. Dennis showed me the dosimeter he carried – it registered twenty microsieverts per hour – he smiled sardonically, and said 'I guessed that,' as if he were gifting the decadent Westerner the jolt he'd paid for. It wasn't *that big* a jolt – about the same as receiving a chest X-ray, if, that is, we'd stuck around for a couple of hours – but the confirmation of its presence was enough to tint the perfectly ordinary scene – the overgrown railway line and the stacks of ties wreathed with weeds – with the same numinous tint you see in photos of the railways that terminated in the Nazis' death camps: the banal coloration of evil. Hitler understood about time. Following a trip to Rome in 1938 he promulgated an order known as the *Theorie vom Ruinenwert*. Henceforth, all Nazi buildings were to be of marble, stone and brick alone – steel and ferro-concrete were too perishable – so that even if the 1,000-year Reich were to fall, evidence of its mightiness would remain.

Back in Kiev, Dr Yuri Saienko had presented me with his statistics. He sent out exhaustive questionnaires to the Chernobyl displaced as often as he could – money for social science research was, unsurprisingly, in short supply. The results were in some ways predictable – in others wildly counter-intuitive. As, over the years, people's fear of another nuclear accident had declined, so their anxiety about that staple Ukrainian disaster – famine – had increased. In the last set of results Dr Saienko had tabulated – those for 2010 – his sample feared hunger twice as much as radiation. And why wouldn't they? The famine during the Russian civil war, then the still more devastating genocide inflicted by Stalin on Ukraine through forced collectivisation – these were deep scars on the collective memory. Then there were the Nazis. Babi Yar is a suburb of Kiev – a hecatomb that's a subway ride away. Chernobyl itself was marked by death before the reactor blew. At the tip of one of the trails of maximum contamination that extend westward from the doomed reactor like fingers warding off the evil eye, lies Buriakivka, the site of a wartime mass grave of Soviet soldiers; it's here that the corpses of vehicles used in the Chernobyl clean-up were also interred – dumpsters, earthmovers and lead-sheeted armoured personnel carriers rusting behind barbed wire. And elsewhere in the Zone are other mass graves of Jews killed by the Nazis' *einsatzgruppen* during the 1941 invasion, graves that in places abut the contaminated villages buried by these same dumpsters after the disaster. In Ukraine, death has a geological stratigraphy.

Time drips in the stairwell – it's been raining outside and I can hear the drops that have percolated through the warped joists and cracked concrete falling on the debris strewn throughout the nursery school. Rain falling inside a building was the signature motif of the great Russian film director Andrei Tarkovsky; he used it again and again in his movies to symbolise the inexorability of time, its erosion of all human aspirations – whether noble or pathetic. Before leaving for Ukraine I had sat up late one night watching again Tarkovsky's *Stalker*, an adaptation of the Strugatsky brothers' classic science fiction novel *Roadside Picnic*. The book was written in 1971, but was refused publication in the Soviet Union in its original form – only versions bowdlerised by the censor appeared in Russian for many years, and the first unexpurgated edition was published in English, in the US in 1977. *Stalker*, the credits of which list the Strugatskys as joint screenwriters, was released in 1979; both works, of course, antedate the Chernobyl disaster by several years, yet both uncannily prefigure the particular ambience of the Zone of Alienation, with its Modernist ruins and perimeter fence manned by armed and uniformed guards.

In *Roadside Picnic* we are told that the zone was caused by an alien visitation – but *Stalker* is utterly opaque; all the viewer discovers is that the stalker of the title is a man others pay to lead them into this wilderness of rampant nature and mouldering concrete, lead them in search of a mysterious room where their innermost wishes will come true. Lesya, as became a good child of the Soviet intelligent-sia, had told me she had seen *Stalker* 'at least twenty times' – I couldn't claim that level of immersion in Tarkovsky's water-world, but my recent late-night communion with the movie had certainly been the right entrée to Pripyat's warped time zone. Particularly uncanny was the moment when the party of three – known only as the Stalker, the Writer, and the Scientist – are on the brink of entering the wish-fulfilling room, and a telephone rings. A telephone! The intrusion of the outside world, of functioning technology, to this seemingly illimitable realm of flooded tunnels and rusting machinery is chilling. The Stalker gestures sharply: don't answer it. But after it's stopped ringing, the Scientist picks up the receiver and makes an outgoing call. We hear the voice on the end of the line – but we have no idea who it is. The Scientist says he is in 'the old building, Bunker Four . . .'

Bunker Four where wishes are fulfilled – Reactor No.4 where nightmares came true. You would need to be a lot less credulous a writer than me not to feel that prescience was involved here . . . And now, turning away from Doctor Ouch-Hurts's floating clinic, I crunch into a large room where there seems a disturbing artfulness to the destruction – a child-size gas mask is arranged by a picture of Lenin just so, a rotten doll is propped up in a pedal car, a plastic duck on wheels has been manoeuvred into an escape lane of fallen plaster chunks – and there, on the filthy wall, is a spray-painted graffito of a flung bolt trailing a length of cloth: the Stalker's way finder – his equivalent of Dennis's radiation dosimeter. This is the method he uses in the movie to move through the zone, chucking it ahead of the party to check for invisible and unearthly mantraps.

Does it matter, I wonder, that others so precisely like me have been here before? Does it matter that Pripyat is a palimpsest that has been worked over with these troubling cultural references? No, of course not, the idea that anyone can approach ruins de novo is absurd – even Modernist ones. And besides, Chernobyl cries out for such mysticism – demands it, even. The very word '*chornobyl*' means 'wormwood' in Ukrainian and the herb of the same name grows in great profusion throughout the Zone of Alienation. That the star called Wormwood is, in the Book of Revelation, the harbinger of the sinful world's imminent destruction was lost on no one at the time of the disaster. The biblical quotation has even been posted by the door of the small museum of the disaster just opened in the town of Chernobyl, a door that takes the chilling form of the whole-body Geiger counter you must pass through in order to enter and leave the thirty-kilometre Zone.

Still, the amount of radiation visitors to the Zone receive is negligible – between 0.03 and 0.2 microsieverts for the duration of a stay – it's said that you sop up more flying from London to Kiev. Even sleeping the night in the government's hostel in Chernobyl, as we did, is no big deal. After all, we were only spending a couple of days in the Zone – some people remained there, at least in spirit, for their entire lives. People like Anatoly, who, the previous evening, we had met at his painfully neat apartment in Kiev, his district a Brutalist wasteland of Soviet-era blocks on the eastern bank of the Dnieper. A fit-looking man in his mid-fifties with iron-filing hair, Anatoly led us into a plain white room dominated by enormous stereo speakers and a shrub-choked balcony, then made us coffee. When the coffee arrived he got out a bottle of cognac and offered us a tot: 'I have low blood pressure,' he explained through Irina, 'and this helps.'

I declined, but Irina and Lesya obliged. Clearly, Anatoly was an emotional man – he got out a neatly compiled dossier of government documents in order to support what he was about to tell us, then asked for my reassurance that it would be helpful – I said: just tell us. And so he told us about the six and a half days that had dominated his entire life, days that began on the evening of 28 April 1986 when he was visited by an army captain and a policeman who informed him that martial law had been declared and he was being conscripted into a special formation bound for Chernobyl. So Anatoly became one of the so-called 'liquidators', part of the first batch of 350 who were installed by hastily erected helipads on the banks of the Pripyat river a couple of miles from Reactor No.4. Here, as the reactor continued to belch out contamination, he and his comrades had laboured to fill parachutes full of sand, dolomite and lead ingots, so these could be dropped by helicopters onto the pile to damp it down.

'We had no tents,' he said, 'we slept on the bare ground and worked for sixteen hours a day breathing in the dust whipped up by the helicopters. The first couple of days there was no food – but anyway, our commanders had told us we would not be coming back alive.' As he spoke, even through the medium of a translator, I could tell that there was no bitterness in Anatoly. True, after he had collapsed on the seventh day, the authorities marked on his discharge card that he had only been exposed to 20 roentgens of radiation – because this was the maximum allowable; true, he had received medical follow-up for only a few years after the disaster; true, he had never worked again, while his pension – especially now that inflation was rampant in Ukraine – was inadequate; true, of the 700 first-wave liquidators that he knew of, only 93 were still alive; true, his best friend, Sasha, had died of cancer only the previous week – yet, when I put it to him that he couldn't be certain that all these deaths were caused by Chernobyl he readily concurred. And when I raised the spectre of Fukushima, Anatoly shuddered with sympathy then said: 'If it happened here again and they called me, I would go.'

A chill wind soughs through the symbol of the hated regime. I'm up on top of a sixteen-storey block in Pripyat, hanging on to a scaffolding of rusting steel that holds aloft a massive hammer and sickle. Lesya is on top of this, her camera whirring away as she captures the desolate scene: the pines, spruces and birches infiltrating the streets and squares of the empty city. In the mid-distance crouches the Sarcophagus; a crane's arm dallies over the building site beside it and an ominous clanking bash resonates rhythmically – over there another, still bigger, concrete container is being built; and so it will have to go on, container containing container, like a monumental matryoshka doll for all the millennia that the ghost of Reactor No.4 continues to haunt us – if, that is, we're still around to be haunted.

I'm up on top of the block, but naturally, I also remain standing in the stairwell of Kindergarten No.7, transfixed by time – and timing. As my British Airways flight to Kiev took off from Heathrow Airport outside London and headed east, I looked down through pellucid air on a land that over the decades has become legible to me from 20,000 feet. Where, I wondered, would we be crossing the east coast of England? Then I saw it, the stark white dome of the Sizewell B nuclear power plant, which sits on the shore a few miles north of the Suffolk coastal town of Aldeburgh. I had lived near Sizewell for a couple of years in the mid-1990s, and on summer days I would drive there then walk along the beach to swim in the artificial marine micro-climate created by seawater used to cool the reactor. Floating on my back in the choppy waters I would look back, awed by the massive reactor building, its childlike geometry of white dome and iridescent blue plinth.

Fission is the most mysterious of processes, an ineffable moment when a particle is also a wave. The decay of radioactive isotopes is measured in half-life – the average time it takes half the material to decay – because it can only be apprehended statistically, no given particle can ever be fixed or located. No wonder nuclear energy has always inspired such a fierce awe in humans, whose time on this earth is so definitively circumscribed. I had set out for Ukraine hoping for what, an answer to the question of the safety of nuclear power? I hardly think so. The Japanese government may have announced the closure of one plant in the wake of the tsunami, and a slow-down on their nuclear programme, but other countries will do what they do regardless. No, it was always about time for me, holding the small measure of my own life against these vast half-ones. And in this respect, the stairwell of Kindergarten No.7 hadn't let me down – this room had granted my innermost wish and made time visible. I'm standing there still – and perhaps I always will be.

2011
Playboy

Kafka's Wound

I am guilty of an association of ideas; or rather: I am guilty – that's a given, and in casting about for the source of my guilt I find I cannot prevent myself from linking one idea with another purely on the basis of their contiguity, in time, in place, in my own mind. It's not only ideas I connect like this, I do it with images, sensory impressions and the most epiphenomenal of mental glitches. Hume writes in his *An Enquiry Concerning Human Understanding* that the imagination is best conceived of as a combinatorial faculty: there is nothing intrinsically imaginative about the idea of 'gold', nor the idea of 'mountain', but join them together and you have a fantastically gleaming 'gold mountain'. And might not that gold mountain be the Laurenziberg in Prague? After all, it looms over the contemporary city – under its Czech-language moniker, the Petřín – just as it loomed in the consciousness of Franz Kafka, whose earliest surviving narrative fragment, 'Description of a Struggle', is in part an account of a phantasmagorical ascent of its slopes: 'But now the cool light which precedes the rising of the moon spread over the mountain and suddenly the moon itself appeared from beyond one of the restless bushes. I on the other hand had meanwhile been gazing in another direction, and when I now looked ahead of me and suddenly saw it glowing in its almost full roundness, I stood still with troubled eyes, for my precipitous road seemed to lead straight into this terrifying moon.'

Written during the winter of 1903–4, by a young man of 19, the story postdates by only a few years the intimations concerning his life ambitions that Kafka had had as a schoolboy – also on the slopes of the Laurenziberg – and which he set down in a 1920 letter to his Czech inamorata Milena Jesenská: 'The most important or charming was the wish to achieve a view of life (and – this was necessarily bound up with it – to convince other people of it in writing), in which life maintained its natural heavy rise and fall, but at the same time would be recognised, no less clearly, as a void, a dream, a floating.' The adult Kafka – the Kafka vermiculated by tubercular bacilli after having been played on for decades, as a demonic organist might press fleshy keys and pull bony stops, by his own relentless neurasthenia – reached a mystical appreciation of his youthful velleity, characterising it as a desire both to expertly hammer together a table and at the same time 'do nothing'. The inanition would validate the craftsmanship involved, freeing it to become 'even bolder, even more resolute, even more real and, if you like, even more insane'. I too have wished for this Dionysian timpani. I too have appreciated that nothing comes of nothing. While for the avuncular Kafka, patting the shoulder of his younger self, it was self-evident that 'his wish was not a wish, it was only a defence, an embourgeoisement of nothing'.

After a night's dreamless sleep in a conifer wood, the narrator of 'Description of a Struggle' encounters an obese and litter-borne Buddha-like figure whose 'face bore the artless expression of a man who meditates and makes no effort to conceal it' – an uncharacteristically taut one-liner for Kafka; he soon put paid to such callow excesses. The holy man inveighs against the Laurenziberg: 'Mountain, I do not love you, for you remind me of the clouds, of the sunset, of the rising sky, and these are things that almost make me cry because one can never reach them while being carried on a small litter. But when showing me this, sly mountain, you block the distant view which gladdens me, for it reveals the attainable at a glance. That's why I do not love you, mountain by the water – no, I do not love you.' As if the mundane urban hillock were golden, it takes on these elemental characteristics: vaporous, gaseous, luminescent. But even as a dross of medieval masonry and Renaissance stucco – the Hunger Wall, the Strahov Monastery, the Hradčany Castle – it still represents a rigid piece of stage dressing, occluding what for Kafka, until the last few months of his active life, would always remain unattainable: the world beyond Prague.

I am guilty of an association of these ideas: on the turn of the year between 1916 and 1917, Kafka wrote to his on–off fiancée Felice Bauer, 'You are acquainted with my two years of suffering, insignificant compared to the world's suffering

during that period, but bad enough for me.'* Like an opio-
mane in a Wilkie Collins novel, for Kafka the least sound
was an exquisite torture. So, despite the pleasant modern
rooms afforded him by his parents' new apartment at the
Sign of the Golden Pike (from the window he had a good
view of the golden Laurenziberg), Kafka was tormented by
the neighbours' maid hanging up their washing in the attic
space above his head, whereupon she would, 'quite inno-
cently, put the heel of her boot through my skull'. Much of
the letter is taken up with Kafka's apartment hunting: 'A
vast subject. It scares me; I won't be able to cope with it.
Too much for me. I can't describe more than a thousandth
part of it in writing.' But he breaks off from this kvetching
to hymn the diminutive house that has been lent to him
by his youngest and favourite sister, Ottla, as a writing
bolthole: 'Today it suits me perfectly. In every respect: the
pleasant walk up to the house, the silence; only a very thin
wall separates me from a neighbour, but the neighbour is
quiet enough; I take my evening meal up there, and usually
remain there until midnight; and then the advantage of the
walk home; I have to remind myself to stop, then I have
the walk to cool my head.' That winter was particularly

---

* A copy or draft of this letter was found in Kafka's papers after his
death and then published by the indefatigable Max Brod. We do not
know whether Felice Bauer ever received it. If not, there may have been
a considerable hiatus between the terminal self-laceration of a letter
dated 20 December 1916 ('My life is monotonous and proceeds within
the prison of my innate, as it were threefold, misfortune') and one dated
9 September 1917, in which he announces 'four weeks ago, at about
5 a.m., I had a haemorrhage of the lung. Fairly severe, for ten minutes
or more it gushed out of my throat; I thought it would never stop.'

chilling; but in the little house, 22 Golden Lane (also known as Alchimistengasse, 'the Alchemists' Street'), Kafka was experiencing the frictional heat of his combinatorial powers. Between December 1916 and the next April – with the exception of the fragmentary 'Guardian of the Tomb' – he wrote all the short prose fictions that were published during his lifetime. Among them were: 'Jackals and Arabs', 'The Great Wall of China' (inspired, perhaps, by the nearby Hunger Wall), 'Report to an Academy', 'The Hunter Gracchus', and the superficially more coherent – more finished, more enclosed in narrative circularity – 'A Country Doctor'.

In 1916 the German equivalent of the pyrrhic victory, *'sich zu Tode siegen'* ('to commit suicide by winning'), entered the language. The Russians' Brusilov offensive was finally halted in October, but it shattered the Austrian armies on the Eastern Front. More than 350,000 soldiers had been captured, and total casualties have been estimated at as high as a million men. Eight divisions of the Austro-Hungarian forces were Czech.** The Austro-Hungarian Army Handbook issued by the British War Office in 1918 gives the acute perspective of an enemy: the Czech troops are described as 'united in their opposition to the Western Bohemian Germans', who themselves are characterised as anti-Slav, 'vigorous and unpleasant'. The Czechs are 'intensely nationalistic, energetic and forceful' but also

---

** 97 per cent of Czechs were literate – on a par with figures for Britain at the time. This made these armies the most literate ever to be fielded. A diarist on the Western Front recorded the atmosphere of concentration in a BEF dugout where all the officers and men were reading, most of them various novels by Joseph Conrad.

'poor fighters who are generally willing to surrender unless their resolve is stiffened by a large proportion of Teutonic officers and NCOs'. In April 1915 the 28th (Prague) regiment deserted in its entirety, going over to the *druzhina* (or 'retinue') battalion that had been raised from among the 70,000 Czechoslovaks living within the Russian empire. The *druzhina* targeted their countrymen, who often came to meet them waving white flags and singing the anthem of the pan-Slavic movement, *Hej Sloveni*. In May 1915 the 8th regiment deserted, and during the Brusilov offensive two more Czech regiments went over to the Russians. These men went on to form the core of the Czech Legion, which after the war became the basis of the new state's national army. But in 1916 the officer corps of the Czech divisions of the Austro-Hungarian army still represented the ethnic and linguistic tensions of Kafka's Prague. While the Jewish population of the Dual Monarchy was only about 5 per cent, Jews made up almost 18 per cent of the reserve officer corps, and one of those reservists was Kafka.

It has been characteristic of the Kafka industry not so much to neglect the social, cultural, political and historical dimensions of the writer's life but to sideline them, except insofar as they contribute to one or other paradigmatic view of the writer. Even a biography as nuanced as Ernst Pawel's *The Nightmare of Reason* foregrounds the headaches, the agonising over the *mésalliance* with Felice Bauer, the office grind and the strident cheeping of the Modernist cuckoo still – at this time in his early thirties – occupying the patriarchal nest. The commonplace problem of taking a writer at his own word(s) always seems compounded in the case of Kafka by the queered provenance of those words: the unfinished novels and unpublished stories, the copious journals saved from oblivion by Brod;* and the letters to Felice Bauer and Milena Jesenská that surfaced in the years after the writer's death. These are taken to form the purlieu of Kafka's citadel of consciousness, on the basis of his perceived ability to cast a dark shadow forward over the middle decades of the 20th century. The canard is in part that of his genius being constituent of our climate quite as much as making its own weather, and in part that of a refusal to allow a writer whose vowels howl out towards the universal – through the purgation of the particular, the specific and their psychic consonants – to exist within a matrix of ephemera: a member of a German-speaking Jewish minority within a German-speaking minority within a Czech minority within the turbidly disintegrating Austro-Hungarian empire.

But I am guilty of an association of ideas: that winter, Prague, already supporting a large refugee population of *Ostjuden* fleeing the 1914 advances of the Russian army into Galicia, was further swamped by wounded and shell-shocked troops returning from the Eastern Front, and a series of defensive battles against the Italians along the Isonzo River. Fuel and food supplies ran low, with each of the city's moieties

---

* Benjamin's concluding remark in his essay 'Max Brod's Book on Kafka', that Kafka's 'friendship with Brod is to me primarily a question mark which he chose to put in the margin of his life', says nothing at all about Kafka – let alone Brod – and everything about Benjamin's own weird jealousy.

accusing the other of hoarding. Even the well-to-do Kafkas were subject to privation, and Kafka's mother wrote to Felice Bauer's mother in the New Year that at Yom Kippur: 'The fasting came easy, since we've been in training for it all year.' Her etiolated and vegetarian son was always match-fit for privation, but while many commentators have seized upon Kafka's journal entry of 6 August 1914 as confirmation of his disengagement from the European Götterdämmerung: 'I discover in myself nothing but pettiness, indecision, envy, and hatred against those who are fighting and whom I passionately wish everything evil.' I am minded to look to the words he wrote in the tiny house in the lee of the Hradčany Castle, and in particular to his description of the wound the eponymous narrator of 'A Country Doctor' finds in 'the right flank' of his young patient, a wound described with a combination of forensic precision and lubricious eroticism: 'at around hip-height, he has a fresh wound as big as my hand. Pink, in many shades, a deep carmine at the centre, lightening towards the periphery, with a soft granular texture, the bleeding at irregular points, and the whole thing as gapingly obvious as a mineshaft.'

If anything is gapingly obvious, it's associative thinking, unless, that is, like Kafka (and myself), you have come to suspect still more the metaphor's detachment from, and modification of, its metaphrand. The fugitive quality of Kafka's seeming metaphors, which, in common with the directives of the Castle's inexorable bureaucracy, are 'as shy as young girls', must derive in part, as one of his translators, Joyce Crick, has observed, from the near obsolescence

of the subjunctive in contemporary English. In Kafka's
German it is omnipresent: it always seems to be the case that
such-and-such was, which is by no means the same as the
wooden modality of 'would', let alone the bedevilling similitude implied by 'as if' and its sluttish coeval 'like'. And yet,
when, in Michael Hofmann's 2006 translation of 'A Country
Doctor' I read this description of the wound, it was as if a
light had gone on in my mind. I was writing an introduction
to the Folio Society's edition of *Metamorphosis and Other
Stories* (which includes 'A Country Doctor'), I had returned
to these texts with a heavy sigh; occluding my view was the
Laurenziberg-sized heap of objections to Kafka in translation piled up by Milan Kundera in his essay 'A Sentence'.
Kundera was writing about translations from German into
French, but his remarks on the willed sparseness of Kafka's
vocabulary, its precise employment of repetition, and the
rhythmic flow of this prose – achieved by pruning articula-
tions to the bare minimum – which in itself constitutes an
untranslatable and unique violation of 'good German style',
seemed to me, a non-German reader, unassailable barriers to
a proper appreciation of Kafka in any translation. Then there
were Hofmann's own more nuanced remarks on Kafka's
style: on the significance of the little words rather than the
big, on the expressiveness of German word order – contra
English – and how the punctilious encoding of these semantic
bytes allowed the prose to become 'drily controlling'. He also
observes that translating Kafka is difficult because '(he) has
already translated himself' from the Prague German which
Hofmann quotes Klaus Wagenbach characterising as 'dry and

papery . . . incapable of conveying the unhesitating intimacy and immediacy of ordinary or dialect German speech'. This would account for the otherworldliness of Kafka's prose, for its strange penumbra of ultra-realism, which imparts a sense of fidelity to the commonplace it simultaneously undermines. But there are contrary views of this: others speak of Prague German as a chewy dialect, leavened with Czech and Yiddish loan words, a sort of strange 'mockney' (*Mauscheln*), spoken by a derided commercial elite aping their own helots.

Whichever the case: it was all up with me. Nine months of relatively fruitless French lessons had recently convinced me that, bar scanning headlines in *Le Monde* and ordering food, I would always remain a miserable monoglot; and so I resolved to write the introduction, and then descant no more on the properties of texts written in languages I don't understand. I might read translations of foreign-language works for the associations of ideas they provoked in me, but I could no longer convince myself that I understood the writer's own associative faculty as it was instantiated in his or her prose.*

* One of those most troubling aspects of reading Kafka in English, for me, was the extent to which German speakers – and in particular his peers – seemed to find his work funny. Brod writes of Kafka reading the opening sections of *The Trial* aloud to him and a group of their friends, and the writer corpsing himself as the others also doubled up. Personally, I've never found Kafka particularly funny at all – except in a bleakly absurd vein – and I convened a City University meeting of Kafka translators, in part, to try and get to the bottom of this humorousness in German. Anthea Bell and Joyce Crick were enlightening about many things – but on the matter of humour, I found them unconvincing, speaking as they did of the amusement implicit in the shift between '"Will you save me?" the boy whimpers, dazzled by the life in his wound' and 'That's the way people are in this parish. Always demanding the impossible from their doctor.' More helpful was an Englishman who approached

Then came the wound. 'Metamorphosis' was the text that I thought of as the beacon lighting the way into my own crepuscular fictional realm: 'One morning, when Gregor Samsa awoke from troubled dreams, he found himself transformed in his bed into a horrible vermin.'** This was all it had taken – or so I romanticised – to show me, at age 16, the reality-transforming powers of narrative prose. There was no need of chemical aids or technical inventions: a few simple words could usher you into a world mutated out of this one; all it required was your assent.

I had been reading read Paul Fussell's *The Great War and Modern Memory*. I found his thesis beguiling: In the contrast between the jinglingly innocent jingoism of the Great Powers' armies as they trotted off to a short war, confident

me after the session and said that after having lived for many years in Germany, he came to understand how formal even humour was for the Germans, sometimes even announcing itself thus: 'I am going to tell a joke now, and you are going to laugh.' In his view, Kafka's humour derives from his undermining of these situational cues: the joke, like the country doctor, or the lad's wound, comes out of nowhere.

** With my limited faculties I nonetheless dissent here from Michael Hofmann's translation – which employs 'cockroach' – and turn to that of David Wylie offered by Project Gutenberg. Kafka employs the term '*Ungeziefer*', itself an intensified – by the prefix '*un-*' (which he uses no less than three times in this sentence) – form of '*Geziefer*', or 'vermin'. I agree with those who argue that the lack of specificity is important to our ability to suspend disbelief in Gregor's transmogrification, although I wouldn't go as far as Nabokov, who argued that Kafka's very precise description deliberately failed to correspond to any known insect. But certainly a more likely candidate than a cockroach for Gregor's invertebrate counterpart would be a bedbug. Its morphology corresponds more closely to Kafka's account, and besides, this would have been the vermin he was most exposed to: he was tormented by them during the night he spent at the Askanischer Hof Hotel in Berlin, after the dreadful 'trial' to which he had been subjected by Felice Bauer that ended their first engagement.

in August 1914 that it would all be over by Christmas, and the subsequent assembly lines of death that snaked their way across Europe* lay the very crucible of modern irony. Indeed, this grandly horrific reversal, from evanescent hope to intransigent despair, was for Fussell a sort of irony factory. He adduces many examples to support his thesis, but the one that reared up from the page at me was the climactic scene from Joseph Heller's *Catch-22*, in which the protagonist Yossarian attempts to succour the wounded gunner Snowden, who's been hit by flak during a bombing mission. Heller first describes Snowden's wound thus: 'the *wrong* wound [my italics], the yawning, raw, melon-shaped hole as big as a football in the outside of his thigh, the unsevered, blood-soaked muscle fibers inside pulsing weirdly like blind things with lives of their own, the oval, naked wound that was almost a foot long and made Yossarian moan in shock and sympathy the instant he spied it and nearly made him vomit.'

We have already had this episode with Snowden implanted in our minds far earlier in the novel, but in the closing pages of *Catch-22* both reader and protagonist are thrust into its full, gory revelation. Yossarian, lying in the night-time darkness of the hospital where he has taken refuge, is unable any longer to repress the memory: 'The wound Yossarian saw was in the outside of Snowden's thigh, as large and deep as a football, it seemed. It was impossible to tell where the shreds of his saturated coveralls ended and the ragged flesh

* Fussell concentrates particularly on the terrible stasis of the Western Front, but it seems to me that his thesis is also applicable to the more mobile Eastern Front.

began.' After he discovers that the morphine has been stolen from the first-aid kit, Yossarian gains control: 'His mind was clear now, and he knew how to proceed. He rummaged through the first-aid kit for scissors.'

Yossarian cuts away Snowden's clothing, and although 'stunned at how waxen and ghastly Snowden's bare leg looked, how loathsome, how lifeless and esoteric the downy, fine, curled blond hairs on his odd, white shin and calf,' he is nonetheless heartened by this: 'The wound, he saw now, was not nearly as large as a football, but as long and wide as his hand and too raw and deep to see into clearly. The raw muscles inside twitched like live hamburger meat.' That the unit of comparison should be a football – with all the apple pie resonance of high school sports – is given still more ironic intensification by the metaphoric 'live hamburger meat'. Having applied a tourniquet and sprinkled copious amounts of sulfanilamide**

** The so-called 'sulfa' drugs have a 'bacteriostatic' action – preventing bacteria from multiplying in the host, so permitting the patient's immune system to kill them – and were isolated and tested by Gerhard Domagk during his time as research director of the German chemical combine I. G. Farbenindustrie. Domagk was awarded the Nobel Prize in 1939, but prevented by Hitler from receiving it (he did eventually in 1947). By 1941, 1,700 tons of sulfa drugs were given to 10 million Americans. Yossarian's liberality with the 'white crystalline powder' thus reflects a wholesale development in biotherapeutics at this time: penicillin and other antibiotics were being simultaneously produced by British drug companies, and by D-Day would be available in unlimited quantities to treat battlefield wounds. The irony of the 20th century's medical advances is, as ever, given the darkest shading by the experiments of the Nazi doctors, who, in Ravensbrück concentration camp between 1942 and 1943, deliberately wounded inmates, then infected these wounds with streptococci, gas gangrene and tetanus, and tied off the blood vessels to simulate the conditions of a battlefield wound, before applying sulfa drugs to determine their effectiveness.

into the wound and also tucked in 'shreds of drying flesh', Yossarian binds it up in a compress.

But the wounded young man carries on whimpering, 'I'm cold. I'm cold,' until 'with just the barest movement of his chin' he points towards his armpit, and Yossarian sees 'a strangely coloured stain seeping through the cover-alls just above the armhole of Snowden's flak suit'. That the grotesque wound in Snowden's thigh is, in fact, the lesser of his injuries, is served up to the reader in two distinct spasms; first when Yossarian rips open his flak suit and screams wildly as, 'Snowden's insides slithered down to the floor in a soggy pile and just kept dripping out.' Then there is a brief hiatus as Yossarian contemplates the mechanics of this second and far worse wound – the result of a three-inch chunk of flak tearing laterally through the young man's thorax – before 'Yossarian screamed a second time and squeezed both hands over his eyes. His teeth were chattering in horror. He forced himself to look again. Here was God's plenty, all right, he thought bitterly as he stared – liver, lungs, kidneys, ribs, stomach and bits of the stewed tomatoes Snowden had eaten that day for lunch. Yossarian hated stewed tomatoes and turned away dizzily and began to vomit, clutching his burning throat.'

To return to Kafka's wound, which we left boring into the page 'as gapingly obvious as a mineshaft', we then learn that, from the country doctor's perspective, this was only the case: 'From a distance, at any rate. Closer to, there's a further complication. Who could take in such a thing without whistling softly? Worms, the length and thickness of my little finger, roseate and also coated with blood, are writhing against the inside of the wound, with little white heads, and many many little legs. Poor boy, it's not going to be possible to help you. I have found your great wound; the flower in your side is going to finish you.' You don't need to be that guilty of the promiscuous association of ideas to discover unnerving parallels here between these roseate worms 'writhing against the inside of the wound, with little white heads,' and 'the unsevered, blood-soaked muscle fibers inside [Snowden's wound] pulsing weirdly like blind things with lives of their own.' Especially since Heller offers a wormy image of his own: 'The raw muscles inside twitched like live hamburger meat.'

In Kafka's story, the patient, like Snowden, is preternaturally aware of his own mortal condition: 'the lad pulls himself up in his bed, drapes his arms round my neck and whispers into my ear: "Doctor, let me die."' And the practitioner shares Yossarian's numbed confidence, and when compelled by the lad's relatives to make an examination finds, 'I am confirmed in what I thought already: the boy is perfectly healthy, his circulation a little sluggish, plied with coffee by his anxious mother, but basically healthy and needing nothing more than a good kick to get him out of bed.' In both narratives a mounting ironic tension is effected between an optimistic healer and a fatalistic patient, a tension that finds a sort of anti-catharsis – confirmatory, but with wholly negative psychic consequences – in the revelation of the wounds. Looking for the real-life correlate to Kafka's wound, many commentators go to his journal entries of December 1911, where, recounting his nephew's circumcision, Kafka writes: 'One sees blood and raw flesh, the *moule* bustles about briefly with his long-nailed, trembling fingers and pulls skin from some place or other over the wound like the finger of a glove.'* And then goes on to explain the 'dreams or boredom' of those present who listened to the prayers: 'I saw Western European Judaism before me in a transition whose end is clearly unpredictable and about which those most closely affected are not concerned, but, like all people truly in transition, bear what is imposed on them.'

I am not insensible to those analyses and interpretations of 'A Country Doctor' that place the story within a context provided by Hassidic parable and then undercut by Kafka's sceptical engagement with his own Jewishness. To accept this you do not have to go to the extreme represented by Max Brod's remoulding of Kafka as a Jewish saint, nor the one that comes from Kafka's own notorious – and in my view notoriously misinterpreted – notation of 8 January 1914, 'What have I in common with Jews? I have hardly anything in common with myself and should stand very quietly in a corner, content that I can breathe.' But other journal entries from this period suggest a Kafka alive to the new ironies generated by the war. A tense skit

* In this case the baby was held on his grandfather's lap – possibly by the much excoriated (by his sole surviving son) Hermann Kafka – but the only stipulation is that the lap belongs to the closest available Jewish male relative other than the father. I myself have held a nephew prone so that the *moule* can ply his knife, and there's no doubt that the immediate sympathy occasioned by the alignment of genitals places the ceremony foursquare within a psychosexual cradle.

on a 'patriotic parade' witnessed in Prague at the beginning of August sees him inveigh against its organisers: 'Jewish businessmen who are German one day, Czech the next; admit this to themselves, it is true, but were never permitted to shout it out as loudly as they do now.' The deadpan coda is: 'Naturally they carry many others along with them. It was well organised. It is supposed to be repeated every evening, twice tomorrow and Sunday.' Is it fanciful to find an echo of this political observation in the twentieth of the so-called Zürau Aphorisms, composed by Kafka in the winter of 1917–18: 'Leopards break into the temple and drink all the sacrificial vessels dry; it keeps happening; in the end, it can be calculated in advance and is incorporated into the ritual.'

In November 1914 Kafka devotes a journal entry to a Fussellian anecdote told him by his brother-in-law on his return from the front: 'Story about the mole burrowing under him in the trenches which he looked upon as a warning from heaven to leave that spot. He had just got away when a bullet struck a soldier crawling after him at the moment he was over the mole – His Captain. They distinctly saw him taken prisoner. But the next day found him naked in the woods, pierced through by bayonets.' The form of the vignette is of a series of falsely secure surfaces beneath which yawn oubliettes of excavated irony: the captain is shot but survives to be taken prisoner, however, 'the next day found him naked in the woods, pierced through by bayonets. He probably had money on him, they wanted to search him and rob him of it, but he

– "the way officers are" – wouldn't voluntarily submit to being touched.' His death results from social mores rather than mortal threats, and Kafka then digs out still more ironic traps, by relating how his battle-shocked brother-in-law 'met his boss (whom in the past he had admired ridiculously, out of all measure) on the train, elegantly dressed, perfumed, his opera glasses dangling from his neck, on his way to the theatre.'* With slapstick timing Kafka then tells how his brother-in-law slept one night at a castle, a second in front of the Austrian batteries, and a third in an overcrowded peasant cottage. He completes the entry with the laconic observation: 'Punishment given to soldiers. Stand bound to a tree until they turn blue.'

Decocted into these few short lines are all of the magical thinking that Fussell – and many others – identified as the very essence of the miasma that blew across the battlefields of the First World War: the preoccupation with omens, both ill and good; the obsessive linkage of events, objects and persons into numerological strings – often of threes; the profound alienation felt by those at the front from those at home; and of course, the ceaseless ironic reversals signalled by the drum fill of machine gun, rifle and artillery: b'boom-boom-chhhh! There are entries in Kafka's journal that amply confirm a hermetic reading of 'A Country Doctor' – one purely in terms of the author's

---

* A further three ironic pitfalls yawn when Kafka tells us that his brother-in-law: subsequently went to see the play himself; with a ticket provided by his boss; and it was a comedy – *Der ungetreue Eckehart* (*The Unfaithful Eckhart*).

self-generated worldview, which he himself characterised as 'a talent for portraying my dreamlike inner life' – but they depend for their force on the same purgation of the particular, the temporal and the contingent that his prose enacts. Thus, on 16 September 1915 there are three short entries that put forward a dialectic that begins with this thesis: 'The Polish Jews going to Kol Nidre.** The little boy with prayer shawls under both arms, running along at his father's side. Suicidal not to go to temple.' It is followed by a turn in which Kafka, after consulting 'the unjust Judges', concludes: 'I am never visibly guided in such things, the pages of the Bible don't flutter in my presence.' Finally, the somewhat paradoxical resolution comes in the form of a vision of a vision of a suicide – Kafka imagines that 'between throat and chin would seem to be the most rewarding place to stab', but concludes, 'this spot is probably rewarding only in one's imagination. You expect to see a magnificent gush of blood and a network of sinews and little bones like you find in the leg of a roast turkey.'***

The hallucinogenic quality of this image – no one expects a gush of blood when they cut into a fowl, not even Henry Spencer in Lynch's *Eraserhead* – only serves to make of the self-murder a hazily collective one. In 'A Country Doctor', the doctor inveighs against the people of the parish: 'They

** The legalistic Aramaic formula recited at the beginning of Yom Kippur, and which gives its name to this evening service.
*** Kafka's writings – intimate and fictional – are full of wounds and the sharp objects that cause them. Wounds that shape-shift from biblical or torahic punishments to the secularly self-harming.

have lost the old faith; the priest sits around at home, ripping up his altar garments one after another; but the doctor is expected to perform miracles with his delicate surgeon's fingers.' One such miracle might be to suture the gaping wound in traditional religious belief and sew it scientifically up. The patient's family together with the village elders undress him, while a choir of school children sing the words: 'Undress him, and he will heal you, / If he doesn't heal you, kill him! / He's just a doctor, a doctor!' Lain in the bed beside his faithless patient, the two quibble with one another, pained and marital in their unity. The doctor accuses the lad of lacking perspective: 'I, who have been in sickrooms far and wide, tell you: your wound isn't so bad as all that. A couple of glancing blows with an axe. There are many who offer their flanks, and barely hear the axe in the forest, never mind it deigning to come any nearer to them.'

In the harsh midwinter of 1916–17, Kafka ceased to make entries in his journal just as he stopped his epistolatory head-butting at Felice Bauer. Kafka, who favoured literary biography over fiction, perhaps found it possible to free himself from remorseless self-examination only when he was engaged in imagined worlds. But a liberation from providing psychic bulletins doesn't necessarily imply an immunity to the news. 7 November 1916 saw the re-election of Woodrow Wilson and the death of the 85-year-old Emperor of Austria and King of Hungary Franz Josef.* Many Prague Jews feared the

---

* Whose valedictory words, 'I am behindhand with my work,' his namesake would doubtless have appreciated.

worst: the city had been subjected to periodic anti-semitic riots, while only days before, the son of the Austrian socialist leader – himself a Jew – had assassinated the prime minister, Count Stürgkh. In Prague at least, the worst didn't happen, although elsewhere it already had: the 16,000 operational German machine guns on the Western Front and the 16,000 deployed by the Russians on the Eastern Front had spent the entire year ripping up flesh. The battle of the Somme had enacted the most savage single annihilation of human life heretofore: the 50,000 British casualties in the first morning's offensive. The corpses were so densely slumped along the German wire that observers thought they were praying. But arguably it was at Verdun that the most gaping wound was torn. General Falkenhayn's assault on this pocket-sized salient had resulted – by the time it was called off that November – in 800,000 casualties. General Pétain had shovelled men into 'the furnace' as the French called the battle; and although Falkenhayn's own strategy for this obscene attrition – to 'bleed the French army white' – is now viewed as an ex-post facto justification, there's no gainsaying that the experience of Verdun cut the French nation to its cleft centre. It was no longer the France Kafka had known: in September of 1912, on a visit with Brod and his brother to Paris, they had seen *Carmen* at the Opéra Comique and also Racine's *Phèdre*. Kafka had confided to his journal a 'lonely, long, absurd walk home' from a brothel where he noted of the girl offered that her 'clenched fist held her dress together over her pudenda'.

I cannot speak for other writers of fiction, but for myself I can divide my fiction reading between the instrumental, and that vanishingly small category: the rest. I must have read the balance of Kafka's fiction by the time I was 21 – the three unfinished novels in their first translations by Edwin and Willa Muir, 'Metamorphosis' and a fair selection of the shorter pieces and fragments. I read them concerned particularly with technique: how did Kafka achieve suspension of disbelief? How did he suffuse his milieus with the uncanny? How did he impel his narratives forward, while simultaneously applying the brakes?* I was sublimely unconcerned by symbols, themes – meanings, or their context. I read neither the letters to Felice, nor those to Milena; I had no familiarity with Kafka's journals or aphorisms. Over the years I returned to Kafka intermittently, picking up and letting fall texts insofar as they chimed with things I was working on. When I was writing my novel *Great Apes*, I puzzled over the narrator of 'A Report to an Academy', but not to any great purpose. No, my relationship with Kafka took place within the compass of the Kafkaesque.

It's a peculiar apotheosis: the adjectival. It is widely held that the 20th century was Kafkaesque rather than Joycean, let alone Proustian. Kafkaesque, and latterly

* If Kafka's 'Metamorphosis' drew my attention to the mechanics of suspension of disbelief, at around the same time I was breaking *Catch-22* down into its constituent parts – treating Heller's novel as a pattern book for the production of satirical tropes, ploys and manoeuvres: comic exaggeration, deadpan surrealism, bureaucratic parody – it had them all, and in abundance. I barely noticed that it was an antiwar diatribe.

Orwellian, another adjective slapped on to practices, institutions, innovations to evoke the alienating dimension of mass, authoritarian, technologically mediated society. My sense of the rise and fall of the Kafkaesque is that it mirrored the solidification then dissolution of the Soviet bloc. Kafka, characterised relentlessly in the three decades after Yalta as the secular prophet of totalitarianism, lent his name to this catchall, which in turn was deployed by the West against itself. When I was young every instance of bureaucratic arbitrariness, vaguely sinister intent, or paradoxical norms – 'Everything not forbidden is permitted' read a popular 1980s graffito – was deemed 'Kafkaesque'. The reasons for this were, I think, akin to those that explain the ideological floundering of the Western left since 1989: the Kafkaesque, like the utopian socialist, required the lowering presence of the Soviet doppelgänger. For the leftist liberals where I grew up in London it was sufficient – since the Stalinist Terror for some, the Hungarian Uprising for others, and the Prague Spring for virtually all – to believe in what they were not, and would never become: which was the perverse mutation of socialism in the East. It was less pressing to present coherent ideological solutions to the intractable problems of nationalism versus internationalism, or parliamentary gradualism versus revolutionary change. In a similar fashion, to label a minor abuse of power or judicial doublethink 'Kafkaesque' was to indulge in a sort of psychic legerdemain: sneaking a little of the East's oppression for one's own, and so justifying jejune anomie – or, as Kafka himself might have termed it, 'the embourgeoisement of nothing'.

That the world is now girdled by slick and translucent info-panels on which glow all the data you would need to have to confirm the rise and fall – among English speakers and writers – of the Kafkaesque is at once liberating and unpleasantly constricting. Think of the sharp attention the writer himself paid to human gesture and movement. For Kafka the action of any given narrative largely consists in just this: actions, painstakingly described. These, together with his use of montage and the dissolve have been interpreted as his responses to the new medium of cinema, but they seem to me quite as anticipatory of the condition of the contemporary extended mind, smeared from a static – and compulsively gestural – body into a virtual, and frictionless, space. 'Kafkaesque', then, with some minor peaks and troughs, steadily proliferates in English texts after 1945. It would be nice – in the sense of exact – if the data set was precise enough to identify a partial stagnation in the early 1980s, in line with a general *tedium vitae* in the West when it came to the Cold War, or perhaps a sharp peak in the term's use immediately following the fall of the Berlin Wall that would bear out my general contention, but what we can see is a precipitate decline throughout the 2000s. The instances in English texts of the name 'Kafka', on the other hand, display an altogether spikier profile that does indeed seem to mirror wider phenomena in the political and cultural realms.

It was Robert Musil, an early and consistent champion of Kafka's writing, who in *The Man Without Qualities* wrote of asylums for the insane that 'they have something of hell's lack of imagination'. When I visited Theresienstadt, walking out from the tunnel that leads under the ramparts of the Small Fortress, our guide Susannah pointed out the swimming pool the SS concentration camp guards had had built for them and their families to frolic in while a few yards away inmates were being shot or hanged. The Nazis were great *bricoleurs* of the exterminatory – but imagination was not their forte. I'm not the first to observe that the Theresienstadt camp – condensed into its kilometre-square grid pattern of streets lined with 18th-century Italianate buildings – represents the most extreme example of the Nazis' genocidal improvisation; their equivalent of the Wagnerian *Gesamtkunstwerk.** The vast bulk of Prague's Jewish population either died in Theresienstadt, or was deported further east to Auschwitz, Treblinka and other camps to be killed. Among those sent to Auschwitz was Ottla David (née Kafka), who insisted on accompanying a group of orphaned children

---

* The most beautifully entranced of Kafka's successors is W. G. Sebald, who puts the lightly fictionalised 'Dr K' at the centre of *Vertigo* (itself a structural embellishment of Kafka's 'The Hunter Gracchus'); in *Austerlitz*, he places the Theresienstadt concentration camp at the core of both the narrative and a German-inflicted Europe, the memory of which has been repressed by its traumatised protagonist. Working on my novel *Umbrella*, which concerns the aftermath of the *encephalitis lethargica* epidemic that swept Europe at the end of the First World War, I sought to avoid Theresienstadt, but then I discovered that the camp was one of the few places where an outbreak of the unusual disease had been recorded after 1917–18.

who had become attached to her, although there was no necessity that she herself go. The Theresienstadt camp became notorious as an example of the Nazis' monstrous perfidy: specially selected wealthy Jews were encouraged to pay for housing in what was advertised as a sort of garden city resettlement zone. Instead, they were interred in the militarily obsolete fortress-town, in conditions that were a parody of the worst of the old Eastern European ghettos, such as Prague's own Josefov, which before its 1917 demolition was described by one of its own Jewish inhabitants as 'a suppurating ulcer on the face of the Mother of Bohemian towns'.

Was the recapitulation of the ghetto in the Holocaust an instance of irony, or merely coincidence? The jibing and disjunction between texts and the worlds they are born out of always allows for plenty of coincidence: imprisoned in Theresienstadt during the war his assassination had instigated, Gavrilo Princip languished in cell no.1 in the Small Fortress.* He had failed, twice, to commit suicide in the days following his arrest for the murder of the Crown Prince, and was too young to be executed. He instead fell victim to tuberculosis: weighing less than 40 kilos, one arm amputated, Princip died in April 1918, attended by a Jewish doctor who two decades later himself died in Theresienstadt. The impulse to view Kafka's two minatory novels, *The Trial* and *The Castle*, as prophetic of the Nazi and Soviet regimes, is also a queered variant

* At that time employed by the Dual Monarchy as a jail for political prisoners.

of either dramatic or situational irony. Dramatic, if we consider the novels to be aimed at forestalling the oppressive conditions they describe; situational, if we consider Kafka himself as a player in a historical scene and ourselves an audience privileged with hindsight. The rising curve of the 'Kafkaesque' suggests the dramatic variant, as each new confirmatory event throws into starker relief the predicament of the neurotic and latterly moribund writer, struggling to forestall the inevitable. The super-saturation in the detail of a writer's life and works afforded by contemporary media, and seen in the steady rise in the incidence of the word 'Kafka', inclines towards the situational variant. Both ironic perspectives propagate happily in a late capitalist world that, as Fredric Jameson has observed, is now wholly constituted by the human and its manufactures.**

The same impulse might lead one to feel that had Walter Benjamin not written on Kafka, it would have been necessary to write his essay 'Franz Kafka: On the Tenth Anniversary of His Death' for him, then build a time machine to go back to 1934 and implant it in his papers. The perfection of the fit between the loose affiliate of the Frankfurt School and the soi-disant 'Prophet of Prague' can also be viewed as culturally necessary, coincidental – or dramatically ironic, given Kafka's own resistance to

** E.O. Wilson suggests that the next great era to be visited on the earth will be 'the Eocene', in which humans exist alone in the world they have denatured. I see in Kafka's 'animal tales', with their narrators possessed of self-consciousness but no viable ecological niche, a foreshadowing of this condition.

the decipherment of a symbolism that he himself always took on emotional trust. Benjamin retells an anecdote concerning Catherine the Great's chancellor, Potemkin, his paralysing depressions, and the hapless intervention of a minor official, Shuvalkin. The pay-off line: 'This story is like a herald racing two hundred years ahead of Kafka's work' encapsulates the thrust of Borges's fragmentary essay 'Kafka and His Precursors'. After enumerating various writings – among them Zeno's paradox, Kierkegaard's *Either/Or*, and Robert Browning's poem 'Fears and Scruples' – in which he detects a 'resemblance' to Kafka's work, Borges says: 'In each of these texts we find Kafka's idiosyncrasy to a greater or lesser degree, but if Kafka had never written a line, we would not perceive this quality; in other words, it would not exist.' Borges's argument is by no means specific to Kafka: 'The fact is that every writer creates his own precursors. His work modifies our conception of the past, as it will modify the future. In this correlation the identity or plurality of the men involved is unimportant.'

The worms in the wound in the lad's side have the character of bacilli magnified by the writer's microscopic gaze. The lesions Kafka was suffering in August 1917, he wrote in a letter to Max Brod, were a 'symbol' of the greater 'wound' – a manifestation of a deep-seated malaise. The proleptic quality of the wound examined by the country doctor closes the first of the rings that ripple out from the fact of Kafka's tuberculosis, through his writings, and into the wider world. Rings of coincidence – or situational irony, since the impact that caused them occurred years before, as is attested by their precursors in Kafka's writings *before* his diagnosis. That Kafka should suffer and die from tuberculosis would be ironic were it not that so many others did as well. Kafka initially saw his illness not as a tragedy but as a 'Blighty wound', allowing for his speedy return home from the frontline of workaday toil and suffering to a *Heimat* of pacific preoccupation. That Kafka's death in 1924 comes at a sort of fulcrum point in time between the dissections of the Parisian doctors René Laennec, Gaspard Bayle* and Pierre Louis – whose combined efforts established both a prospective aetiology and epidemiology for the disease – and the discovery of streptomycin as an effective therapeutic drug in the 1940s, would seem to be just another of those ironic rings. In the autumn of 1923, finally having struggled over the Laurenziberg and tucked up in the Berlin suburb of Steglitz** with his lover Dora Diamant, Kafka witnessed Germany's hyperinflation, and was compelled by poverty to read the newspapers through shop windows. Together with Diamant he burnt some of his notebooks,*** and admitted in a letter to Brod that 'concealment has been my life's vocation.' He was visited by his uncle Siegfried Löwy, the country doctor, whose anxieties about Kafka's health set in train

---

* Both of whom also died of tuberculosis.
** The Heimatstil houses of which – when I toured the area in April 2012, visiting the sites where Kafka and Diamant lived – I found oppressively reminiscent of those in the Hampstead Garden Suburb of North London where I grew up.
*** Although she kept some, together with letters – the cache was, in due and predictable course, seized by the Nazis.

the phased withdrawal to the sanatorium outside Vienna where Kafka would die the next year.

I could go on – and on: linking together the enthusiasm for *Naturheilkunde* and vegetarianism that Kafka shared with Hitler; or the neurasthenia and phonophobia he shared with Proust. Once bitten by a mania for associative thinking, you can't tell where you might end up. Alternatively, I could survey the referential underpinnings of 'A Country Doctor' that any academic literary critic will already have noticed are conspicuously absent from this essay, but then I am not an academic literary critic. In my teens, I was introduced to the rudiments of the then modish applications of structuralism and deconstruction to literary theory. I recoiled. I dimly perceived that this development represented a shockwave (or perhaps more accurately 'dullwave') radiating out from the collapse of the Western tradition of metaphysics: it might no longer be possible, after Wittgenstein, to use pure reason to say anything certain about the world. But theoreticians could perhaps preserve their profession by shifting the locus of enquiry to fictional texts that would stand as proxies for what had been ceded to psychotherapy, anthropology, neurology and cognitive science. Yet I could tell that such studies – when it came to the business of writing fiction – were utterly beside the point. And so I went to university to study philosophy, where I learnt about the combinatorial nature of the imagination.

I remained aware of the pullulating nature of literary critical theory, and took hurried and shocked glances into its gaping maw, much as Yossarian glimpses the wound in Snowden's thigh and looks away. It wasn't until I embarked on this essay that I looked it full in the face, and realised that if there were a primary site of infection identifiable, it might well be the works of Franz Kafka. Michael Hofmann in his spare way notes the same phenomenon: 'Kafka's writing is a remarkable instance of something coming out of nowhere and, in the space of a human generation, attaining in its reception the condition of inexhaustible intractability he was so often drawn to describing within it . . . As long ago as 1975, one of the great authorities on Kafka, Hartmut Binder, declined to get involved in the making of a complete bibliography running even then to some thousands of titles; instead he merely referred readers to a book that captured the state of the industry in 1961 (suggesting that was the last moment such a thing was possible).' But then as early as 1947 Max Brod said: 'One can hardly survey the gigantic essay literature that is concerned with Kafka.' Kundera wrote of Brod's admittedly bathetic novel *The Enchanted Kingdom of Love*: 'What a marvellous paradox: the whole image of Kafka and the whole posthumous fate of his work were first conceived in this simpleminded novel . . . which, aesthetically, stands at exactly the opposite pole from Kafka's art.' Kundera further charges that Kafkaology has removed Kafka and his works from the domain of Modernism: 'Kafkaology is not literary criticism . . . [it] is an exegesis.' Kundera means that it does not assess the value of the works or what they say about the world, still less the evolution of fiction, but rather attempts to decode their hidden messages by applying to them one or other interpretative paradigm. He cites psychoanalytic, existential and Marxist strains, and one could add the Lacanian. Kundera's central point is that these are all, hermeneutically speaking, equivalently religious.

Hannah Arendt said of Walter Benjamin: 'his basic approach, decisive for all his literary studies, remained unchanged: not to investigate the utilitarian or communicative functions of linguistic creations, but to understand them in their crystallised and thus ultimately fragmentary form as intentionless and noncommunicative utterances of a "world essence".' Benjamin was the first ranking critical theorist to survey the *corpus delicti*, and he had the gift of thinking poetically about this 'world essence', rather than seeking to define it in terms of a system; after him have come legion upon legion of Kafka interpreters, who, far from thinking poetically, think prosaically and instrumentally both about his work and their own interpretations. Reaching the head of a lengthy queue, they zip their symbolic order into Kafka's and then bungee jump into the oblivion of academic publication, bouncing back up to receive tenure. As for these symbolic orders, they are not personally striven for, but issued off the peg courtesy of their own university educations. Everyone understands that this state of affairs is a scandal, and an abuse of scholarship that makes the pinpoint deliberations of medieval schoolmen appear positively utilitarian. In academia it's customary not to critique the work of your peers, so, presumably once you've got through the early-career choppy waters, floating on your own frail origami of Kafka, you can look forward to plain sailing, and showing the next whey-faced generation how to open the wound in their side and zip it to the wound in Kafka's. And just as the marriage between Kafka and the postgraduates seems to have a degree of necessity, so the marriage between Kafka and the web has the nightmarishly dysfunctional air of one arranged between parties oblivious of one another. Kafka himself was viscerally repelled by marital domesticity, recoiling from the sight of his parents' nightshirts folded on the bed; but then how much worse is this, the embourgeoisement of nothing? We end up being the relationship counsellors, sitting on the other side of the one-way glass, watching the ceaseless and asexual replication of blog after essay after update, one symbolic order ceding to the next, as Kafka's long shadow percolates darkly through the glass of the screen you're currently staring at. In his 'Letter to My Father', Kafka wrote: 'To marry, to start a family, to accept all the children that come, and to help them in this insecure world, is the best that a man can do.' And so it transpires that these spurious issues are his only ones. And if Kafka's precursors were Zeno, Lewis Carroll, Lord Dunsany, then his successors are these: the inedible cookies that themselves chomp through virtual space as you flick from info-panel to info-panel, in the process absorbing into their maggot bodies all the information necessary to tell the proper authorities where you live, where you go, what you look at and what you buy.

Resuming his journal on 6 April 1917, after a five-month fiction-writing furlough, Kafka set down a 150-word fragment that he would subsequently incorporate in what, for me, is the most haunting of his shorter pieces, 'The Hunter Gracchus'. Condemned to wander the earth unceasingly, trapped in a limbo that is coextensive with the world of the living, 'I am,' Gracchus says, 'always on the great stairway that leads upwards. On this infinitely broad flight of stairs now up, now down, now to the right, now to the left, always on the move.' I see him there, trapped in a characteristically Kafkaesque pose of fluid inanition – and I see you there, also, peering into this world, your hand moving now up, now down, now to the right, now to the left, always on the move while you yourself remain static. I am reliably told that some people now hold races using Google Street View: they go online, sitting side by side, and race across America – or wherever – frantically clicking, going to the right and to the left to circumvent obstacles while maintaining a straight line. You might very well 'go' now to Prague, the city where the robot was invented, and organise a little race out from the Old Town and over what was once the Laurenziberg – a very leaden hill, now transformed into a virtual and golden cloud by this alchemy. I would go with you, but I am guilty of associative thinking, and I am sentenced to be my own search engine.

2 August 2012
London Review of Books

A Care Home for Novels:

The Narrative Art Form in the Age of

Its Technical Supersession

If you happen to be a creative worker, one of the great benisons of having children is that your personal culture mine is equipped with its own canaries. As you tunnel relentlessly on into the future, these little harbingers either choke on the noxious gases released by the extraction of mere decadence, or they thrive in the clean air of what we might – for want of any better expression – call progress. A few months ago one of my canaries, who's in his midteens and harbours a laudable ambition to be the world's greatest ever rock musician, was messing about on his electric guitar. Breaking off from a particularly jagged and angry riff, he launched into an equally jagged diatribe, the gist of which was already perfectly familiar to me: Everything in popular music had been done before, and usually those who'd done it first had done it best – moreover, the instant availability of almost everything that had ever been done stifled his creativity, and made him feel it was all utterly hopeless.

A miner, if he's any sense, treats his canary well, so I began gently remonstrating with him: Yes, I said, it's true that the web and the internet have created a permanent Now eliminating our sense of musical eras; it's also the case that the queered demographics of our longer-living, lower-birthing population mean that the middle-aged squat on top of the pyramid of endeavour, crushing the young with our nostalgic tastes. Moreover, the decimation of the revenue streams once generated by analogues of recorded music have put paid to many a musician's income, but my canary had to appreciate this: if you took the long view, the advent of the 78 rpm shellac disc had also been a disaster for musicians who in the teens and twenties of the last century made their daily bread by live performance. I repeated to him – repetition being the essence of dialoguing between miner and canary – one of my favourite anecdotes: When the first wax cylinder recording of Chaliapin singing the 'Song of the Volga Boatmen' was played, its auditors, despite a lowness of fidelity that would seem laughable to us (imagine a man holding forth from a giant bowl of snapping, crackling and popping Rice Krispies), were nonetheless convinced the portly Russian must be in the room, and searched behind drapes and underneath chaises longues for him.

So, recorded sound blew away the nimbus of authenticity surrounding live performers – but it did worse things. My canaries have also oft heard me tell how back in the

1970s heyday of the pop charts, all you needed was a writing credit on some loathsome chirpy-chirpy-cheep-cheeping ditty in order to spend the rest of your born days lying by a guitar-shaped pool in the Hollywood Hills hoovering up cocaine. Surely if there's one thing we have to be grateful for it's that the web has put paid to such an egregious financial multiplier being applied to raw talent-lessness. Put paid to it, and also returned musicians to the domain of live performance and arguably reinvigorated musicianship in the process. Anyway, I was saying all of this to my canary when I was suddenly overtaken by a great wave of noxiousness only I could smell – I faltered, I fell silent, then I said: Sod you and your creative anxieties, what about me? How do you think it feels to have dedicated your entire adult life to an art form only to see the bloody thing dying before your eyes?

My canary is a compassionate and perceptive song-bird: he immediately got my point and ceased his own cheeping, except to chirrup, I see what you mean. In my experience older and less tuneful canaries aren't nearly so perspicacious. In what follows I hope to convince you that the literary novel as an artwork and a narrative art form central to our culture is indeed dying before our eyes. Let me refine my terms at the outset so you know exactly what I'm talking about here: I do not mean narrative prose fiction *tout court* is dying – the kidult boywizardsroman and the soft sadomasochistic porn fantasy are clearly in rude good health – and nor do I mean that serious novels will either cease to be written or read, but what is already no longer the case is the situation that obtained when I was a young man. In the early 1980s, and I would argue throughout the second half of the last century, the literary novel was perceived to be the prince of art forms, the cultural capstone and the apogee of creative endeavour. The capability words have when arranged sequentially to both mimic the free flow of human thought and investigate the physical expressions and interactions of thinking subjects; the way they may be shaped into a believable simulacrum of either the commonsensical world, or any number of invented ones; the capacity words have to move between the imagistic and the concretised, expressing all shades in between; and the diacritical capability of the extended prose form itself, which, unlike any other art form is able to enact self-analysis, to describe other aesthetic modes and even mimic them. All this, given the particular productive forces and technological processes embodied in the codex during this period, led, I would argue, to a general acknowledgement: the novel was the true Wagnerian *Gesamtkunstwerk*.

This is not to say that everyone walked the streets with their head buried in *Ulysses* or *To the Lighthouse*, or that popular culture in all its forms didn't hold sway over the psyches and imaginations of the great majority. Nor do I mean to suggest that in our culture perennial John-Bull-headed philistinism wasn't alive and snorting: 'I don't know much about art, but I know what I like.' However, what didn't obtain is the current dispensation, wherein those who reject the high arts feel not merely entitled to their opinion, but wholly justified in it. It goes further: the hallmark of our contemporary culture is an active resistance to difficulty in all its aesthetic manifestations, accompanied by a sense of grievance which conflates it with political elitism. Indeed, it's arguable that tilting at this papery windmill of artistic superiority actively prevents a great many people from confronting the very real economic inequality and political disenfranchisement they're really subject to, exactly as being compelled to chant the mantra 'choice' drowns out the harsh background muzak telling them they have none.

Just because you're paranoid it doesn't mean they aren't out to get you. Simply because you've remarked a number of times on the concealed fox gnawing its way into your vitals, it doesn't mean it hasn't this moment swallowed your gall bladder. Ours is an age in which omnipresent threats of imminent extinction are also part of the background noise. The paradigm for this is the threat of nuclear annihilation visited on this country for the half-century following Hiroshima. In the wake of its apparent dissolution, Spartan boys and Trojan Cassandras went looking for other doom-laden prophesies. Guy Debord, the French Situationist observed that 'the perfect democracy fabricates its own inconceivable enemy; it wants to be judged by its enemies rather than its results.' He meant 'perfect democracy' ironically, because its perfection consists in a wholly apathetic consensus: convinced, for example, of the omnipresent, imminent and deadly threat of terrorism, the majority will find everything else, in his words: 'rather acceptable, in any case more rational and democratic'. The omnipresent, imminent and deadly threat of environmental disaster has long since been subsumed to this dialectic of top-down willed ignorance, and so the mounting rhythms of flooding and fracking acquire a character of creeping normalcy.

Given all this, it's easy to understand how we can be blinkered when it comes to tectonic cultural shifts as well. The omnipresent and deadly threat to the novel has been imminent now for a long time – getting on I would say for a century – and so it's become part of the culture's background noise; after all, during that century more books of all kinds have been printed and read by far than in the entire preceding half-millennium since the invention of moveable-type printing. By the beginning of this century a book was printed somewhere in the world every 45 seconds – if this was death it had a weird pullulating way of expressing itself. The saying is that there are no second acts in American lives; the novel, I think, has led a very American sort of life: swaggering, confident, brash even – and ever aware of its world-conquering manifest destiny. But unlike Ernest Hemingway or F. Scott Fitzgerald, the novel has also had a second life. By reason of its internal dissolution and external supersession the form should have been laid to rest at about the time of *Finnegans Wake*, but in fact it's continued to stalk the corridors of our minds for a further three-quarters of a century. Many fine novels have been written during this period; novels of true significance, beauty and – adopting the ghastly modern idiom

– relevance, but I would contend that for all that, these were, taking the long view, zombie novels, instances of an undead art form that yet wouldn't lie down.

Literary critics – themselves a dying breed, a cause for considerable schadenfreude on the part of novelists – make all sorts of mistakes, but some of the most egregious ones result from an inability to think outside of the papery prison within which they conduct their lives' work. They consider the codex almost wholly in terms of the codex; and they are – in Marshall McLuhan's memorable phrase – the possessors of Gutenberg minds. The school of practical criticism founded here in Middle England by white, male, middle-class, ideologically middle-of-the-road and largely middle-aged academics, contended that texts could be evaluated solely by reference to their internal qualities and how they measured up against the timeless veracity constituted by a literary canon they were themselves the arbiters of. This closed loop of value, allegedly purged of such sordid referentia as sex, class and all cultural specificities or psychological contingencies, finds its analogous expression in their Gutenberg minds' inability to perceive the twilight of their idols: they screw their eyes up, they squint hard – in short, they do anything they can to keep reading, because that's all they can do.

There is now an almost ceaseless murmuring about the future of narrative prose in the age of bi-directional digital media; you can switch on your radio or television and hear pundits discourse on the subject at any time of the night or day; should you be antediluvian you can pick up your newspaper and read reams of speculation. Most of it is at once Panglossian and melioristic: Yes, these experts assert, there's no disputing the impact of digitised text on the whole culture of the codex; fewer paper books are being sold, newspapers fold, bookshops continue to close, libraries as well . . . But . . . but, well, there's no substitute for the experience of close reading as we've come to understand and appreciate it, so if we only reassert the values associated with the Gutenberg mind – the capacity to imagine entire worlds from parsing a few lines of text; the ability to achieve deep and meditative levels of absorption in others' psyches; the skill of committing to memory not only one text, but a whole series of them, and combining these word-bodies within our own thoughts – then all will be well. This circling of the wagons comes with a number of public-spirited campaigns: children are given free books (as if they weren't cheap enough already); book bags are distributed with slogans on them urging readers to put books in them; books are hymned for their physical attributes – their heft, their appearance, their smell – as if they were the bodily correlates of all those Gutenberg minds, which of course they are.

The seeming realists among the Gutenbergers say such things as: Well, clearly the codex is going to become a minority technology, but the beau livre will survive. The populist Gutenbergers prate on about how digital texts linked to social media will allow readers to take part in a public conversation while engaged in the formerly private practice. What none of the Gutenbergers are able to countenance, because it's quite literally – for once the jaded intensifier is justified – out of their minds, is that the advent of bi-directional digital media is not simply destructive of the codex, but of the Gutenberg mind itself. There is one question and one question alone that you must ask yourself in order to establish whether the serious novel will still retain cultural primacy and centrality in another 20 years. This is the question: If you accept that by then the vast majority of text will be read in digital form on devices linked to the web, do you also believe that those readers will voluntarily choose to disable that connectivity? If your answer to this is no, then the death of the novel is sealed out of your own mouth.

We don't know when the form of reading that has supported the rise of the novel form began, but there were certain obvious and important way-stations. We think of Augustine of Hippo coming upon Bishop Ambrose in his study and being amazed to see the prelate reading silently while moving his lips. We can cite the introduction of word spaces in seventh-century Ireland, and punctuation throughout medieval Europe – then comes standardised spelling with the arrival of printing, and finally the education reforms of the early 1900s which meant the British Expeditionary Force of 1914 was probably the first (and possibly the last) universally literate army to take to the field. Just one of the ironies that danced macabre attendance on this most awful of conflicts was that the conditions necessary for the toppling of solitary and silent reading as the most powerful and important medium were already waiting in the wings while Sassoon, Graves and Rosenberg dipped their pens in their dugouts.

In *Understanding Media* Marshall McLuhan writes about what he terms the 'unified electrical field'. This manifestation of technology allows people to 'hold' and 'release' information at a distance; it provides for the instantaneous two-way transmission of data; and it radically transforms the traditional relationship between producers and consumers – or, if you prefer, writers and readers. If you read McLuhan without knowing he was writing in the late 1950s, you could be forgiven for assuming he was describing the interrelated phenomena of the web and the internet that are currently revolutionising human communications. When he characterises 'the global village' as an omni-located community where vast distances pose no barrier to the sharing of intimate trivia, it's hard not to believe he himself regularly tweeted. In fact, McLuhan saw the electric light and the telegraph as the founding technologies of the 'unified electrical field', and rather than being uncommonly prescient, he believed all the media necessary for its constitution – broadcast radio, film, television, the telephone – were securely in place by the time of, say, the publication of *Finnegans Wake*.

McLuhan, having enjoyed his regulation 15 minutes of fame in the unified electrical field of the 1960s has fallen out of fashion; his rigorous insistence that content of any given medium is an irrelevance when it comes to understanding its psychological impact is unpopular with the very people who first took him up: cultural workers.

No one likes to be told their play/novel/poem/film/TV pro-gramme/concept double-album (delete where applicable) is wholly analysable in terms of its means of transmission; such a reduction of the message to the medium smacks of other discredited ideologies dependent on a technological *primum mobile* – although McLuhan was far from being a Marxist. Marxists, notoriously, have to tinker with history (and often completely rewrite it) so as to force it into con-formity with their eschatological dialectic; with McLuhan the reverse is the case: *Understanding Media* tells us little about what media necessarily will arise, only what impact on the collective psyche they must have. The pullulating codex publication of the late twentieth century, in line with the efflorescence of many other newer media, con-vinced a culture typified by a consumerist ethic that they – that *we* – could have it all. This 'having it all' was even ascribed its own cultural era: the postmodern. Modernism, with its messily paradoxical – and frankly unreadable – response to the condition of modernity could be happily set aside; we postmoderns were savvier by far. We weren't overtaken by new technologies, we simply took what we wanted from them and collaged these fragments together, using the styles and modes of the past as a framework of ironic distancing, and hence reasserted the primacy of the message over its medium.

The main objection to this is, I think, at once pro-foundly commonsensical and curiously subtle. The literary critic Robert Adams observed that if postmodernism was to be regarded as a genuine cultural era then it made of

Modernism itself a strangely abbreviated one. After all, if we consider that all other Western cultural eras – Classicism, the medieval, the Renaissance – seem to average about half a millennium apiece, it hardly matters whether you date Modernism's onset to Rousseau, Sturm und Drang or *Les Demoiselles d'Avignon*, it clearly still has a long way to go. By the same token, if – as many seem keen to assert – post-modernism has already run its course, then what should we say has replaced it, post-postmodernism, perhaps? A post-postmodernism soon to give way in turn to post-post-postmodernism, and so on ad nauseam. It would seem better all round to accept the truth, which is that we are still solidly within the Modernist era, and that the crisis registered in the novel form in the early 1900s by the inception of new and more powerful media technologies continues apace. The use of montage for transition; the telescoping of fictional characters into their streams of consciousness; the abandonment of the omniscient narrator; the inability to suspend disbelief in the artificialities of plot – these were always latent in the problematic of the novel form, but in the early twentieth century, under pressure from other, juvenescent narrative forms, and partly in response to philo-sophic thinking that either conflated semantics with logic, or sited meaning in socially specific contexts, the novel began to founder. The polymorphous multilingual pervers-ities of the later Joyce, and the extreme existential asperities of his fellow exile, Beckett, are both registered as authentic responses to the tedium vitae of the form, and so accorded tremendous, guarded respect – if not affection.

After Joyce we continue to read; we read a great deal – after all, that's what you do when you're wheeled out into the sun porch of a care home: you read. You may find it difficult to concentrate, given the vagaries of your own ageing Gutenberg mind, while your reading material itself may also have a senescent feel, what with its greying stock and bleeding type – the equivalent, in codex form, of old copies of the *Reader's Digest* left lying around in dentists' waiting rooms; yet read you do, closing your ears obstinately to the nattering of radio and television, squinting so as to shut out the bluey light from the screens that surround you, turning your head in order to block out the agitation of your neighbours' fingers as they tweezer info-panels into being. I've often thought that Western European socialism survived as a credible ideological alternative up until 1989 purely because of the Soviet counterexample: those on the left were able to point east and say, I may not altogether know how socialism can be achieved, but I do know it's not like this. So it was with the novel: we may not have known altogether how to make it novel again, but we knew it couldn't go the way of Hollywood. Now film too is losing its narrative hegemony, and so the novel – the cultural Greece to its world-girdling Rome – is also in ineluctable decline.

I repeat: just because you're paranoid it doesn't mean they aren't out to get you. When I finished my first work of fiction in 1990 and went looking for a publisher I was offered an advance of £1,700 for a paperback original edition. I was affronted, not so much by the money (although pro rata it meant I was being paid considerably less than I would've been labouring in McDonald's), but by not receiving the sanctification of hard covers. The agent I consulted told me to accept without demur: It was, he said, nigh-on impossible for new writers to get published – let alone paid. At that time the reconfiguration of the medium was being felt through the ending of the net book agreement, the one-time price cartel that shored up publishers' profits by outlawing retailer discounting. In retrospect the ending of the agreement was simply a localised example of a much wider phenomenon: the concertinaing of the textual distribution network into a short, wide pipe. It would be amusing to read the novel's diehard boosters if it weren't also so irritating; writing a few months ago in the *New Statesman*, Nicholas Clee, a former editor of the *Bookseller*, no less, surveyed all of the changes wrought by bi-directional digital media – changes that funnel together into the tumultuous word-stream of Jeff Bezos's Amazon – before ending his excursus where he began, with the best of all possible facts implying we were in the best of all possible worlds: 'I like,' Clee wrote, 'buying books on Amazon.'

Groucho Marx once said to a man with six children taking part in his TV show: 'I like my cigar, but I know when to take it out.' By the same token: I also like buying books on Amazon, but I'm under no illusion that this means either the physical codex, or the novel – a form of content specifically adapted to it – will survive as a result of my preferences; because I'm also very partial to sourcing digital texts from Project Gutenberg, then word-searching them for a quotation I want to use. I like my typewriter as well, a Groma Kolibri manufactured in the German Democratic Republic in the early 1960s, but I'm under no illusion that it's anything but a soggy old technology. I switched to writing the first drafts of my fictions on a manual typewriter about a decade ago because of the inception of broadband internet. Even before this, the impulse to check email, buy something you didn't need, or goggle at images of the unattainable instead of labouring at the work within grasp was there – but at least there was the annoying tocsin of dial-up connection to awake you to your time-wasting; with broadband it became seamless: one second you were struggling over a sentence, the next you were gossiping, or buying oven gloves. Worse, if, as a writer, you reached an impasse where you couldn't imagine what something looked or sounded like, the web was there to provide instant literalism: the work of the imagination, which needs must be fanciful, was at a few keystrokes reduced to factualism. McLuhan writes: 'The effects of technology do not occur at the level of opinions or concepts, but alter sense ratios or patterns of perception steadily and without any resistance.' And surely here too he's right: all the opinions and conceptions of the new media amount to nothing set beside the way they're actually used. McLuhan also states: 'The serious artist is the only person able to encounter technology with impunity, just because he is an expert aware of the changes in sense perception.'

I'm not sure that I agree with this; possibly I'm an insufficiently serious artist, because while I may've registered the effect of bi-directional digital media on my sense perception, I by no means feel immune from them; on the contrary, I've come to realise that the kind of psyche implicit in the production and consumption of serious novels (which are what, after all, serious artists produce), depends on a medium that has inbuilt privacy: we must all be Ambroses. In a recent and rather less optimistic article in the *New Yorker* on the Amazon phenomenon, George Packer acknowledges the impact on the publishing industry of digital text: the decline in physical sales; and the removal of what might be termed the 'gatekeepers', the editors and critics who sifted the great ocean of literary content for works of value. He foresees a more polarised world emerging: with big bestsellers commanding still more sales, while down below the digital ocean seethes with instantly accessible and almost free texts. Packer observes that this development parallels others in the neoliberal economy, which sees market choice as the only human desideratum. The US court's ruling against the big five publishers in the English-speaking world and in favour of Amazon was predicated on this: their desperate attempt to resist Amazon's imposition of punitive discounting constituted a price cartel. But really this was only the latest skirmish in a long war; the battles of the 1990s, when both here and in the US chain bookstores began to gobble up the independents, were part of the same conflict: one between the medium and the message, and as I think I've already made perfectly clear, in the long run it's always the medium that wins.

I've no doubt that a revenue stream for digitised factual text will be established: information in this form is simply too useful for it not to be assigned monetary value. It's novels that will be the victims of the loss of effective copyright (a system of licensing and revenue collection that depended both on the objective form of the text, and defined national legal jurisdictions); novels and the people who write them. Fortunately institutions are already in existence to look after us. The creative writing programmes burgeoning throughout our universities are exactly this; another way of looking at them is that they're a self-perpetuating and self-financing literary set-aside scheme, purpose-built to accommodate writers who can no longer make a living from their work. In these care homes erstwhile novelists induct still more and younger writers into their own reflexive career paths, so that in time they too can become novelists who cannot make a living from their work and so become teachers of creative writing.

If you think I'm exaggerating, as part of my duties at Brunel University where I teach I have just supervised a doctoral thesis in creative writing; this consists in the submission of a novel written by the candidate, together with a 35,000-word dissertation on the themes explored by that novel. My student, although having published several other genre works, and despite a number of ringing endorsements from his eminent creative writing teachers, has been unable to find a publisher for this, his first serious novel. The novel isn't bad – although nor is it Turgenev. The dissertation is interesting – although it isn't a piece of original scholarship. Neither of them will, in all likelihood, ever be read again after he has been examined. The student wished to bring the date of his viva forward – why? Well, so he could use his qualification to apply for a post teaching – you guessed it – creative writing. Not that he's a neophyte: he already teaches creative writing, he just wants to be paid more highly for the midwifery of stillborn novels.

If you'll forgive a metaphoric ouroboros: it shouldn't surprise us that this is the convulsive form taken by the literary novel during its senescence; some of the same factors implicated in its extinction are also responsible for the rise of the creative writing programme, specifically a wider culture whose political economy prizes exchange value over use value, and which valorises group consciousness at the expense of the individual mind. Whenever tyro novelists ask me for career advice I always say the same thing to them: think hard about whether you wish to spend anything up to twenty or thirty years of your adult life in solitary confinement; if you don't like the sound of that silence, abandon the idea right away. But nowadays many people who sign up for creative writing programmes have only the dimmest understanding of what's actually involved in the writing life; the programme offers them comity and sympathetic readers for their fledgling efforts – it acts, in essence, as a therapy group for the creatively misunderstood. What these people are aware of – although again, usually only hazily – is that some writers have indeed had it all; if by this is meant that they are able to create as they see fit, and make a living from what they produce. In a society where almost everyone is subject to the appropriation of their time, and a vast majority of that time is spent undertaking work that has little human or spiritual value, the ideal form of the writing life appears gilded with a sort of wonderment. The savage irony is that even as these aspirants sign up for the promise of such a golden career, so the possibility of their actually pursuing it steadily diminishes; a still more savage irony is that the very form their instruction takes militates against the culture of the texts they desire to produce. W. B. Yeats attributed to his father the remark that 'Poetry is the social act of the solitary man'; with the creative writing programmes and the Facebook links embedded in digitised texts encouraging readers to 'share' their insights, writing and reading have become the solitary acts of social beings. And we all know how social beings tend to regard solitary acts – as perversities, if not outright perversions.

As I said at the outset: I believe the serious novel will continue to be written and read, but it will be an art form on a par with easel painting or classical music: confined to a defined social and demographic group, requiring a degree of subsidy, a subject for historical scholarship rather than public discourse. The current resistance of a lot of the literate public to difficulty in the form is only a subconscious response to having a moribund message pushed at them. As a practising novelist do I feel depressed about this? No, not particularly, except on those occasions when I breathe in too deeply and choke on my own decadence. I've no intention of writing fictions in the form of tweets or text messages – nor do I see my future in computer games design; my apprenticeship as a novelist has lasted a long time now, and I still cherish hopes of eventually qualifying. Besides, as the possessor of a Gutenberg mind it's quite impossible for me to foretell what the new dominant narrative art form will be – if, that is, there's to be one at all. What I can do is observe my canary: he doesn't read much in the way of what I'd call serious novels, but there's no doubting that he's alive, breathing deep of a rich and varied culture, and shows every sign of being a very intelligent and thoughtful songbird indeed. On that basis I think it's safe for us both to go on mining.

6 May 2014
Delivered as the Richard Hillary Memorial Lecture for 2014 at Trinity College, Oxford

The Last Typewriter Engineer

It's disgusting, really – at best a nasty habit, at worst a full-blown fetish. I'm repulsed when my peers begin cooing about writing paper as if it were a lover's skin, or perving over their favourite pens and pencils, or mooing amorously in the direction of their Moleskine notebooks. Loathe it, because of course I'm one of the worst offenders. Still, we all know why we do it – and it isn't because we've missed our metier as stationers; for me there's nothing intrinsically beautiful about this stuff at all, and when I hear someone say how arousing they find the aroma of pencil shavings, or the stiff flexion of a new A4 ream I think, 'Poor blinkered behaviouristic you, to be so conditioned by this association of ideas that when a bell rings you start salivating – then eat the bell.' Either that, or 'Poor Stockholm-syndrome-afflicted you, not to grasp that the only reason you've developed an obsession with writing equipment is because you're held captive with it for year upon year.'

Yes, imprisoned with it, and – which isn't usually the case, even with the most manipulative kidnappers

– compelled to look fixedly at it as well. For how long have we stared at the titivating nib, or the blinking cursor? Do we not know every whorl in the grain of our desktops? Surely we can be forgiven if we invest these picayune things with great importance, for they are the tools of our mystery with which we make our thoughts and imaginings transmissible. I've always believed this – believed also that since to be a writer is to be a corporation of one, whatever little rituals and protocols are required to get the job done should be encouraged: for us there is no management flowchart, no plastic-laminated mission statement, no team-building exercise; unless, that is, we create them for ourselves.

In common with any PLC our corporate culture alters with the years. When I was a child I perved over my mother's typewriters; first her beautiful olive-green Olivetti Lettera 22 with the American keys, then later on over her IBM golf-ball electric which seemed to explode into kinesis if you touched it. I picked up an ancient Underwood of my own in a junk shop and used it to hammer out comedic plays – but when I'd grown to be a man and wanted to write less childish things, my mother had died, and since she'd been a relatively early adopter I'd inherited her primitive Amstrad PC 9512 word processor. I wrote my first five books (and plenty of journalism) on that machine and thought it perfectly adequate to the task, but then in the mid-1990s its printer packed up. I invested in a proper PC that could connect to the internet with a loud noise of whistling timpani, suggestive of Alberich forging the ring of the Nibelung. Still, I didn't find this too much of a distraction, because I only used the internet to file my journalistic copy.

In general I judged computers to be unlovely things, their functionalist design yet more evidence of the worrisome convergence between the British built environment of the period and all the actual – as opposed to virtual – desktops it aspired to encapsulate. As for the computer screen that nowadays is ever before us, I can recall perfectly the primitive holotype with its horse-trough depth and greenish luminescence; surely its lineal descendants' capacity to display almost infinite imagery has resulted in this unintended consequence: a leeching of aesthetic interest or engagement from its immediate purlieu; the duff skeuomorphic icons denoting folders and programmes have encroached, rendering all local space planar: 'And the heaven departed as a scroll when it is rolled together; and every mountain and island were moved out of their places.' Sometimes, when I worked for too long without a screen-break, on turning away from the screen the blinking cursor would go with me, and hover, heralding, above an ashtray or a mug. Naturally I desired computers – who didn't? Shinier ones, smaller ones, slimmer ones, more powerful ones; the problem was I didn't really know what to do with their myriad emergent capabilities. So, during this period I reserved my perving for notebooks and propelling pencils, Post-it notes and file cards.

Then, in 2004, I was invited by the artists Neville Gabie and Leo Fitzmaurice to contribute to a project in Liverpool:

they had persuaded Liverpool Housing Action Trust, the body responsible for dynamiting the city's council high-rises and rehousing their tenants, to let them have a number of flats in a 22-storey block in Kensington, up the road from Lime Street Station. The idea was that various creative types would take up occupancy for a period of months and be inspired by the experience. I was allocated a flat on the 21st floor with astonishing views across the Mersey and all the way to Snowdonia, 70 miles distant. I didn't have any firm ideas on what I was going to write about in my strange new atelier, but I knew I wanted to mediate living in the building, since the remaining tenants – perhaps a hundred or so, in a street-in-the-sky that had once housed five times that number – were being encouraged to get involved. For some time an urge had been growing in me to write on a manual typewriter. I didn't know why exactly but it felt a strangely inappropriate lust, possibly a form of gerontophilia. I disinterred my mother's old Olivetti, dusted it off, and resolved to type my daily word count, Blu-Tack the sheets to the scarified wallpaper of my Liverpool gaff, and invite the other residents up to view them. This I duly did. I found working on the Olivetti indecently pleasurable; I can't touch-type, but even so, my stick-fingers produced satisfying percussive paradiddles, in between which came blissful fermatas, devoid of electronic whine and filled instead with the sough of the wind on the windows, down the lift shaft, and wheedling through the Vent-Axias. The new instrument altered my playing style; instead of bashing out provisional sentences, as I would on a computer, the knowledge that I was going to have to re-key everything in the future caused me to stop, think, formulate accurately, and then type.

It was laborious to begin with, and I had the nagging suspicion that, as so often in the past (I feel confident many will identify), I was seeking a technological fix for a creative problem. But I persisted, and after I'd completed the story in Liverpool (it's called '161' and appeared in my collection *Dr Mukti and Other Tales of Woe*), I wrote my next book entirely on the Olivetti. In retrospect, although the decision to revert to a redundant writing technology may have been prompted by the valetudinarian tower block, there was an underlying and more significant cause: wireless broadband had been installed in our house, and now whenever I was writing I was only a few finger-flicks away from all the deranging distractions of the worldwide web. Much later I began to understand why exactly the new technology was so inimical to writing prose fiction, but to begin with my revulsion was instinctive: and I recoiled from the screen – straight into the arms of Shalom Simons. I'm not quite sure how I acquired Shalom – although quite likely it was a web search – but as soon as I had him I began to worry about losing him. He must've been in his late fifties then (he's 69 now), and while he's never spoken of retiring, he has in recent years conceded: 'I'm not looking for work.' Apparently there is one other like him down in Surbiton, but I've never been tempted to make any overtures, while Shalom seems curiously antagonistic towards this nameless conspecific. I suppose it's the cosmic irony one would expect; just as the nanny and the billy Shem selected to preserve their goatish lineage probably butted and bored each other all the way into his father's ark, so the last two typewriter repairmen in London are wholly antipathetic.

Over the decade Shalom and I have consorted I've at times been visited with a terrible (and reasonable) anxiety: he'll shut up shop before I do, leaving me with these battle-field wounded machines and no one to perform triage. My Wikipedia entry says that I 'collect and repair vintage typewriters'; the very idea of it! The repairing, that is – a child of cack-handed epigones who never got over the 'servant problem', I wouldn't know how to repair a potato for printing purposes, let alone a typewriter; however, collecting them I did do. Soon after Shalom began working on my Olivetti I started buying more typewriters; in part this was because my nasty habit was steadily turning into full-scale fetishism, but I also wanted to give Shalom as much work as I could, simply to keep him at it. I've always been like this with artisans and workmen I viscerally need: manufacturing employment for them out of trans-generational anxiety and personal ham-fisted desperation. I speedily acquired a second Olivetti and a brace of 1930s Imperial 'Good Companions'; a friend gave me a serviceable 1970s Adler, and, after long hours spent perving over a US website called The Vintage Typewriter Shoppe, I splashed out and bought an early 1960s Groma Kolibri for $500. This latter machine attracted my lustful gaze when it had a cameo part in the film *The Lives of Others*, a tale of East

German dissidents whose anachronistic existence behind the Wall in the 1980s included jiving to bebop jazz and typing samizdat.

In the film, the Groma is celebrated by one character as 'the thinnest typewriter ever made'; this means it can be neatly concealed from the Stasi under a door lintel. I didn't need my Groma for reasons of dissidence – I needed it because I hadn't seen anything quite as beautiful since my youngest child was born. Yes, it had got that bad already: I mooned over the things, I caressed them, and I thrilled to the counterpoint between their blocky inertia and their percussive eruption into creative being. I wanted older and older machines – and seriously considered trying to acquire an example of Rasmus Malling-Hansen's proto-typewriter of the 1860s, the so-called 'Writing Ball' (due to its globular appearance with the keys emerging from the core as pins do from a pincushion), a machine that was used by Nietzsche, among others. Throughout this pell-mell race into the past Shalom was my trainer, offering counsel, wisdom and expertise; although I never really felt he altogether grasped the seriousness of my obsession, how for me the manual typewriter was coming to be more than a mere writing instrument, but rather a reification of the fictive act itself.

Shalom grew up in an Orthodox family in Stamford Hill. His father, who ran an office furniture business, had intended him for a synagogue cantor, and when Shalom finished school he was sent to the yeshiva. However, Shalom said to me, wryly, 'I was a good Orthodox boy and didn't like the idea of working on Shabbat.' Instead, he went to train as a typewriter engineer with Smith Corona in Osnaburgh Street then worked for a dealer with premises near Liverpool Street Station. After that he was employed by various other typewriter dealers: 'The last one was in Camden Town, but then I got ill, and when I came back they didn't want to know.' Never one to be defeated, Shalom went round various stationery suppliers and picked up work that way. Throughout the 1970s and 1980s he kept on: 'I did a fax machine course and one on electric typewriters, but I had enough work and I really couldn't get my head round computer technology.' When he told me this I developed a strange image in my mind's eye: Shalom's typewriter world shrinking and shrinking, but always able to contain him – he was a microorganism swimming in this droplet of obsolescence, one that plummeted through fluvial time until, in 2004, it met me: a writer wilfully submerging himself in bygones.

Not that Shalom's life is quite as bounded by typing as my own; now he's in semi-retirement he can devote more energy to his singing. He's the lead tenor for the Shabbaton Choir, which tours extensively; recent highlights include concerts in Israel and Los Angeles. You might have imagined that Shalom and I would clash politically – he being of the Orthodox and Zionist persuasion, me being a Jewish apostate who supports a two-state solution – but in fact we never have; Shalom is one of those folk given to the homespun homiletic: 'A happy person is a person who's happy with his lot,' he'll say – or, to vary the terms of endearment: 'Food on the table and your family happy, that's all you need.' It's at this very basal layer of comity that we tend to communicate, all other potential disputes being incorporated into the tinking, clanking matter at hand: how is this or that half-century-old machine going to be coaxed back into utility? And not just my own burgeoning collection, but writer friends' old typewriters I've encouraged them to let me give to Shalom. They're often piqued by the idea of manually reverse-engineering their own compositional practices, but I know perfectly well that once serviced and cleaned their Remingtons and Hermes Babies will end up back in the cupboards and attics they were disinterred from, because, let's face it, apart from the ageing, hardly anyone writes books on a typewriter anymore.

Even so, as the technology takes its final bow there's been quite a flurry of interest: Cormac McCarthy auctioning his Olivetti Lettera 32 for a quarter of a million bucks made big news, while I was approached by Patek Philippe to write about them for an advertorial feature. I could see the synchrony of watches and typewriters: both beautifully efficient devices wholly animated by human power, object lessons – along with the bicycle – of what truly sustainable technologies should be. Less enticing was the offer from Persol, the Italian sunglasses manufacturer, to advertise their eyewear with a little film that would depict me frenziedly typing my 'great novel' on my 'iconic' typewriter – true, the money was good (€80,000 for a single day's work), but the destruction of my sense of myself as a writer would've been complete and utter: 'The End' in blood-red Courier to the accompaniment of a firing squad of keystrokes.

Beryl Bainbridge, who typed all her first drafts on an Imperial Good Companion (a delicious, steam-punky 1930s machine, take a look on Google images), went to her grave in 2010, preceded a year earlier by J. G. Ballard, the last writer I'd known personally – besides myself – who took his books all the way to typesetting as manually generated typescripts. One of the last services I performed for Jim Ballard was to obtain a ribbon for his 1970s Olympia; then, after his death, his partner, Claire Walsh, gifted me this machine. It's an unlovely thing, its textured beige-mushroom plastic casing anticipating the coming CPU towers and printers, rather than hearkening back – like Beryl's and my own Good Companions – to the steel and glass engineering of Joseph Paxton. I meditated on the Olympia for some time, wondering if working on my dead mentor's typewriter would either gift me some of his imposingly strange vision, or, on the contrary, rob my prose of whatever originality it might possess. In the event, after I'd written one piece on the Olympia I had a letter from Jim's daughter, Fay, who said she was distressed to learn I had the machine, since it had been such an integral part of her childhood; and despite the fact that her chronology was way out (she must have been thinking of its predecessor), I conveyed the Olympia to her with something like relief.

Relief, I now realise, because just as I'd subliminally registered the inception of wireless broadband by changing my solo corporate culture, so another transformation was now underway. During the completion of my last novel I'd had various problems with the Groma, and since the right parts were apparently no longer obtainable I'd bought a second machine. Watching Shalom fiddle about with the deteriorating Gromas I'd begun to have unworthy thoughts: how did I know he was actually any good as a typewriter engineer? It might be argued that the last living individual of a given species should be the fittest – after all, they've managed to survive the others' extinction; but an alternative view is that the others underwent mutagenesis, becoming part of the burgeoning IT genotype, while Shalom, the poor dinosaur, roved the clashing, bashing, hammering lost world of obsolescence. But really my suspicions about Shalom – I'm sure entirely unfounded – were symptomatic of a deeper malaise: I was falling out of love with the typewriter because I'd found a new old writing method to fetishise.

In truth, for some time I hadn't really been manually retyping my first drafts (let alone *all* of them), but instead had begun to key them into a computer for reasons of speed and editorial convenience. Moreover, while I still thought of the typewriter draft as the 'first', I'd discovered a certain resistance to bashing the keys first thing in the morning, and so had taken to handwriting at least a couple of hundred words which I would then type up. In time the amount I was handwriting increased until I realised I was effectively composing a proto-first draft this way. The realisation dawned uneasily on me that I could very well cut out the typewriter stage altogether – and what a relief that would be: no more lugging the machine about when I wanted to work somewhere else; no more – entirely justifiable – complaints from my wife, who sleeps in the room below where I work; and who, despite the interposition of several layers of rubber matting, was still rudely awoken by my early morning drumming; and of course, no more anxiety about keeping the damn things working after Shalom finally retires. I mean, what was I going to do when that day inevitably came? Wander the leafy back roads of Surbiton calling out tremulously for a new saviour?

I haven't as yet started the next novel, and it may well be that once I begin I'll recoil from the hard handy-graft, but for now my mind is made up and my heart has begun to sing: for years I've had a twinkle in my eye when I gaze upon the slim, silvery forms of the propelling pencils I customarily use to take notes – finally I've decided to go all the way with them. There's only one problem, as far as I can tell from a cursory web search: this particular model has been discontinued. I'll have to ask Shalom if he can introduce me to a propelling-pencil engineer before he bows outs.

23 October 2014
London Review of Books

Isenshard

Shortly after the topping-out ceremony for Renzo Piano's skyscraper, the Shard – which at the time of writing is at 308 metres the tallest building in Europe – a squib appeared in the British satirical magazine *Private Eye*. There's a regular feature in the *Eye* called 'Lookalikes' that invites readers to send in two photographs which foreground a resemblance between disparate people. Usually one of the individuals will be a politician or similar worthy and the other a popular entertainer, so the intent is obvious: to denigrate the former by association with the latter. The images are always accompanied by the reader's letter which follows a stock formula: 'Has anyone else noticed the resemblance between X and Y, I wonder if by any chance they may be related?' So it was that a postage-stamp-sized photo of the Shard appeared, next to an equally grainy illustration of the four-pronged tower inhabited by the wizard Saruman in J. R. R. Tolkien's fantasy novel, *The Lord of the Rings*; and the reader's letter of course read: 'Has anyone else noticed the resemblance between the Shard and Isengard, I wonder if by any chance they may be related?'

Setting to one side fantastical nit-picking – Isengard is the name of the entire fortress, the central tower is in fact called Orthanc – this struck me as a very funny trope indeed, and I'm still laughing. Like all the best visual jokes this one establishes an antinomy: perceptually the two objects are indeed startlingly similar, but conceptually they couldn't be further removed. Or could they? What makes the joke continue to resonate is the way the mind goes on bouncing between the two towers, delineating a complex interlacing of correspondences, until forced to the conclusion that, yes, they must indeed be related.

When it comes to skyscrapers I am, in the proper sense of the word, ambivalent: I hate them for all the obvious reasons – sometimes a cigar may be just a cigar, but a skyscraper is always a big swaying dick vaunting the ambitions of late capitalism to reduce the human individual to the status and the proportions of a submissive worker ant. Architecturally skyscrapers are the most meretricious of structures; predicated not on the possible realisation of any aesthetic ideal, but on the actualisation of specific construction technologies. In syllogistic lock-step with Mount Everest – which was climbed simply 'because it was there' – they are there . . . simply because. And following on from the cast-iron-frame method that allowed for the first skyscrapers to be raised in the late 19th century, each successive wave of innovation has been incorporated into further erectile capability. The current architectural zeitgeist, whereby form invariably follows finance, finds its purest expression in the skyscrapers *de nos jours*, which, with their parametrically designed waveforms positively billow with opportunism.

Yet I also love them – truly, I do. I love their Promethean swagger and their crystallisation of the urbane; I love their ability to transform our perception of the city by proposing a new parallax around which we instantly reorient as we tunnel along at ground level. And I love the way that they are seemingly purpose-built to accompany what Marshall McLuhan limned as the 'instantaneous medium' of electricity. By day the Shard is an almost frantically undistinguished building; far from being the mirrored sliver thrust into the skyline its designer envisaged, its dirt-dappled haunches hunker down on top of London Bridge Station, surely straining even the notable credulity of the City commuters who, morning and evening, gaze up at the prosaism of its exposed giant bolts. But by night, through the window of the bedroom where I sleep – a room I have moved to simply to enjoy it – I thrill to the sight of this Orion's dagger, dropped from the jet-howling darkness to quiver and wink in the sodium-lit belly of the urban beast; and I hearken – like the good global tribalist that I am – to the message of this medium, which is that to look upon the Shard is, perforce, to worship it.

I am a child of two cities with markedly different edifice complexes. My mother was a New Yorker who grew up in Queens – my father, a Londoner, born in the southern suburb of Blackheath. As they were growing up in the 1920s and 30s, both would have had good long-distance views of their respectively burgeoning metropolitan centres, with this key difference – until the late 1960s, Wren's St Paul's remained far and away the most salient building on the London skyline: a baroque salver cover beneath which lay church and state disjointed. London had an early flirtation with the skyscraper: Queen Anne's Mansions in Petty France, Westminster, was raised at first to 12 storeys in 1873 and a further two were added in the early 1890s. Equipped with hydraulic lifts by its enterprising developer, Henry Alers Hankey, the Mansions were at once a cynosure of the new urban lifestyle – tenants included Sir Edward Elgar – and a focus of the most intense disapproval, not least from Queen Victoria, whose royal prerogative, she felt, included an unobstructed view of the Houses of Parliament from her own back garden. The architectural historian Harold Clunn said of the Mansions, 'it is for real ugliness unsurpassed by any other great building in all London.' The 1894 London Building Act, with its 80-feet height limit, was a direct result of this genteel disapprobation; an ordinance that remained in place until it was waived in 1963 – essentially by Harold Wilson's prime-ministerial fiat – so as to allow Conrad Hilton to raise his Park Lane hotel to 28 storeys (313 feet). When I was a child, in the 1960s and 70s, central London remained a mostly low-rise zone, with Millbank Tower, the Shell Centre and Harry Hyams' Centre Point (designed by Richard Seifert) being the notable exceptions.

Whereas in the US the popular perception of the

skyscraper coalesced in a nimbus around the International Style office block, in Britain the field remained clear for the late arrival of Le Corbusier's machines for living: system-built structures (many prefabricated by the French engineering company Camus) that came stalking ashore in the late 1950s and early 60s. Initially hailed in the spirit their planners intended – as harbingers of the new, the classless and the progressive – the collapse of Ronan Point, a 22-storey residential tower in Newham, East London, in 1968, marked a definitive break between optimistic post-war futurism and the subsequent enduring association in British popular culture between the high rise and high levels of social anomie – a linkage that had already been welded by Anthony Burgess's 1962 dystopic novel *A Clockwork Orange*, with its urine-smelling and graffiti-bedizened high rises. This seems woefully unfair: Ronan Point collapsed almost certainly because of construction errors, but underlying any consideration of the practical merits of these buildings lay the deep-rooted conflict between Ebenezer Howard's bucolical – and low-rise – Garden City movement and its Modernist rivals; a conflict that goes back to at least the period when Queen Anne's Mansions humped up above the horizon, when, in cultural form, it was played out in the oppositional views of the city enshrined on the one hand in the scientific romances of H. G. Wells, and on the other by the retro-feudal fantasising of William Morris's *News from Nowhere*.

No Wellsian prospect of the distant future is complete without a full complement of mega-structures; he

understood with deep and intuitive force that the technological extension of human capabilities would brook no
opposition: an urbanism defined by the high-piling of the
species was a propositional inevitability of the form 'Have
pile-driver – will drive piles.' Wells's recasting of vertical
living arrangements as expressive of vertiginous social
hierarchies – which is seen most famously in his time
traveller's confrontation with the surface-dwelling Eloi
and their troglodytic nemesis, the Morlocks – becomes a
familiar trope in the European popular culture of the early
20th century. Fritz Lang's beautifully realised *Metropolis*
is as much a celebration of the penthouse and the roof
garden as it is a bitter conflation of Taylorisation with
child-sacrificing despotism. The British disaffection from
the high rise as an instrument of social change – up-thrust-
ing the proletariat – becomes, post-Ronan Point, subject
to a spatial *bouleversement* by the razing of these skyscrapers. To take Merseyside as just one example, some
80 blocks were demolished in a twenty-year period from
the mid-1980s to the mid-2000s. For a while, in 2004, I
had the tenancy of the highest flat in Liverpool; from the
21st storey of this block in back of Lime Street Station
I could see as far as Mount Snowdon, 70 miles to the
south. All around me extended the echoic emptiness not
only of the block itself – that by then had fewer than 100
residents – but the city itself, which had lost over half its
population since 1945.

Typing a novella on my manual machine in its gutted
shell, I was conscious of acting out an adaptation of

J. G. Ballard's *High Rise* (1975). Ballard's novel recasts the spatial analogue of class warfare ingrained in the British popular imagination of the skyscraper as a picaresque for the age of evolutionary psychology. The opening line is a synecdoche: 'Later, as he sat on his balcony eating the dog, Dr Robert Laing reflected on the unusual events that had taken place within this huge apartment building during the previous three months.' The eponymous high rise – in a familiar instance of Ballard's prescience – has been built on the Isle of Dogs site soon to be occupied by One Canada Square (popularly known as Canary Wharf); the blank-faced 50-storey block designed by César Pelli that became in the 1990s the concretisation of London's financial Big Bang, synonymous with the full alignment of British society with neoliberal finance capitalism – and the concomitant eastward expansion of the City of London – and which remained the tallest building in Britain until the completion of the Shard. Ballard's building is socially stratified, with the less affluent tenants on the lower floors, and the penthouse occupied by the architect-developer himself. As class warfare breaks out between lower and upper floors, and the building becomes wilfully sealed off from the surrounding city, the protagonist, Laing, embarks on a journey upwards that is less an exercise in social climbing than a phylogenetic descent from the crown of the evolutionary tree to its roots in primitivism. Hence the dog-roast.

Ballard's understanding of the role played by the sky-scraper in the collective unconscious is that it cannot help

– because of its alteration of the traditional proportions of domestic life – subsisting in an explicatory mode. In this he follows Lévi-Strauss who observed that 'all distortions in scale sacrifice the sensible in favour of the intelligible'. Whether very small – an architect's model of a skyscraper; or very large – the skyscraper itself – the important factor is the loss of the felt experience. Of course, the actual myths that enshroud the cloudy summits of multi-storey buildings are necessarily banal in secular Britain, quite as much as they are in the more plangent and religiously revanchist climate of the US. Nevertheless, Huxley, when he opens *Brave New World* by limning the central London Hatchery as: 'A squat grey building of only thirty-four storeys'; Orwell, when he embeds the Ministry of Truth in a repurposed version of London University's Senate House (the tallest unconsecrated building in pre-war central London), Wells, Morris, Burgess – Ballard himself; all are operating within the unified field of the same foundational myth:

> And the whole earth was of one language, and of one speech. And it came to pass, as they journeyed from the east, that they found a plain in the land of Shinar; and they dwelt there. And they said one to another, Go to, let us make brick, and burn them thoroughly. And they had brick for stone, and slime had they for mortar. And they said, Go to, let us build us a city and a tower, whose top may reach unto heaven; and let us make us a name, lest we be scattered abroad upon the face of the whole earth. And the LORD came down

to see the city and the tower, which the children of men builded. And the LORD said, Behold, the people is one, and they have all one language; and this they begin to do: and now nothing will be restrained from them, which they have imagined to do. Go to, let us go down, and there confound their language, that they may not understand one another's speech. So the LORD scattered them abroad from thence upon the face of all the earth: and they left off to build the city. Therefore is the name of it called Babel; because the LORD did there confound the language of all the earth: and from thence did the LORD scatter them abroad upon the face of all the earth.

A myth that remained indissolubly bound up with all Westerners' apprehension of the multi-storey until the morning of September 11th 2001. Any and all skyscrapers were at one and the same time worthy anthropic subver-sions of the Godly perspective – attempts to realise the entirety of human life within the built environment – and hubristic affronts to our Maker and his transcendent Will, for: 'now nothing will be restrained from them, which they have imagined to do.' The British dichotomies bucolic/urban, high-rise/low-rise, proletarian/bourgeois – all are mere spin-offs, subsumed to this primary one: our will/His; and its moral concomitant: good/evil. Naturally it follows, mutatis mutandis, God's razing of the Tower of Babel recapitulates that earlier toppling from a peak perspective: Lucifer's jump, and its sequel: the apple of knowledge plummeting from a higher branch of the phylogenetic tree down into Eve and Adam's moistened mouths as they loiter between its roots.

The starts and fits with which skyscrapers were raised in the US may have been a response to boom-and-bust economic cycles, while the Metternich-inspired floor plans of the late-19th-century skyscrapers – featuring individual worker-bee cells, each equipped with its own electric lighting, window and ventilation – served a sanitary conception of social advance; the buildings' hydraulic elevators literally lifted their clerkly tenants out of disease. However, New York's 1916 Zoning Resolution – unlike London's late Victorian stricture – imposed only formal patterning on skyscrapers, and a fixed ratio between plot size and tower footprint, rather than restricting height per se. From the top-floor observatory of hindsight we can see the evolution of the set-back design of New York and then Chicago skyscrapers not as a response to the problem of human air rights, but as the unconscious construction of a staircase fit for King Kong. True, the giant ape swarms up the façade of the Empire State, yet once he nears the top he is able to hold Ann Darrow out in front of him, all the better to perform his snuffling inter-specific *Totenlieder*. In my memory Kong is always enormous, fully the equal of the manmade peak he scales. Still, every time I review the scene I am shocked by how he is dwarfed by the Empire State Building far more than Ann Darrow is by him. Kong is us – or, rather, Kong is the prototypical superhuman of 20th-century myth, and at least fleetingly the skyline of Manhattan is his jungle gym.

Kong is thus the way-finder for all the bat-, super-, iron- and plastic men that will follow on behind; each of whom is, in their various ways, attempting to re-apprehend the intelligible with their magically enhanced sensibilities. Indeed, flipping through back issues of Marvel and DC comics it is impossible to avoid the conclusion that the entire genre exists largely as an unconscious response to the skyscraper. Frame after frame features these limber figures leaping, back-flipping and curvetting over row after row of Mies van der Rohe; that Kong himself was a personification of the re-insemination of the machine age by the primitive necessitates his own penetration by .50-calibre machine-gun bullets synchronised to fire through diaphanous aeroplane propellers. He falls – or perhaps jumps – and takes with him the Edenic and irenic reverie of a city that can still be enjoyed haptically rather than visually. The superheroes that succeed him are the humans we wish we were; whereas the lowly apes that grub up the news in the offices of the *Daily Planet* or knuckle-walk along the slot canyons of Gotham are condemned to an unthinking and bestial existence in a built environment over which they can exert no management – let alone control.

Like a window cleaner's cradle dangling from a davit in high wind, American popular culture can't help letting it all hang out. The recrudescence of the Athenian polis in the spatialisation of the Manhattan skyline – a solid block of concrete, steel and masonry neatly sliced into democratically accountable chunks – brought with it the original Grecian sin: hubris. The super-charged sexual lucubrations of Ayn Rand's *Atlas Shrugged* are entirely beside the point here – 'It was like a phallic symbol . . .' Tom Waits groans about the Empire State Building in the song 'King Kong', but as I think we've already established, there's no need to stretch to similitude. As the fuse cupboards explode and flames wasp-waist the 138-storey tower, Doug Roberts, the architect played by Paul Newman asks Fire Chief Mike O'Halloran – mummed by Steve McQueen – 'Just how bad is it?' to which O'Halloran replies: 'Depends how good your imagination is.' The answer is, of course, not terribly good at all – because it doesn't need to be. The so-called 'Master of Disaster' Irwin Allen, ushered in the counter-weight to all those Lycra-clad leapers with *The Towering Inferno* (1974), a film whose release lagged only twenty months behind the completion of the World Trade Center.

Corrupt developers and their senatorial shills mill around in the Promenade Room; their celebratory party has been abandoned and now they must fight to gain access to the scenic lifts scooting down the glassy flanks of the world's tallest skyscraper. With blue-collar probity etched into every angle of his face, Chief O'Hallorhan sneers, 'Architects!' To which smooth Doug Roberts can only rejoin, 'Yeah, it's all our fault.' Over the next three decades, and now on into the new century, the bonfire of the vanities has never wanted for more fuel; the raising of one actual skyscraper is effectively twinned with the destruction of its cinematic doppelganger. J. G. Ballard's 1981 novel *Hello America* features an expedition mounted from Europe in 2114 to visit the ecologically ravaged remains of the former superpower; and which rediscovers the skyscrapers of Manhattan sticking out – like the bones of a dinosaur – from 100-foot-high sand dunes. Ballard's fervid skill in conjuring up the sensation of silica on silicate was about to be eclipsed; indeed, if the medium is CGI, its message is 'Get a kick out of those two vast and trunkless legs'. Best case is that the rapacious appetite Hollywood imagineers display for deluging, flaming, death-raying, exploding and otherwise laying waste to the central business districts of American cities is an ironic comment on the short specs of some of their signature skyscrapers. But irony isn't Hollywood's major key.

No, whereas in *The Towering Inferno* there are only close-ups, mid- and long-shots – the mastery of the disaster consists in their effective harmonisation – with the advent of CGI it becomes possible, at least in theory, for disbelief to remain suspended high above the skyscrapers, an all-seeing eye that contemplates *The Day After Tomorrow* for its entire nauseating duration. But by creating the super-viewer – taller, faster and stronger than a collapsing skyscraper – the imagineers have simply reconfigured the problem at a different scale; now we are too big to experience our cities' destruction feelingly, just as before we were too small to inhabit them empathetically: lunch(ing) atop a skyscraper, we were, each of us with his baloney sub in waxed paper and his soda bottle, part of a Renaissance group reclining on a girder, one that wouldn't have been any more or less comfortable were that girder to have been lain on the ground in front of a half-built basilica. And surely, that was the entire point of what was intended to be a publicity shot for the RCA Building, a skyscraper that was completed in the same year *King Kong* was released.

If Hollywood doesn't mete out brimstone to go with the fire it rains down on the hubristic sinners of Babel it's only because Smell-o-Vision never caught on. It's certainly not to do with any restraint on their part. Following the destruction of the Twin Towers by Al Qa'eda backed terrorists in 2001 you might have expected some compunction about the vivid portrayal of skyscrapers being destroyed. Not a bit of it – if anything, the frequency of their cinematic annihilation has only increased as competing teams of visualisers do battle with one another for the wilting credulity of the viewers. How could it be otherwise, when the phenomenon itself is so devoid of manifest content, but only responding to a brute fact: the number of mega-structures going up keeps on . . . going up. I say free of manifest content, yet what I really want to say is that the willed destruction of the Twin Towers by religious fanatics steeped in Judaeo-Christian eschatology made this latent content so very manifest that the myth became a tale the telling of which was effectively over. After 9/11, in a very important sense, the skyscraper simply ceased to exist. Just as my teenagers defend their first-person shooting of virtualised Nazi zombies on the grounds that 'They're Nazis *and* they're zombies', so the zombie skyscrapers continue to stalk the globe, but their raison d'être dispersed through the cloud of toxic dust that billowed out from Lower Manhattan throughout that endless and apocalyptic day.

How to show the storied skyline after 9/11 became a problem for the visualisers. Steven Spielberg ended his slick amorality fable, *Munich*, by having one of his Mossad assassins cast a monitory glance over his shoulder at the Twin Towers, but a film director this accomplished should've known that prolepsis – the film is set in the mid-1970s – can never compel catharsis; after all, how can anyone feel better about the state-sanctioned murders deemed necessary revenge for crimes that have yet to happen? The release in 2008 of James Marsh's *Man on Wire*, a feature-length documentary about Philippe Petit's 1974 guerrilla high-wire walk between the Twin Towers, was a cause not for the celebration of the indomitable human spirit – which would, anyway, have been another prolepsis – but for a faux-reconnection with an earlier and more naïve age, one when it was possible for a gang of renegade circus artists to breach security without too much trouble, all in the cause of a spectacle whimsical rather than world-shattering. Pertinently, the wire walk remained un-filmed, so it disappeared into a still more profound lacuna than the towers themselves; while Petit, interviewed on camera, had the definite feel of a man who had surpassed his wildest expectations while still in his relative infancy. He may have kept his footing on the wire, but for the rest of his life he was in freefall.

How could it be otherwise? This was a stupendous feat of bravery and conquest; Petit himself became during the hour-long walk – throughout which he frolicked and struck attitudes – a real-life Superman, apprehending the skyscrapers directly through his own twanging form. That he subsequently found himself unable to comment on the destruction of the WTC (which Marsh's film also makes no mention of) is a pure and Coleridgian involute: the buildings that he had so romantically linked had ceased to exist, not simply now – but in 1974 as well. This is also why the presence in the opening sequence of *The Sopranos* of the Twin Towers, which are glimpsed over Tony Soprano's shoulder as he exits the Holland Tunnel en route to his mafia fiefdom of North Jersey, seems quite so *unheimlich*: in the face of the painful verisimilitude of the drama series – which inaugurated a renaissance in American television drama that endures to this day – it is the World Trade Center that confirms its true status as pure fiction. The same might be said of the opening sequence of *Mad Men*, another lavishly produced television drama series that, in the manner of Balzac's *Comédie humaine* attempts to link together, through drama, the unravelling strands of American culture and society in the decades following the Second World War.

This sequence uses spare graphics of the style employed by the 'mad men' of the title (a self-ascription of cynically self-congratulatory Madison Avenue advertising executives of the 1950s and 60s) to show a white-shirted, dark-suited man plunging downwards in mute supplication – arms outstretched, legs akimbo – past the cubism of sparsely sketched skyscrapers. Although strenuously denied by its creators, this forces on the informed viewer's mind, quite unavoidably, the image of the so-called 'jumpers', those most benighted individuals, who, facing either immolation in the fires raging after the hijacked planes smashed into the North and South Towers, or certain – but possibly less painless – death upon impact with the ground, chose to fling themselves from the upper floors. In particular the *Mad Men* sequence recalls the most famous image of them: the 'Falling Man' shot of a still-unidentified man plunging from the North Tower taken by the veteran AP photographer Richard Drew. Head down, arms at his sides, legs half bent as if in the act of walking within the blurring lines of the skyscraper's graticule, the Falling Man became the focus of intense speculation – and even theorising – in the months and then years after the terrorist attack. His apparent Petit-like insouciance in the face of death – and by extension his domination of the built environment that was an accessory to his (self) murder – was, of course, just that: a trick of the lens.

For some, the unsettling, willing-victim feel of the Falling Man became just another reason to airbrush those who had jumped from the Twin Towers out of history. The NYC Medical Examiner's Office is on record as stating that it does not consider those who fell from the WTC to be 'jumpers' as ordinarily understood – for this implies the premeditation of a commonplace(!) suicide. Still, setting intentionality to one side for the moment, it is easy to see that the jumpers are a complete confirmation of the submerged but still dominant mythos of the Western skyscraper. In *The Towering Inferno* the adulterous businessman is immolated – the first actual death we witness on

screen – as he tries futilely to find a way out of the conflag-
ration for him and his lover; shortly after this, the woman
taken in sin jumps from the skyscraper. That the people
killed in the Twin Towers were a believably representative
sample of the world's population, while the buildings they
worked in were, in turn, credible icons of transnational
capital flows, only serves to complete the apotheosis:

> Go to, let us go down, and there confound their lan-
> guage, that they may not understand one another's
> speech. So the Lord scattered them abroad from
> thence upon the face of all the earth: and they left off
> to build the city.

In the years since the violent opponents of usury (a prohi-
bition contemporary Salafist jihadis share with medieval
Christians) launched their attack on the Babel-that-was-
Mammon, the skyscraper has struggled to maintain any
salience at all. In 2008, on a two-day hike across the auto-
plutocratic city state of Dubai and into the Empty Quarter
of Arabia, I marvelled at skyscraper after skyscraper, built
by indentured labour, and each seemingly a more bowdlerised example of that inherently bowdlerising architectural
style, postmodernism. Hypertrophied mansard roofs supported by gargantuan Corinthian columns; Pantagruelian
porticos leaning out over six-lane expressways planted
with wastes of begonias drenched in costly desalinated
water – the spectacle Dubai presents is of a last-chance
saloon at which all the formal decadences of the West have

come home to die. And then there's the matter of scale: by elevating detailing more suited to a sports shoe or an SUV thousands of feet into the sky, the Dubai skyscrapers themselves apotheosise those first Chicagoan up-thrusts, whereby the belle époque was blasted into inner space. Now, the new International Style is that of the desktop toy or bibelot writ horribly large.

Here in my hometown of London it isn't only the Shard that instantiates in the skyscraper a tendency the English architectural critic Owen Hatherley has noted, which is to elide icon and logo in a single structure. The nicknames for these vast promotional devices follow ineluctably: 'the Quill', 'the Walkie-Talkie' and 'the Cheese Grater' are joining the Gherkin and the Shard itself in altering for the foreseeable future the skyline of the city and the parallaxes it enjoins on its traditionally earthborn inhabitants. And while there may be desultory coverage of these pharaonic undertakings – in and of themselves confounding the much-loved Skyscraper Index, since the country as a whole remains resolutely in recession – the popular and collective apprehension of them is more or less nonexistent; apart, that is, from *Private Eye*'s squib. It was said of J. R. R. Tolkien that, while a devout Catholic himself, he laboured carefully to expunge the Judaeo-Christian worldview from *The Lord of the Rings*, putting in its place what he saw as an older and deeper moral eschatology. That may well be; and it may also be true that the Two Towers of Isengard and Barad-dûr (the Dark Tower) were inspired by a pair of particularly ugly Victorian water towers close to his boyhood home in Birmingham, but the meticulous scholar of Anglo-Saxon – and wild fantasist – nonetheless managed to zero in on the popular cultural consciousness of the 21st century with uncanny prescience.

Shortly before I sat down to write this essay, the latest in a whole series of Arab mega-structures was completed. Largely ignored in the West – which, as you recall, has no need even of a bad imagination – these include the crazed bodkin of the Kingdom Centre in Riyadh, and of course the Burj Khalifa in Dubai. In the next two decades even this uppermost peak is set to be over-topped by at least ten more vast skyscrapers in the region; but the Abraj al-Bait Towers in Mecca are undoubtedly the purest expression of the deep correspondence between the Shard and Isengard. An engorged hulk of pseudo-neoclassicism only 11 metres shorter than the Burj Khalifa, the Towers do indeed tower over the Masjid al-Haram and its meteoric core, the Kaaba. Many of the 3,000 hotel rooms and suites in the seven towers that make up this manmade massif are positioned so that their windows look right down into the holy-of-holies, so encouraging devotion in their temporary tenants. But it is the giant clock set in the Mecca Royal Clock Tower forming Abraj al-Bait's summit that cements together those two seemingly disparate lookalikes, the Shard and Isengard. Underneath the iconic logo of the horned moon sit four clock faces, each 6 feet larger in diameter than London's Big Ben, and bearing a distinct resemblance to that most imperialist of timepieces.

Mohammed al-Arkubi, general manager of the hotel, is reported as saying that 'Putting Mecca time in the face of Greenwich Mean Time, this is the goal.' It's a fruitless goal if he expects the inhabitants of Middle Earth – sorry, I mean the West – to pay any attention. We don't so much as look upon our own tower of Isengard, whose designer's stated aim it was to create a skyscraper that disappeared vaporously into the surrounding atmosphere – and we know better than to even glance at the compound eye of Saruman that floats atop the Dark Tower of Barad-dûr (sorry, I mean Abraj al-Bait). And if you were to tell us that this sky-scraping nemesis, like so many of the Arabian towers, had been built by the Saudi Binladin Group, why, we'd only shrug our shoulders and observe, Why not? After all, they are the biggest construction company in the world.

23 June 2015
Originally published in *The Future of the Skyscraper*,
edited by Philip Nobel

How Should We Read?

How should we read? The S-word makes it sound, like it or not, like a moral injunction – deep, passionate and enthusiastic readers we may well be, there nonetheless remains something about the way we transform marks on a page or screen into images and ideas in the mind that leaves us feeling like failures. Modish neuroscience may provide at least some of the answers: the ability to read and write – unlike speech – isn't hard-wired into the human mind-brain, but rather, such is our neural plasticity, that we're constantly changing in our very essence so as to refine these skills. Perhaps this is why reading always feels a little like striving – unless we've mastered the facile trick of reading entirely for pleasure, a subject to which I'll return.

So, there's always this quality of endeavour about reading – and at the same time, in cognitive terms it's hard work. When someone reading complex passages of prose – ones, say, that attempt to convey human lives in all their manifold sensuous and intellectual complexity – is placed in an MRI (Magnetic Resonance Imaging) scanner, we can see on the machine's visual display that almost all of their brain is lit up like the proverbial Christmas tree. Not only that, but the parts of the brain employed when actually talking, walking or making love are illuminated by the very act of reading about talking, walking or making love.

Long before such data was available, the French literary critic René Girard argued that portrayal of characters' behaviour and motivations in novels was just as valid a study for psychological theorists – now science seems to have borne him out. Fancifully, I imagine a reader in an MRI machine reading about a man reading . . . in an MRI machine – and I wonder how this *mise en abyme* might appear to the literary technicians of the future, and whether it could turn the 'is' into an 'ought', thereby telling us – at long last – how we should read. Because I have to confess: I no longer have that sense of security in my own methods that I once did – one which, in retrospect, I based on my empirical study of a single subject: myself.

Raised by bookish but undisciplined parents, I always felt I had just about the best introduction to reading imaginable: my American mother's modish novels and zeitgeisty works on psychology mingling on the shelves with my English father's English canonical tastes and his motley collection of philosophic texts (many of which came from my autodidactic grandfather's own extensive library). And there were plenty of other books as well – acquired by my brothers or me at second-hand stores and flea markets. Nobody was remotely precious about these volumes: they were there to be read, not revered. And since my parents had also decreed – in order to inculcate us with their own bookish tendencies – that we could have no television, reading was pretty much all we had to do: there was no street life in leafy middle-class English suburbia in the 1960s, unless you liked watching lawns grow.

I didn't. I read – and I read, and I read some more. I read what was to hand – and since there was no prescription for how to do it, I read promiscuously, mixing fiction and non-, children's and adult's books. My ascent from the twee confines of *The Secret Garden* into the terrifying ones of Yossarian's bomber as it circled over Bologna was altogether vertiginous. And if I didn't altogether understand the full satirical intent of Heller's masterpiece (I first attempted *Catch-22* when I was 12 years old), the opening line of the novel nonetheless hooked me in with its appeal to my own warped romanticism: 'It was love at first sight . . .'

My mother loved to read with an almost sensual intensity – trips to the local lending library, where we squeaked on waxed floors between shelves at once sunny and sepulchral, had the air of religious rituals – my library card was equivalent to a party one, a catechism, or both. When my father left, my brother and I, aged eleven and nine, would find ourselves attending 'reading suppers' with our depressed and only intermittently communicative mother. By this stage the words on the page encoded not simply the thoughts and imaginings of their author, but the yet deeper intelligence that this was a way out – a time tunnel into the past, or a space one, projected across the interstellar immensities and into as many worlds as could be imagined.

I favoured the plain bright-yellow jacketed Gollancz science fiction editions when borrowing books from the library – and I'd usually leave with my full allowance: seven volumes. I first read the novels of J. G. Ballard this way. I was far too young for his sexualised car accidents and other exhibitions of atrocity – but his minatory vision compelled me, stayed with me, and many years later the writer himself became a friend and a sort of mentor to me: quite possibly this was one of the fruits of having learnt how to read. I was, of course, taught to read – if, by this, is meant the basic decoding of the alphabet. My mother, good American that she was, used flashcards and the thick velvety nap of the material covering the sofa, which she'd write on with her finger then erase with the back of her hand. Such magic inspired precociousness, and I could indeed read fluently by the time I went to nursery school.

But merely being able to decipher texts isn't really reading in its fullest sense – any more than reading so-called 'page-turners' teaches you much besides how to turn a page. True, there is a pleasure to be gained from un-demanding works that hustle you along their lines, luring you on with little resolutions to equally picayune conun-drums. But let's face it: reading a Dan Brown novel is to literature as playing Candy Crush is to advanced strategic thinking – and while 'reading for pleasure' may encompass a huge variety of texts, given one person's whodunit is another's why are we here?; as an answer to the ques-tion 'How should we read?', 'For pleasure' has no more substance than hedonism ever does in what we must, per-force, call the real world.

Which brings me back to that promiscuity animad-verted to above: a promiscuity born of fidelity rather than its dereliction; a fidelity not to a given work or its author, but to the great palimpsest of texts, worked up, worked over, interleaved and woven with one another, that con-stitutes literature in its entirety. To read promiscuously is to comprehend the caresses of one work in the arms of another – and the promiscuous reader is a pedagogue par excellence. How should we read? We would read as gourmands eat, gobbling down huge gobbets of text. No one told me not to pivot abruptly from *Valley of the Dolls* to *The Brothers Karamazov* – so I did; any more than they warned me not to intersperse passages of *Fanny Hill* with those written by Frantz Fanon – so I did that, too. By reading indiscriminately, I learned to discriminate – and learned also to comprehend: for it's only with the acquisi-tion of large data sets that we also develop schemas supple enough to interpret new material.

How should we read? We should read not expecting to comprehend all that we read: if we come across a signifier we don't understand, or something signified we cannot clearly discern, we should read on, secure in the knowl-edge that either the context will supply the answer, or the writer will use the same words again in a different one. As it is to the individual morpheme, so it is to the magnum opus: understanding, engagement and enjoy-ment all rest on an ability not only to suspend disbelief, but also suspend comprehension – to allow oneself, as one reads on, the sweetest luxury, that of doubt. One of the many problems digital reading brings with it is its drive to make all texts as transparent as the screens upon which they're displayed: a touch of the finger and a definition appears – a swipe then we're given annotations, glosses and exegeses in terrifying abundance. Yet when I think back, it was always in my more negative capability that I found the deepest engagement: I learned more by resisting the effort to get up and consult a dictionary or an encyclopaedia than I did by doing so – for I carried on learning how to read by doing just that.

To reproduce the circumstances under which I was able to achieve such levels of literary absorption a contemporary reader would have to go on some sort of retreat, to a destination without any internet connection, and sufficiently remote to replicate a child's distant view of worldly concerns. Then there's ennui – out of boredom we call forth invention, and there's nothing more inventive than reading, save possibly for writing. If there's one thing our culture, with its relentless cultural commoditising, cannot abide, it's that even the smallest portion of tedium should be left unperturbed or not monetised. I believe it was my indiscriminate browsing among my parents' books that enabled me, once I reached university, to absorb most of the punitive reading lists that my professors set – for each essay, often ten volumes or their equivalent; and we had to read for two essays every week of the semester. It was an elite education – no doubt: but its elitism for the most part resided simply in this three-year workout of Broca's and Wernicke's areas: those portions of the brain most involved in the decipherment of text.

I took these pumped-up and hyperactive neurones with me into a life of indolence – I used to joke that I spent all of my twenties lying in bed reading novels, and as Freud so nicely observed, there are no such things as jokes. I've no wish for this to conclude as some sort of diatribe against screen-based reading – to do so would seem a little, um, rich, given you, dear reader, in all likelihood are doing just this, right now. But I wonder if this state of affairs represents a conundrum quite as capable of being infinitely regressed as that reader in an MRI machine, reading about a reader reading in an MRI machine. This is only to say that just as the digital readers' eyes slide across the screen too quickly, and on to another screen – quite possibly one displaying images rather than words – so their analogue counterparts' saccades are arrested by boards and bindings.

This is the chaste reclusion required as a counterpoint to all that promiscuity: keeping faith with a single text, toughing it out until the very end, regardless of either longueurs or those purple passages whereby it seems to be being unfaithful to its reader. And of course, in an era when pretty much the entirety of the world's literature is available more or less instantaneously, such fixity can be difficult – if not impossible – to achieve. By the time our culture reached 'peak paper' – in the late 1990s – my bedside table boasted a teetering stack of books I was reading simultaneously. Twenty years on, there's only an e-reader, loaded up with perhaps as many as seventy texts I'm concurrently carrying on with. Don't get me wrong: I still find the time – and possess the guile – to have clandestine rendezvous with particularly alluring works; and I still cleave just as strongly to the idea that it's in the oscillation between textual monogamy and polygamy (or polyandry) that we find our true love of – and engagement with – reading.

But the new technologies of reading have had a significant impact on what we read, quite as much as how we do it – and it's this topic that I wish to turn to in my next article for *Lit Hub*, confident that by exploring the contentious issue of the canonical, we will gain still more insight into the practical.

14 January 2021
Literary Hub

Junky

I have it on the desk beside me as I write – the first edition of *Junky* by William S. Burroughs. The world has changed a great deal in the fifty-odd years since it was originally published, and some of those changes are evident in the differences between the first edition of this memorable work and the one you are currently holding in your hands.

Entitled *Junkie: Confessions of an Unredeemed Drug Addict* and authored pseudonymously by 'William Lee' (Burroughs's mother's maiden name – he didn't look too far for a nom de plume), the Ace Original retailed for 35 cents, and as a 'double book' was bound back to back with *Narcotic Agent* by Maurice Helbrant. The two-books-in-one format was not uncommon in 1950s America, but besides the obvious similarity in subject matter, A.A. Wyn, Burroughs's publisher, felt that he had to balance such an unapologetic account of drug addiction with an abridgement of these memoirs of a Federal Bureau of Narcotics agent, which originally appeared in 1941.

Since, in the hysterical, anti-drug culture of post-war America, potential censure could easily induce self-censorship, it's remarkable that *Junky* found a publisher at all. Despite its subhead, Wyn did think the book had a redemptive capability, as the protagonist made efforts to free himself of his addiction, but he also insisted that Burroughs preface the work with an autobiographical sketch that would explain to the reader how it was that someone such as himself – a Harvard graduate from a Social Register family – came to be a drug addict. The same cautious instinct led Wyn to interpolate bracketed disclaimers after most of Burroughs's (often factually correct but radically unorthodox, and sometimes outright wacky) statements about the nature of intoxication and chemical dependency. Thus, when Burroughs stated: 'Perhaps if a junkie could keep himself in a constant state of kicking, he would live to a phenomenal age.' The bracket reads '(Ed. Note: This is contradicted by recognized medical authority.)'

Burroughs's preface (now restyled as a 'prologue') still stands first in the current edition, but relegated to the rear of the text is the glossary of junk lingo and jive talk with which he sought to initiate his square readership to the hip world. And for Burroughs the term 'hip' referred resolutely to the heroin subculture. The bracketed editorial notes have been excised.

Both *Junkie* and *Narcotic Agent* have covers of beautiful garishness, featuring 1950s damsels in distress. The blonde lovely on the cover of Helbrant's book is being handcuffed (presumably by the eponymous 'Agent', although his face and figure is hidden in the shadows), while clad only in her slip. The presence of ashtray, hypodermic and spoon on the table in front of her goes a long way to explain her expression of serene indifference. However, on the cover of *Junkie* we are given a more actively dramatic portrayal: a craggy-browed man is grabbing a blonde lovely from behind, one of his arms is around her neck, while the other grasps her hand, within which is a paper package. The table beside them has been knocked in the fray, propelling a spoon, a hypodermic, and even a gas ring, into inner space.

This cover illustration is, in fact, just that: an illustration of a scene described by Burroughs in the book. 'When my wife saw I was getting the habit again, she did something she had never done before. I was cooking up a shot two days after I'd connected with Old Ike. My wife grabbed the spoon and threw the junk on the floor. I slapped her twice across the face and she threw herself on the bed, sobbing . . .' That this uncredited – and now forgotten – hack artist should have chosen one of the small handful of episodes featuring the protagonist's wife to use for the cover illustration, represents one of those nastily serendipitous ironies that Burroughs himself almost always chose to view as evidence of the magical universe.

From double book to standalone; from Ace Original to Penguin Modern Classic; from unredeemed confession to cult novel; from a cheap shocker to a refined taste – the history of this text in a strange way acts as an allegory of the way the heroin subculture Burroughs depicted has mutated, spread and engrafted itself with the corpus of the wider society, in the process irretrievably altering that upon which it parasitises. Just as – if you turn to his glossary – you will see how many arcane drug terms have metastasised into the vigorous language.

Burroughs observed a discrete – if international – urban phenomenon, confined to the physical as well as the psychic margins of society: 'Junk is often found adjacent to ambiguous or transitional districts: East Fourteenth near Third in New York; Poydras and St. Charles in New Orleans; San Juan Létran in Mexico City. Stores selling artificial limbs, wig-makers, dental mechanics, loft manufacturers of perfumes, pomades, novelties, essential oils. A point where dubious business enterprise touches Skid Row.'

Today junk is everywhere, on housing estates and in penthouses; sniffed, smoked and shot up by models and model makers alike. Heroin chic has been and gone as a stylistic affectation – and will doubtless return again. Countless books and films have been predicated on the use and abuse of the drug. The heroin addict has become a stock figure in soap operas. Conservative estimates of the numbers of heroin addicts in Britain indicate a thousand-fold increase in the past half-century.

Burroughs wrote *Junky* on the very cusp of a transformation in Western culture. His junkies were creatures of the Depression, many of whose addictions predated even the Harrison Act of 1922, which outlawed the legal sale of heroin and cocaine in the USA. In *Junky* the protagonist speaks scathingly of the new generation: 'The young hipsters seem lacking in energy and spontaneous enjoyment of life. The mention of pot or junk will galvanize them like a shot of coke. They jump around and say, "Too much! Man, let's pick up! Let's get loaded." But after a shot, they slump into a chair like a resigned baby waiting for life to bring the bottle again.'

Is it too much to hypothesise that as it was to the demi-monde, so has it been for the wider world? That as addicts have increased in number and become more tightly integrated into society, so has the addictive character of the collective consciousness become more horribly evident. The mass obsessions with polymorphous sexuality, and the awesome death of affect implied by the worship of celebrity, are matched by a compulsive consumerism, characterised by the built-in obsolescence not only of products, but also the 'lifestyles' and the 'mindsets' within which they are placed. And, of course, there is the 'War on Drugs' itself, which has lopped off arm after arm after arm, only for six more, then twelve more, then thirty-six more to grow from their stumps, all of them being shot up into.

Certainly, Burroughs himself viewed the post-war era as a Götterdämmerung and a convulsive re-evaluation of all values. With his anomic inclinations and his Mandarin intellect, Burroughs was in a paradoxical position vis-à-vis the coming cultural revolution of the 1960s. An open homosexual and a drug addict, his quintessentially Midwestern libertarianism led him to eschew any command economy of ethics, while his personal inclinations meant he had to travel with distastefully socialist and liberal fellows. For Burroughs, the re-evaluation was both discount and markup, and perhaps it was this that made him such a great avatar of the emergent counter-culture.

Janus-faced, and like some terminally cadaverous butler, Burroughs ushers in the new society of kicks for insight as well as kicks' sake. In the final paragraph of *Junky* he writes: 'Kick is seeing things from a special angle. Kick is momentary freedom from the claims of the ageing, cautious, nagging, frightened flesh.' He might have added that kicking is what you do to God's ribs once he's down on the ground and begging for mercy.

By all of which you can take it as stated that in a very important sense I view Burroughs's *Junky* not to be a book about heroin addiction at all, any more than I perceive Camus' *The Fall* (1956) to be about the legal profession, or Sartre's *Nausea* (1938) to be concerned with the problems of historical research. All three are works in which an alienated protagonist grapples with a world perceived as irretrievably external and irredeemably meaningless. All three are trajected at the reader in the form of insistent monologues. As Burroughs writes of the hoodlum 'Jack' in *Junky*: 'He had a knack of throwing his voice directly into your consciousness. No external noise drowned him out.' The same could be said of 'William Lee' himself, or Clamence or Roquentin.

But before grappling with the existential lode of *Junky*, let's return to that cover illustration with its portrayal of 'William Lee' as Rock Hudson and his common-law wife, Joan Vollmer, as Kim Novak. When I say Burroughs himself must have regarded the illustration – if he thought of it at all – as evidence of the magical universe he conceived of as underpinning and interpenetrating our own, it is because the first draft of the book was completed in the months immediately preceding his killing of Vollmer on 6 September 1951 in Mexico City. Burroughs himself wrote in his 1985 foreword to *Queer* (which was completed in the year after Vollmer's death, but remained unpublished until thirty-four years later), 'I am forced to the appalling conclusion that I would never have become a writer but for Joan's death, and to a realization of the extent to which this event has motivated and formulated my writing.'

Much has been written and even more conjectured about the killing. Burroughs himself described it as 'the accidental shooting death'; and although he jumped bail, he was only convicted – *in absentia* by the Mexican court – of homicide. However, to my mind this rings false with the way he characterised his life – and his writing – thereafter: 'I live with the constant threat of possession and the constant need to escape from possession, from Control.' Burroughs saw the agent of possession implicated in the killing as external to him, 'a definite entity'. He went further, hypothesising that such an entity might devise the modern, psychological conception of possession as a function of the subject's own psyche: 'since nothing is more dangerous to a possessor than being seen as a separate invading creature by the host it has invaded'.

Personally, I think Burroughs's definition of 'possession' was tantamount to an admission of intent. Certainly, the hypothesis of murderous impulsiveness squares better with the impromptu 'William Tell act' (whereby he called upon Vollmer to place a glass on her head which he would then shoot off), than his own bewilderment in the face of an act of such cruel stupidity and fatal rashness. (He knew the gun to shoot low, and what would've happened to the glass shards even if he had succeeded? There were others in the room.)

I belabour these events for two reasons. First, because I think an understanding of the milieu within which Burroughs and Vollmer operated, and the nature of their life together, is essential in disentangling the *post hoc* mythologising of the writer and his life from the very grim reality of active drug addiction that constitutes the action of *Junky*. When Burroughs was off heroin at all he was a bad, blackout drunk (for evidence of this you need look no further than his own confirmation in *Junky*). However much he cared for Vollmer, their life together was clearly at an impasse (their sexuality was incompatible – she was even beginning to object to his drug use); and what could be more natural – if only momentarily – than to conceive of ridding himself of an obvious blockage?

Second, although the bulk of *Junky* was in place before the killing, Burroughs continued to revise the text at least as late as July 1952, including current events such as the arrival from New York of his old heroin-dealing partner Bill Garver (whose name is changed to 'Bill Gains' in the text). Indeed, such is the contemporary character of what Burroughs was writing about that at one point in the book (and this remains uncorrected in the present edition), he actually lapses into the present tense: 'Our Lady of Chalma seems to be the patron saint of junkies and cheap thieves because all Lupita's customers make the pilgrimage once a year. The Black Bastard rents a cubicle in the church and pushes papers of junk outrageously cut with milk sugar.'

The meat of the text of *Junky* is as close as Burroughs could get to a factual account of his own experience of heroin. In a letter to Allen Ginsberg (who had worried that the book constituted a justification of Burroughs's addiction), he inveighed: 'As a matter of fact the book is the only accurate account I ever read of the real horror of junk. But I don't mean it as justification or deterrent or anything but an accurate account of what I experienced while I was on the junk. You might say it was a travel book more than anything else. It starts where I first make contact with junk, and it ends where no more contact is possible.' To analyse the exactness of the correspondence between the text of *Junky* and what is known of the author's life between 1944 and 1952 (the time span of the book), one has only to read through his collected letters for this period,* or Ted Morgan's excellent biography.**

All of which is by way of saying: *Junky* is not a novel at all, it is a memoir; 'William Lee' and William Burroughs are one and the same person. I realise that in the light of what I've said above – positioning *Junky* as an existentialist

* *The Letters of William S. Burroughs 1945 to 1959*, edited by Oliver Harris.
** *Literary Outlaw: The Life and Times of William S. Burroughs.*

text on a par with the work of Sartre and Camus – this must seem bizarre, but I think it's simply another aspect of the author's own schizoid nature that makes fact serve for fiction. Burroughs's own conception of himself was essentially fictional, and it's not superfluous to observe that before he began to write with any fixity he had already become a character in other writers' works, most notably Jack Kerouac's *On the Road*. He also signed his letters to Ginsberg, Kerouac et al. with his nom de plume, as well as using his correspondence as a form of work in progress, peppering his epistles to the Beats with his trademark riffs and routines. By the time Burroughs was living in Tangier in the late 1950s, his sense of being little more than a cipher, or a fictional construct, had become so plangent that he practised the art of insubstantiality with true zeal, revelling in the moniker '*El Hombre Invisible*'.

For Burroughs, with his increasingly fluid view of reality, the confabulation of fact and fiction was inevitable, the separation of life and work impossible. Doubtless, he himself would seek to underpin – if not justify – this with an appeal to metaphysics, but from the vantage of a half-century later, with Burroughs dead, and the counterculture he helped spawn reduced to little more than attitudinising, T-shirt slogans and global chains of coffee shops, it seems about time to accept that his drug addiction was psychologically anterior to all of this, rather than some optional add-on. It's time to take Burroughs at his most truthful and gimlet-eyed, when he writes in *Junky*: 'Junk is not a kick. It is a way of life.' Burroughs was the perfect incarnation of late-twentieth-century Western angst precisely because he was an addict. Self-deluding, vain, narcissistic, self-obsessed, and yet curiously perceptive about the sickness of the world if not his own malaise, Burroughs both offered up (and was compelled to provide) his psyche as a form of Petri dish, within which were cultured the obsessive and compulsive viruses of modernity.

Burroughs never managed to recover from his addiction at all, and died in 1997 physically dependent on the synthetic opiate methadone. I find this a delicious irony: the great hero of freedom from social restraint, himself in bondage to a drug originally synthesised by Nazi chemists, and dubbed 'Dolophine' in honour of the Führer; the fearless libertarian expiring in the arms of an ersatz Morpheus, actively promoted by the federal government as a 'cure' for heroin addiction. In the prologue to *Junky* and the introduction to *The Naked Lunch*, Burroughs writes of his own addiction as if it were a thing of the past, but this was never the case. In a thin-as-a-rake's progress that saw him move from America to Mexico, to Morocco, to France, to Britain, back to New York, and eventually to small-town Kansas, Burroughs was in flight either from the consequences of his chemical dependency, or seeking to avoid the drugs he craved.

But really the die was cast long before, in the dingy apartments of wartime New York, and the ramshackle habitations of his exile, where Burroughs saw 'life measured out in eyedroppers of morphine solution'. By the time he and Vollmer were ensconced in Mexico City, the pronounced deterioration of their long-term addictions (hers to amphetamine) had already taken its heavy toll. Contemporary accounts describe the once pretty Vollmer as 'a large, shapeless woman, with a doughy face and the kind of eyes that used to be placed in antique dolls, made of blue glass and quite vacant . . .' while Burroughs was 'cadaverous-looking – thin lips, bad teeth, yellow fingers and eyes like death'.*

Burroughs was incapable of confronting the real physical degradation implied by their *folie à deux*, and, as with Vollmer herself, the text of *Junky* avoids the subject altogether, or glosses it – as above – with flat untruths and slurred shibboleths about heroin's life-preserving properties. The writer's wife isn't mentioned at all until page 61, and then only in the context of an aside when 'William Lee' is being inducted into the Federal Hospital at Lexington for a 'cure': 'Patient seems secure and states his reason for seeking cure is necessity of providing for his family.' Thereafter, she is allocated a walk-on part when 'Lee' is busted in New Orleans, before evaporating once more, until, in Mexico City 'she did something she had never done before . . .'

In a postscript to a letter to Allen Ginsberg (who was acting as Burroughs's literary agent) written seven months after Vollmer's death, Burroughs said: 'About death of Joan. I do not see how this could be worked in. I wish you would talk them out of that idea. I will take care

* Marianne Elvins, reported by Ted Morgan in *Literary Outlaw*.

of her disappearance. I did not go into my domestic life in *Junk* because it was, in the words of Sam Johnson, "Nothing to the purpose."' In the text Lee and his wife are said to be 'separated', but while being perhaps a little *de trop*, '(taking) care of her disappearance' was more to the purpose.

As for the text itself, it reads today as fresh and unvarnished as it ever has. Burroughs's deadpan reportage owes as much to the hard-boiled style of the detective thriller writer Dashiell Hammett as it does to his more elevated philosophical inclinations. At the time of writing Burroughs was still much in thrall to the proto-Wittgensteinian ideas of Count Korzybski, whose lecture series he had attended at the University of Chicago in 1939. Korzybski propounded a theory of 'General Semantics', which held that it is the gulf between language and reality which fosters so many philosophical conundrums of the either/or form. In eschewing rhetorical flourish or adjectival excess, Burroughs sought to remain silent about what could not be said, just like the drug subculture he was so enchanted by: 'She shoved the package of weed at me. "Take this and get out," she said. "You're both mother fuckers." She was half asleep. Her voice was matter-of-fact as if referring to actual incest.'

But while Burroughs aims at a plain-speaking style, he cannot avoid his propensity for the *mot juste*, any more than he can escape his destiny as a natural raconteur. His later, more free-form works – such as *The Naked Lunch* – were often worked up out of his own conversational routines, and so it is that *Junky* maintains its high level of entertainment by juxtaposing acute descriptions with acutely remembered conversations. Only Burroughs could characterise the movement of a posse of young thugs as being 'as stylized as a ballet'; describe a lie as 'worn smooth' by repetition; or write of an addict's aggression thus: 'Waves of hostility and suspicion flowed out from his large brown eyes like some sort of television broadcast. The effect was almost like a physical impact.' Burroughs's humour is as dry as tinder, so that while he refuses his authorial persona the comfortable clothing of a physical description, we are nonetheless given a frighteningly clear picture of who he is in every snide put-down – 'Affability, however, did not come natural to him' – and snappy one-liner: '. . . a terrific bore once he has spotted you as a "a man of intelligence."' And his apothegms are apt, if revolting, as if La Rochefoucauld were an arrested adolescent: 'When people start talking about their bowel movements they are as inexorable as the processes of which they speak.'

Burroughs also employs his own special version of the pathetic fallacy – for him everyone has the face he deserves: 'He had the embalmed look of all bondsmen, as though paraffin had been injected under the skin.' Moreover, the capacity of someone's face to imprint itself upon the observer is a function of their status in reality; 'If you walked fast down a crowded street, and passed Dupré, his face would be forced on your memory – like in the card trick where the operator fans the cards rapidly, saying, "Take a card, any card," as he forces a certain card into your hand.' And again: 'Some people you can spot as far as you can see; others you can't be sure of until you are close enough to touch them. Junkies are mostly in sharp focus.' Except – please note – when they are withdrawing from the drug: 'His face was blurred, unrecognizable, at the same time shrunken and tumescent.'

These parings of description are sufficient to give the lie entirely to the idea that there is any profound break between the apparent 'objectivity' of *Junky* and the stylistic excesses of *The Naked Lunch*. All of Burroughs's dystopian world picture is here, in this text, in embryo. The milieu of heroin addiction, as described by Burroughs, is one fraught with magical thinking. And indeed, this does correspond to the mentality of most addicts, who, because of their psychological and physical dependence on a commodity viewed by the rest of society as an unmitigated evil, find themselves habitual participants in a form of black mass.

Burroughs's preoccupation with the viral quality of addiction, as if it is an external organism transmitted from heroin user to heroin user, is concomitant with his sublimation of its very real character as an aspect of the individual psychopathology. But he widens the ambit of this metaphor, to include a portrayal of a dystopian community in the section of *Junky* dealing with the Rio Grande Valley, where he and Kells Elvins ('Evans' in the text) unsuccessfully farmed citrus fruit in 1946. 'Death hangs over the Valley like an invisible smog. The place exerts a curious magnetism on the moribund. The dying cell gravitates to the Valley . . .' Burroughs's coinage of 'the cellular equation of junk', with all that it implies, is his synecdoche for all of the ills of the post-atomic age, and it will reappear in this guise throughout many of his later works.

Present too in *Junky* is the unsettling notion of quasi-human organisms that both prefigure and mutate from humanity itself. Burroughs's 'mugwump' makes its appearance: 'He has a large straight nose. His lips are thin and purple-blue like the lips of a penis. The skin is tight and smooth over his face. He is basically obscene beyond any possible vile act or practice . . . Perhaps he stores something in his body – a substance to prolong life – of which he is periodically milked by his masters. He is as specialized as an insect, for the performance of some inconceivably vile function.' Burroughs and Elvins travelled to Mexico in 1946 to take the Bogomoletz serum, an alleged anti-ageing agent, and together with this, there are veiled references in *Junky* to Wilhelm Reich's theory of the 'cancer biopathy'; the idea that cancer – and by extension social ills as well – is a function of sexual repression.

Burroughs's raptor propensity for looting the wilder clifftop eyries of intellectual speculation and mixing their eggs with his own embryonic ideas is what makes *Junky* such a nourishing omelette. When Burroughs says of a stool pigeon (or informer): 'You could see him bustling into Black and Tan headquarters during the Irish Trouble, in a dirty gray toga turning in Christians, giving information to the Gestapo, the GPU, sitting in a café talking to a narcotics agent. Always the same thin, ratty face, shabby out-of-date clothes, whiny, penetrating voice.' He is with this single image evoking the circular historians Spengler and Vico, quite as much as he is describing a real individual. Just as when he writes – of a homosexual – 'I could see him moving in the light of campfires, the ambiguous gestures fading out into the dark. Sodomy is as old as the human species.' Burroughs prefigures his later experiments that 'cut up' and 'fold in' texts, in an effort to annihilate all dualisms and abolish the linear time of conventional narrative.

And in the drunken phantasmagoria that follow his cessation of heroin in Mexico City, Burroughs scrys out the place of dead roads, where all his fictional vehicles will terminate decades hence. 'A series of faces, hieroglyphs, distorted and leading to the final place where the human road ends, where the human form can no longer contain the crustacean horror that has grown inside it.'

These signposts to future fictional topographies may be what makes *Junky* such a key text for the committed Burroughsian, but what will impress the first-time reader is the author's take on the nature of intoxication itself. From Burroughs's first description of a shot of morphine – 'a spreading wave of relaxation slackening the muscles away from the bones so that you seem to float without outlines, like lying in warm salt water' – to his neat encapsulations of using cocaine, marijuana and even peyote, he remains simultaneously deep and sharp about the realities of drug experience. In this vital respect *Junky* is the 'true account' of which he speaks. From the vantage point of my own – not inconsiderable – experience of intoxication, I can say that *Junky* is unrivalled as a book about taking drugs.

What it isn't, for the reasons outlined above, is any kind of true analysis of the nature of addiction itself. Burroughs's own view – 'You become a narcotics addict because you do not have strong motivations in any other direction. Junk wins by default' – is a deceptively thin, Pandora's portfolio of an idea that entirely begs the question: for what kind of person could drug addiction represent a 'strong motivation'? Surely only one for whom alienation, and a lack of either moral or spiritual direction, was inbuilt.

Indeed, this is the great sadness of *Junky* (and Burroughs himself) as I conceive it. You can reread this entire text, assuming the hypothesis of addiction as a latent pathology, present in the individual prior to his having any direct experience of chemical dependency, and everything that Burroughs says about habitual heroin use begins to make perfect sense. But taking him at his own, self-justifying estimation (predicated on a renunciation of drugs that never, ever came), Burroughs's *Junky* becomes the very archetype of the romanticisation of excess that has so typified our era: 'I loosened the tie, and the dropper emptied into my vein. Coke hit my head, a pleasant dizziness and tension, while the morphine spread through my body in relaxing waves. "Was that alright?" asked Ike, smiling. "If God made anything better, he kept it for himself," I said.'

In conclusion, to return to *Junky* as a key existentialist text, it is Burroughs's own denial of the nature of his addiction that makes this book capable of being read as a fiendish parable of modern alienation. For, in describing addiction as 'a way of life', Burroughs makes of the hypodermic a microscope, through which he can examine the soul of man under late-twentieth-century capitalism.* His descriptions of the 'junk territories' his alter ego inhabits are, in fact, depictions of urban alienation itself. And just as in these areas junk is 'a ghost in daylight on a crowded street', so his junkie characters – who are invariably described as 'invisible', 'dematerialized' and 'boneless' – are, like the pseudonymous 'William Lee' himself, the sentient residue left behind when the soul has been cooked up and injected into space.

6 September 2001
Introduction to the Penguin Classics edition of *Junky*
by William S. Burroughs

---

* 'Junk is the ideal product . . . the ultimate merchandise. No sales talk necessary. The client will crawl through a sewer and beg to buy . . . The junk merchant does not sell his product to the consumer, he sells the consumer to his product. He does not improve and simplify his merchandise. He degrades and simplifies the client. He pays his staff in junk.' *The Naked Lunch* (1959)

Being a Character

When I began writing fiction in the late 1980s I already had a profound suspicion of the characters with which novels tend to be populated. These entities – for, as I hope to demonstrate in what follows, fictional characters are worthy of such an ascription – may arouse in us many of the emotions provoked by their flesh-and-blood models, yet they are so easily spun into being out of lexical threads, we'd be wise to treat them with grave suspicion. If you're listening to this broadcast in your home, and you now hear the front door being unlocked and opened in its characteristic way, followed by footsteps heading towards you, then should you really be surprised when the door of the room you sit in swings open, and a bent-backed old woman haltingly enters.

She's leaning heavily on a stick with a rubber ferrule; wearing an old tweed overcoat worn shiny at cuff and elbow, and has a dirty-beige muffler wound around her scrawny neck. You receive an impression of cornflower-blue eyes set deep in wrinkly reticulation, hair white and fine as feathers – a voice rasps, 'My name's Ethel Nairn, I'm sorry to intrude but I've come to speak to you about the residents' association.' Now, if you're capable in the ordinary way of suspending disbelief, you may have lent Ethel Nairn a degree of credibility – actually, even I believe Ethel Nairn exists, such that an entire range of hopes, desires, fears and impulses could readily be ascribed to her – and this despite the fact I myself only conjured this figment into being minutes ago.

As it is with Ethel Nairn, so it goes with the entire community of characters we either create ourselves, or have summoned to exist on our behalf by writers, screenwriters, games designers and a host of other so-called 'creatives'. Even the characters that people advertisements can take on many of the attributes we associate with living, breathing humans – escaping their confinement in these propagandising playlets to stalk the corridors of our mind. The more sophisticated fictional characters become, the more their similarity to us is plainly evident; by the time we encounter the Emma Bovarys and Leopold Blooms of this world, we're altogether comfortable with the sympathy they arouse in us. Fiction offers many pleasures: we may enjoy its capacity to make the world anew for us through its descriptions, or to advance our understanding of science or philosophy through its application of ideas to examples of human behaviour, but although it does – on examination – seem so faint as to be numinous, nonetheless it's our conviction that fictional characters' hopes, fears and desires matter that allows fictions to become facts on the ground; a ground we sympathetically traverse alongside them as they're subjected to the vicissitudes of plot – its sudden reversals and twists, its caprices and its terrible inexorability.

As I say: when I was a young writer I mistrusted these entities, with their slippery claim to have reality – and so I rendered the characters in my own fictions in ways that drew attention to their preposterousness. I made them caricatures, stereotypes or hieratic figures – I denied them the oxygen of believable dialogue, and the nourishment of a credible inner life. I'd tell anyone who evinced an interest my suspicions about these so-called 'characters', and even give them the Ethel Nairn shtick, so demonstrating the airiness of their own disbelief; my fiction – I'd lecture them – is about the exhilaration of ideas, rather than the enervation provoked by these initially seductive – but ultimately nonsensical – simulacra of people. Then, with middle age encroaching, my views radically changed, swerving in the direction of sentiments I associated with slogans in third-rate greetings cards. People who need people – I began to suspect – are the luckiest people in the world.

But the people people need are not necessarily flesh and blood; people also need people who manifest all their own torturous confusions – about life, love and the pursuit of happiness – but whose own existence is quite immaterial. People need people who can show them just how difficult it is to maintain the illusion that one's the author of one's own life. People need people whose lives can be seen to follow a dramatic arc, so that no matter what vicissitudes they encounter, the people who survey them can be reassured that when the light begins to fade, these people – to whose frail psyches we've had privileged access – will at least feel it's all meant something.

To regard an invented scenario as a believable human life is, when you stop to consider it, an astonishing feat: not simply a suspension of disbelief, but a hefting of it into the heavens. The lives – or plots – of fictional characters are fraught with unbelievable coincidences, or blessed by implausible serendipity; fictional characters, even at their most confused and distraught, still have a sort of clarity of thought and self-presentation, for of necessity their incomprehensible situation must be rendered comprehensible for it to exist at all. Fictional characters – unlike the messy organisms from which they derive – float free from the sordid contingencies of the body, because, no matter how convincingly they're portrayed as being embodied, the medium within which they operate is, of necessity, a mental one.

Of course, the dramatis personae of a play have a material existence as marks on a page or actors on a stage – the same is true of the characters in films, although often in our queered reality, the humans that give them embodiment take primacy; so it is that we say we've seen Angelina Jolie or Brad Pitt in a film, whereas, in truth, the only film we could possibly have seen them in is life itself. As for my own art form, the novel, the characters that wander Austenian landscape gardens, or gather in Proustian salons, or stroll Joycean streets, are at once the realest and the most insubstantial, being in truth nothing but combinations of signs, easily capable of denomination and then digitisation into long sequences of zeroes and ones.

Yet there is one aspect of these entities' predicament that I believe explains precisely why it is we find them so affecting, and believe in their self-consciousnesses so whole-heartedly. It would be absurd, of course, to suggest that we think of Anna Karenina as 'real' in the same way we think of people as real; nevertheless we certainly do believe that Anna Karenina believes herself to be a free agent, responsible for making decisions that will alter the course of her life. She could begin the relationship with Vronsky, or she could not. Even when we have thoroughly explored the world she inhabits, and are reading *Anna Karenina* for the third or fourth time, we can still entertain the notion that it need not all end under the wheels of a passing train.

Which is strange, because we've only to turn to the end of the book to reacquaint ourselves with the facts; which are that Anna Karenina's fate – like those of all fictional characters – was, is, and will always be utterly determined: it matters not one jot what she does or says or agonises about, her suicide remains a foregone conclusion, one that we view from outside the timeframe of the novel. In philosophic terms, the vantage we as readers share with the third-person narrators of fictions is sub specie aeternitatis – from the perspective of eternity. We might like to comfort ourselves with the notion that it's this godlike overview which kindles in us such intense sympathy for the destinies of these man- and womanikins; however, I suspect the truth is rather more disturbing.

It occurs to me that it's precisely in fictional characters' conviction – despite all evidence to the contrary – that they are the authors of their own lives, that they resemble us most. We really intuit that, in between the alternative scenarios of chaotic contingency and universal necessity, there can't possibly be any real wiggle-room within which the human will can operate; yet we persist – and cannot help persisting – in the delusion that we too are the authors of our own lives. That we are unable to turn to the last page of the book of our lives then read the fate inscribed there does nothing to counter our suspicion it has already been written; after all, the same is the case for Ethel Nairn and millions of other fictional characters, and as I believe I've already demonstrated, it's precisely this shared predicament which makes them so very worthy of our compassion.

20 February 2015
Broadcast on 'A Point of View', BBC Radio 4

Australia and I

When, early this year, I was asked to give this address, I didn't hesitate to accept – nor did I prevaricate when asked what subject I'd be tackling. Such alacrity on my part is uncommon: my writing room, at the top of my house in south London, hasn't been cleaned since we moved into the house in 1997. Surveying the furred surfaces and far-off-white walls I often recall Quentin Crisp's fine observation that 'dust is peace'. It was a peace my impulsiveness put paid to: for, having said I'd be speaking about my 'vexed relationship' with Australia, I've been bitterly regretting it ever since. In order to explain why – why the impulsiveness, and why the regret – I'll also have to give you a sense of how it is Australia and I have got along. Or not.

I first came to Australia 33 years ago in August 1983. My father, Peter Self, had emigrated a few years prior to this and was already well established with house, job, car and regulation third wife. He was facing mandatory retirement at 65 from his academic post at the London School of Economics – whereas he'd been offered a senior fellowship at the Australian National University with no temporal strings attached. Dad had been out in Australia for a protracted period before and he unashamedly loved the country – in a way, he and his wife were proto-grey nomads, seeking a connection with the island-continent through near-constant travel. They would've appreciated the sentiment of a bumper sticker I saw in Alice Springs a fortnight ago: 'Adventure before Dementia'. Once domiciled here my father's Austrophilia only increased, and in the late 1990s – a year or so before he died – he took Australian citizenship. Perhaps this is part of what vexes me – after all, while it's reasonable to expect someone to switch nationalities in either the morning or the high noon of their lives, it seems a little perverse to do so in your mid-seventies when the violet shades of evening are thronging. Besides, if my father was technically an Australian, does this retroactively render me a demi-Ocker?

The weather in Sydney had been fine and sunny, but in Canberra it was distinctly chilly, and – to employ a green, glistening, globe-girdling idiom – pissing down. My father was a dolmen of a man whose sartorial style had frozen around 1953. He affected a vast and shapeless gabardine macintosh, equally amorphous grey flannel bags, and huge brogues of antique workmanship. He drove us along rain-drenched boulevards to the suburb of Acton, which was where, he told me, he lived. I laughed like a Canberra drain – the 24-hour flight meant nothing anymore, for my father's presence was as one with the pathetic fallacy he was piloting me through; far from lighting out for the territory, as I stared about me at the bungalows and low-rise apartment blocks, I realised the end of my exploring had been to arrive where I'd begun; for I'd been in Acton, west London – which looked not that dissimilar – only a day or so before.

It didn't take me long to realise, contra this sense of déjà vu, that I would indeed be knowing Canberra for the first time. Up early the next morning I went for a jog around Lake Burley Griffin, marvelling at its consummate artificiality – and marvelling still more at the sweeping, po-mo façade of Parliament House, which appeared to be being injected with its own hypodermic flagstaff. In an underpass I laboured through, a sole graffito proclaimed a sentiment I was to hear oft-repeated in the months and years to come: 'They Took the Dreamtime and Turned it into a Nightmare'.

When I got back to Acton I quipped to Dad: 'What does "Canberra" mean? No, no – don't tell me, I know: it's an ancient Aboriginal word meaning Milton Keynes.' But he took this in good part; one of his specialisms was urban and regional planning, and he'd been among the theorists of Britain's post-war new towns – indeed, part of what attracted him to Canberra was its garden city zoning. But for me, in my early and turbulent twenties, a suburb half a world away was a sort of nightmare – Sartre's *Huis Clos* remade with a bureaucrat, an academic and a politician, all Australian, wiling away a hellish eternity. Over the next couple of months my father did his best: we went walking out at Tidbinbilla, and took trips to the Mudgee and the coast at Byron Bay. To a Little Englander the distortions in scale presented by the Australian landscape are yet more overwhelming than oddities of flora and fauna. But you know this – you've imbibed since birth the *unheimlich* qualities of your homeland. The sense of deep familiarity and equally deep estrangement I felt, staring out over the hypertrophied Yorkshire moors you call the Blue Mountains is surely only antipodal to what you must feel on encountering our shrunken and domesticated wilds? I recall a geographic discussion with an Australian in Cologne of all places, which began civilly enough, but ended with her near-bellowing, 'No, *you're* the antipodes!'

I loved Australia – the physical reality of it, that is. As for the people, the culture, the society . . . Well, to return to *Huis Clos*, hell is indeed other people, including one's own alienated self. I chafed and fretted in the cloistral Canberra atmosphere. I was a faculty brat who'd only recently graduated, yet here I was, back at university again. Still, I did my reading – recommended by my father and his colleagues – and everything I imbibed (including Emu Export) convinced me that if I were to stand a chance of enlightenment I needed to encounter Australia *profonde*. I had a degree in economics, and my father was able, through a well-placed friend, to wangle me a job with the Lands Department of the Northern Territory government. So it was I boarded the scheduled Greyhound service and, like Stuart in search of Wingillpinin, headed counter-intuitively southwest. A day later I staggered about Adelaide trying to get the circulation back into my legs, and marvelling at this strange simulacrum of Cheltenham, complete with its cast of blue-blazered retirees from the colonial service. A day after that the bus had emptied out – and I could understand why: there was no air conditioning or toilet, while the suspension struggled to cope with the corrugations on the long sections of un-metalled road. Flies buzzed around my eyes – I'd never felt so acutely the physics of the sun, a hydrogen bomb ever-exploding for aeons. I sat in the fallout and sweated.

Somewhere between Coober Pedy and the Alice, two men who'd been deeply asleep for hours in the seats across the aisle from me, woke up. With no fuss and apparently no sense of discombobulation, they rose and went forward – one said something to the driver and he slewed the bus off the track. The two men got down, the door shut, and as we pulled away I watched them heading off across the fractured saltpan at a steady lope. They carried nothing – no bags, no water even. I was still trying to comprehend their behaviour when, an hour or so later, the bus slowed again then turned off onto a side-track beside a great pile of chucked tinnies, mangled sheets of corrugated iron, discarded engine parts and other trash. A few minutes later we pulled into the settlement, and struggling out from under humpies came people who resembled the men who'd made off into the desert. At last I was vis-à-vis with these obscure objects of desire.

Let me pause here while you're still absorbing that last sentence – trying to figure out if it was in some way offensive, and if so: to whom? I want to do two things during this little fermata – the first is to reassure you: the narrative stops here; I'm not going to camel-drive you through all my Australian travels. Nonetheless, in what follows I am going to ask you to think about what Australia represents specifically for *a writer* from overseas – Australia not only as subject matter, but as potential muse. This is, after all, a *writers'* festival – its very name calling our attention to the absolute primacy of the creative act; for us, the people of the Logos, there can be nothing at all *avant la lettre*.

I said I accepted the festival's invitation with alacrity – but much as I've enjoyed my time here in Melbourne, there wasn't a sorbet's chance in Hades I would've circum-navigated the earth purely to attend a literary festival. Put bluntly: in a literary world where almost everything ever written is instantaneously available anywhere, and most of it gratis, the only remaining fungible literary property is the writer himself. But I didn't come here to be complicit in my own commoditisation, or to push product – which, as I believe I may've implied above, I now believe to be a largely futile enterprise. No, I returned to revisit the Australia *profonde* which entranced me as a young man, and to expose my three sons to the far stranger facts that have underpinned some of my peculiar fictions. We arrived in Darwin on 13 August, and since then have been travel-ling overland to get to here – if I were to pitch forward now over this lectern and expire, I'd be checking out from humanity's hotel both happy and fulfilled.

To me, fundamentally a writer of place, to come here as any other bourgeois might go on a business trip, is a solecism of an order to disrupt the space–time continuum. For years now I've felt the claustrophobia of my own right, tight little isle radiating out to encompass the earth. Eliot was right physically as much as metaphysically: we travel, yes – but only to arrive at a simulacrum of the place from which we've recently departed. We gaze upon the few vistas that still truly have the capacity to estrange us, through lenses ground by the competing pressures of time and money.

I speak only for myself, but when someone from the northern hemisphere tells me they've *been* to Australia, meaning any or all of the following cities – Sydney, Melbourne, Perth, Adelaide and Brisbane together with their environs – I groan in despair. I feel exactly the same way when I encounter young Australians in London and ask them how much they've travelled in their own land, only to discover the answer is rather less than those tourists who believe 'Australia' to be a bridge, a rock, an opera house and a white-sand beach lined with casinos. Of course, an ignorance of one's own hinterland is neither exclusive to Western cultures, nor to our own times – nevertheless, ours is the era and the society which prizes mobility – of goods, of productive economic units (or 'people' as I call them), and of money – above all else. And yet a mobility predicated on a consumption-driven economy forever poisons the well of its own novelty; it creates a desert of branded goods and calls it freedom of choice. And in the era of global positioning technology, we find the spatial equivalent of our avarice, for we have come to know the location of everything, while understanding nothing about our own orientation – so it is we're led by the nose on to the next fabulous retail opportunity.

The second issue I wanted to tackle during this irenic interlude is the matter of offence itself. In William Burroughs's *The Yage Letters*, a collection of his correspondence with Allen Ginsberg written during his travels in South America in the early 1950s, he writes of the relief he experienced on reaching Peru, because it was a country of sufficient size that Peruvians felt free not to be patriotic – indeed, to slag off their homeland. Therefore I ask of you, dear audience, are you big enough? Big enough not only to critique Australia itself, but to listen to someone from overseas – and an epically whingeing Pom to boot – critiquing your motherland? Not, I hasten to add, that Australia – any more than any other nation of millions – is a unitary phenomenon, for there are many Australias. Nevertheless, what seems incontestable is that no matter how fissiparous a society may be, no matter how full of conflicted groups, once a stranger starts some aggro they all rally round to repel him. Dr Johnson considered patriotism to be 'the last refuge of the scoundrel' not because he thought of patriotism as scoundrelly (how could he as a High Tory?), but because he believed there was no greater profanation anyone could commit than to denigrate his own country.

I dissent from this: to me the nation state is a lamentably necessary, territorially defined monopoly on the exercise of violence – and in Britain and Australia alike, this monopoly is accorded a spiritual significance, one annually re-sanctified by rituals designed to maintain its citizenries' awareness of its foundational myths. For Australia, 2015 has been particularly important – the centenary of the mass sacrifice of its young men on the altar of patriotism. Paul Keating and others of the Australian left may decry Gallipolism, but the fact remains it was on the shores of the Bosporus that the emergent Australian state secured its own monopoly on violence. In Britain, 2016 will be equally significant. But whether it was Gallipoli or the Somme which was ritually blood-soaked is beside the point – as General David Morrison said at a religious service held in this city earlier this year: 'We remember, and we are, at least in part, defined by that act of remembrance.' He went on to express the idea that 'in an uncertain future' our recollection of these thousands of young men, machine-gunned to death in ignorance and fear, can remind us of, 'What we have been and can be: courageous, compassionate and brave.'

A novelist can be many things, including courageous, compassionate and brave; but I believe one thing he can't be if he's to use the form as Stendhal intended – as a mirror held up unflinchingly to life – is a patriot, if by a patriot is understood anyone who uncritically accepts the values of their own state or society as innately superior to those of any other. No, the novelist must be – to borrow a phrase coined by the autistic writer Temple Grandin – an anthropologist on Mars: interrogating the most commonplace phenomena as if they're utterly bizarre. In my own fictive practice such hyper-objectivity goes hand in hand with a particular attention to place – something I find easy enough to understand; after all, if you're not at home anywhere in the world, how much more compelling is the psychological requirement to mitigate that estrangement. When teaching at Cornell University in the 1950s, Vladimir Nabokov would commence each lecture by drawing on the blackboard; this might be a floor plan of Mansfield Park, or a map of Proust's 'two ways' at Combray, but in either case he was drawing his students' attention to two interrelated phenomena: narrative prose is particularly well adapted to conveying a sense of place, while all fiction – no matter how otherworldly – is grounded in cold facts. You realise this when you read a novel or story set in a given location, and become insidiously aware the writer doesn't really know the place themselves, even though *you yourself have never been there.*

This is why almost all my own fiction is set in London – and not even in greater London but the irregular triangle of city between Camden Town, Golders Green and East Finchley, the area my knowledge of which expanded and transformed as I grew, from the seeming-panoptic vision of childhood, to the synoptic understanding of an adult. It's like that, growing up, isn't it? We dabble in the crab grass, building mighty cities of twigs, cracking the whip over corvees of ants – and this is a world entire; then, as we grow bigger, the wider world concertinas into our comprehension by reason of its functionality. So it is we say we 'know' London, or Melbourne, or Beijing – when what we really mean is: I know *how to use it*. Of course, while I confidently assert these things now, they were never givens – rather I set my fiction in London because of that other stentorian warning issued to tyro writers: WRITE ABOUT WHAT YOU KNOW. I have set some scenes in some fictions in other parts of England and Britain – I've even set a novella in Zurich. Some made-up stuff has gone down in my mother's homeland, the United States – after all, she could reasonably claim to have given birth to what invention I possess. But after London, the location in which I've set most of my narratives is here – is Australia.

I added it all up before I left home: I've published 16 works of fiction since 1991, and of these I estimate one and a third have been set here, so, around 9 per cent. As for the factual underpinning, between 1983 and now I've spent approximately a year in Australia. For someone as determined to write places they know as I am this disproportion is worrying – I've inflated my experience by at least a factor of three. This isn't perhaps as egregious as the late John Updike, who, after a scant week lazing on Copacabana penned a novel adventitiously titled *Brazil*, but nonetheless it suggests a writer willing to exploit what he perceives as the exotic rather more than he is the commonplace. I stand guilty as charged: as I say, I found your homeland to be transcendently beautiful, while I also discovered its first peoples to be beautiful transcendental idealists. I came to Australia initially to visit my father – that I came back was because I, in the manner of young Westerners the world over, believed I'd encountered the noumenon in this phenomenal place. If you like, Australia was my India, and the Aboriginals my sadhus.

First peoples, first nations, indigenous people, Aboriginals, blackfellas – what, we may ask yet again, is in a name? And the answer is, for us, the people of the book: everything. We excel in euphemising as a means of exclusion, and ironising as a way of ignoring what we ourselves mean. I cannot claim to have spent huge amounts of time with Australia's first peoples, but I know enough to say I've witnessed rehearsals for the initiation of the Jingili, that I've consorted with Tiwi and Groote Islanders, that I've camped out in Pitjantjatjara lands, and seen the bauxite being scraped from those of the Yolngu. I've been a crass idiot in many areas of my life – charging into situations armed with very little knowledge and doing some very dangerous things, but credit where credit is due, even aged 23 I wasn't deluded enough to imagine I could connect with these people, that I could understand – let alone help them.

I was aided in this by white Australians I met during my time in Darwin; members of the 1960s radical generation, who instead of taking a Grand Tour of Earl's Court, penetrated the heart of their own Centralian darkness. They were indeed trying to help the Aboriginal people, but they drew my attention to this cosmic catch-22: to truly help, a whitefella must acquire a defined position in a tribe – but once initiated his usefulness in the balanda world declines proportionately. Writing a few years ago in *The Monthly*, Galarrwuy Yunupingu identified the true compass of the gap between Australia's two principal mobs: 'Who in the senior levels of the commonwealth public service has lived through these things? Who in the parliament? No one speaks an Aboriginal language, let alone has the ability to sit with a young man or woman (. . .) and find out what is really in their heart.' Twenty years ago I visited Yunupingu's homeland for a piece I was writing on Mabo and Land Rights for the London *Observer*. A white political consultant I spoke with in Nulanboy, who had many years of experience, told me he believed such advances as had been achieved were the result of successive Australian premiers being taken off into the bush by tribal elders, and having 'stardust sprinkled in their eyes'. But Malcolm Fraser kept his eyes tightly screwed – and John Howard wouldn't go at all. That's a credulous whitefella's perspective, but Yunupingu sees it differently: so far as he was concerned they all kept their eyes wide shut, with the exception of Hawke and Keating, who couldn't see the future for their own tears of self-pity and remorse.

In the mid-1990s the Land Rights movements seemed to be getting somewhere – and my piece now appears hopelessly optimistic, with its serious considerations of the prospects for true Aboriginal autonomy, guaranteed under the Constitution. The piece may've been optimistic but I don't believe I ever was. I don't think it's possible to fully sympathise with any other individual except those whose being in the world we're vitally connected to, by reason of birth or physical intercourse – how much harder is it to even empathise with those who have a radically different world-view and equally divergent moral and spiritual values? Are these people, with their 45,000-year-old continuous oral culture, and their profound immersion in a magical world, philosophical idealists or animist pragmatists? Both ways of being are profoundly different to the West's mythic underpinning, which, for all our vaunted humanism, remains solidly Abrahamic: our destiny is a songline leading to a determinate future; while the meaning of our lives is to be sought in the history of our adaptation of the natural world. Yet for the Aboriginal – so far as we can determine – there is no destiny, only a duty which takes this form: a ritual rubric essential for the maintenance – in the widest possible sense – of a status quo that must forever remain ante. For us, the world was made a long time ago; our purpose is merely to adapt it to our increasingly expensive tastes. But for them the world is ever-inchoate, while they are the agents of its coming into being.

Of course, such statements are bullshit of the first order. Who am I to descant on what people from these myriad and diverse cultures truly believe – let alone on how it might cause them to act? Moreover, even if it were possible to adequately characterise such a traditional world-view, how almost infinitely complex must be the impacts of deracination. Nevertheless, I am guilty as charged: in my 2001 novel, *How the Dead Live*, I attempted to envisage what the experience of death might be like for an off-the-peg Western secular atheist, who, upon expiring, discovers that the Tibetan Buddhist cosmology obtains. Wandering in the bardo between life and death, her psyche disintegrating

into the personifications of her basest desires, my protagonist is attended by a lithopedion (the minute calcified foetus
of a baby conceived but never born), and a sorcerer or 'big
man' from one of the Centralian tribes. Yes, I wanted a
suitably mystical 'other' with which to contrast the naïve
psychological realism of my protagonist, but I wanted an
'other' a little less clichéd than some enlightened rimpoche.
I based my big man on a real person – because that's what
writers do, no matter how much we assure you readers
of our powers of invention, when it comes to the evanescent subtleties of human being we always draw from life.
Usually the alteration of a few basic facts – sex, class, eye
colour – is all that's required to throw you off the scent;
it never fails to amuse me how blind even close friends
can be to the shameless use I've made of them. 'I enjoyed
the novel,' they'll say, 'but that X is an arsehole.' Clearly,
they've never held up a Stendhalian mirror to where the
sun doesn't shine. True, I have had some comeback from
characters – sorry, I mean 'people' – but only when I make
the criminal error of failing to change their names.

Yes, you heard me: I modelled my fictional big man on
a real one, and while I was writing the novel I retained his
real name. Why? Because I felt it allowed me to engage
more thoroughly with the reality of a being I was in the
process, in all likelihood, of travestying. My intention was
always to change the name before the text went to press,
but mysteriously I didn't. When the finished copies came
back what leapt off the page was this name, the name
of a real big man – the real big man who'd had such an

influence on my oldest Australian friend that after many years of resistance he'd finally given in and been initiated. When I asked a mutual friend how this could possibly have happened, he expostulated: 'He was only living bang next door to the most powerful bloody sorcerer in the Territory.' I phoned my newly Aboriginal friend and asked him what I should do – would X be alright about being name-checked in a literary novel? A day or so later the message stick was returned to me, and the answer was unequivocal: X very much minded – whatever copies of the book were already in Australia would have to be pulped, while I'd have to pay compensation for the offence I'd caused.

When, in the late 1980s, I was making my first tentative forays into the inhospitable, over-exploited and semi-arid country known as literary London there was a tale doing the rounds concerning V. S. Naipaul's younger brother, Shiva, who'd recently died. Also a writer – I can thoroughly recommend his sole novel, *Fireflies* – Naipaul Minor had penned a collection of essays on matters Australian entitled *Black and White*. According to these cognoscenti – most of whom thought the Southern Cross was a pub on the King's Road – the book revealed certain taboo items of Aboriginal arcana, and for this he had been killed, the weapon employed being sympathetic magic. It was the same with Bruce Chatwin, whose offence was to suggest in *The Songlines* that it was absurd for Western museums to have to return sacred artefacts, such as tjuringas, to the descendants of their original owners – let alone for anthropologists to cease studying such lore.

As a writer who, albeit in a glancing way, had witnessed in the outback psychic phenomena I found inexplicable in terms of natural law, these tales had considerable impact on me – especially in combination with the far more plangent anxieties of the white Australians: the consultant who told me my friend had been initiated vouchsafed he was 'terrified' of his Aboriginal employers for just this reason, and that when they told him to jump, he simply asked 'How high?' In a way it doesn't matter what we think about the efficacy or otherwise of sympathetic magic as a means of literary criticism. The important thing is such anxieties track the fault lines in our own psyches – the way we suppress our sense of how uncanny our own consciousness is: we may well have taken the dreamtime and turned it into a nightmare, but then again, we too are such stuff as dreams are made of. It's the same with the camp north of Coober Pedy, up in the desiccated country that's the *fons et origo* of white Australia's sense of manifest destiny – here Stuart groped from waterhole to waterhole, and 110 years later I saw Aboriginal children with pot bellies and streptococcal skin infections, their eyes whited-out by trachoma. The fourth-world conditions indigenous Australian people still live in are a totalising phenomenon; I don't belabour this in order to shame anyone – every modern, democratic, human-rights-supporting nation boasts its own viciously excluded groups; there are no utopias, nor will there ever be – no matter what our leaders tell us. When Stuart reached what he calculated to be the centre of Australia, he raised the Union Jack and gave a

short speech to his two starving and weary companions;
they gave 'three cheers for the Flag, the emblem of civil and
religious liberty, and may it be a sign to the natives that
the dawn of liberty, civilisation and Christianity is about
to break upon them'.

I paid to have the copies of my novel pulped and
reprinted; I paid the compensation demanded: $5,000, two
hunting rifles and a set of cooking pots. I paid because I
was credulous, because – as an English Protestant with
a Jewish knob on me – I felt prey to collective guilt.
When it came time to write a post-9/11 satire on Western
liberal impotence and ethical culpability in the debacles
of Afghanistan, Iraq and all the other wars of material
conquest waged in the name of liberty, civilisation and,
implicitly, Christianity; my own response to the otherness
of Aboriginal Australia became a means of probing our
circumnavigatory hypocrisy. My novel *The Butt* is set in a
country which is an island continent; the overlords, who are
clearly of European descent, have reached different sorts of
accommodation with the various indigenous peoples. My
protagonist – who's equally clearly an American, although
this is never explicitly stated – accidentally flicks his last
cigarette before abandoning the habit, onto the head of an
elderly white man who's married to an indigenous woman.
In what follows, due to the complex entwinement of indigenous distributive justice and statutory law, the offender
winds up having to compensate his victim's in-laws to the
tune of . . . Well, you guessed it: $5,000, two hunting rifles
and a set of cooking pots.

That Australian reviewers couldn't spot the satiric wood for the circumstantial trees, and so pronounced *The Butt* offensive took me as much by surprise as . . . well, as the realisation I'd failed to substitute an alias for a real person's name in *How the Dead Live*. To me, the capacity to step back from the particularities of one's situation and to adopt the perspective of an anthropologist on Mars is the sine qua non of any understanding at all. I found it simultaneously amusing and deranging that a society such as Australia could institute draconian anti-smoking legislation, while failing to fully acknowledge the genocide which was perpetrated on its indigenous peoples. However, this to me was only a particular instance of a wider Western capacity to substitute public health for civic morality; consumer rights for economic equality, and the unfettered exercise of the libidinal imagination for political freedom. Inasmuch as Australia wishes to be included in the great, progressive project, so its citizens must sign up to these still greater, regressive hypocrisies.

In Peter Carey's 1991 short story collection *Exotic Pleasures* there's one entitled 'The Cartographers' which is essentially a gloss on Jorge Luis Borges's celebrated fragment, 'On Exactitude in Science'. Borges writes of an empire in which the cartographers' guild created a map of the empire itself 'whose size was that of the Empire and which coincided point for point with it'. However, successive generations 'saw that the vast Map was Useless, and not without some Pitilessness was it, that they delivered it up to the Inclemencies of Sun and Winters'. And here are the concluding lines I believe fired Carey's imagination: 'In the Deserts of the West, still today, there are Tattered Ruins of that Map, inhabited by Animals and Beggars; in all the land there is no other Relic of the Disciplines of Geography.' Carey's story is set in a recognisable Australia, and told from the perspective of a son whose father was once a cartographer, but who – in common with his colleagues – has abandoned the ceaseless mapping of the giant territory. The consequences of this are that parts of the massive country have begun to disappear – to begin with the remoter, infrequently mapped areas, but then quite substantial landmarks in the major cities start to wink out of existence. The tale ends – so far as I can remember – with the narrator being berated by his own father, who's becoming increasingly insubstantial himself.

The tyranny of distances – both internal and external – may not have shaped Australian national self-consciousness quite as much as Gallipoli, but in a way the most tyrannical aspect of colonisation was the tearing up of a far more ancient map, one that did indeed coincide point for point with the entire Australian landmass. I've stood on the shore of the Arafura Sea at the point where the primordial oyster first jumped up and made landfall – and I've eaten its offspring at St Kilda seafood restaurants. I come from a landmass where not a single feature is without humanity's impress – even the most isolated Scottish moor is the creation of Iron Age slash-and-burn agriculture. The job I had in Darwin in the early 1980s consisted in preparing a report assessing the demand for building land in the

Territory. Initially the necessity for this seemed unclear to me, given the vast land area and the sparse population – but of course, the granting of Crown leaseholds has been intrinsic to the development of Australia, and rests fundamentally, still to this day, on the infamous doctrine of *terra nullius*. I discovered soon enough that, unlike in Britain – where rates of household formation based on a number of demographic factors determine demand – in the Territory there was only one determinant: the size of the federal government's subsidy. Once again, I believe this continues to be the case.

I'm not here to berate white Australia for the genocide perpetrated on its indigenous peoples – how could I? If the sins of our fathers and mothers are to be visited on us, then, unquestionably, we're all to blame. But what I do want to make crystal clear is that I wouldn't have come here at all if it weren't for the physical reality of Australia's astonishing hinterland, and the equally remarkable complexity and sophistication of the traditional Aboriginal world-view. This is not to dismiss the cultural achievements of the majority community here, but for me the long road to the deep north will always be the Stuart Highway. Cultural cringe is, I believe, entirely optional for white Australia – judge yourselves by the criteria of the English-speaking, globalised neoliberal world and you will always be found wanting. As you stand in relation to Britain, so we stand in vis-à-vis the USA. I'm often asked if my books do well in the States, and I usually say this: Not too well; after all, they don't need an extra Will Self – they've already got at least four of their own. By extension, it's no good prosecuting a draconian policy on illegal immigrants while offering up 'multiculturalism' as a sop – England is the native land of the hypocrite, and we enact this sort of bullshit politics far more thoroughly than you ever can. But if Australia, rather than presenting itself as just another so-called 'liberal democracy', one whose relation to place is determined entirely by how it can be marketed or otherwise exploited, instead hearkens to its own unique strangeness, then I believe all Australians, no matter what their heritage, can feel at home in this inhospitable world.

I remember swimming in the pool of the Darwin hostel I first stayed in when I went to the Territory, and over-hearing two white girls whose most common epithet, as they shouted and splashed, was 'gammin'. Everything was gammin – what he said, what she said, what everyone said. I've often asked my Australian friends for the etymology of the term but it wasn't until a couple of weeks ago, around a Darwin dinner table, that I dredged up the answer – and that was courtesy of a Google search. It is, of course, an Aboriginal word – although from which of the estimated 200 language groups there were prior to contact it derives we have little way of knowing. Nevertheless, one of my Darwin friends, a political activist deeply involved with indigenous affairs, gave me a fuller contextualisation of the term, one I'd like to share with you in all its unvar-nished, Australian directness. According to him, he and his mob had a very simple way of dividing up the people they had to deal with in order to live: there were those who are 'true God' (and he further explained that this doesn't relate to a unitary conception of Godhead, but to a collective state of spiritual grace), and those who were 'gammin cunts'. Surely this harsh dichotomy gives us all something to aspire to? We may think being true God lies beyond us, but if the alternative is to be a gammin cunt . . . Well, I think it at least behoves us to make the effort, don't you?

1 October 2015

The Rise of the Machines

Written by Norbert Wiener, an MIT mathematician, and published in 1948, *Cybernetics, or Control and Communication in the Animal and the Machine* is the book which first brought the term 'cybernetics' to public attention. Synthesised from the Ancient Greek – meaning to steer, navigate or govern – the coinage has resonated down the decades ever since; in the process giving rise to all sorts of odd, cyber-prefixed neologisms – my personal favourite being the chain of American-style confectioners dubbed CyberCandy. Wiener, a famously eccentric character, had been driven to develop an overarching theory of the machine by two vital problems that had arisen during the recent war. The first was the need for an automated system that would allow British anti-aircraft gunners to hit German bombers – and by extension make it possible for any gunner to hit a fast and erratically moving target; and the second was the dropping of Little Boy on Hiroshima by the 509th Composite Group of the United States Army Air Forces (USAAF). Wiener, like many scientists of his generation, responded to the split-second incineration of 125,000 Japanese civilians with horror: he had an epiphany in which he saw a future of deadly conflict dominated – and perhaps even initiated – by sophisticated machines. But again: in common with so many scientists of the era, Wiener had already tried to bring about just such a future, by creating a machine that would massively enhance humans' ability to locate, aim and unerringly deliver ordinance.

This Janus-faced – or perhaps more properly, Manichean – inspiration was thereby encrypted into cybernetics' DNA from the outset: on the one hand this was intended to be a general theory of how all possible – not just actual – machines might work, with a view to assisting those intent on building them; on the other hand it was a monitory account of how interaction between humans and human-like machines might lead to the latter becoming firmly ensconced in the driving seat. Given 2016 has already seen the first fatal accident involving a self-driving car, now might seem like the ideal time to take stock and calmly examine the last seventy years of human–machine interaction – possibly with the ulterior motive of discovering whether it's a who or a what in control. On the surface of it, Thomas Rid's book, *Rise of the Machines*, is less ambitious: taking a particular development of the core ideas of cybernetics, one per decade, its main narrative vehicle travels forward, while each of the seven sections loops back so as to place asynchronous developments within an overall timeline. Rid's structure, of course, owes something to one of the core concepts of cybernetics: the feedback loop.

The kinds of machines which inspired Wiener were ones that could self-correct or otherwise modify their own behaviour in response to external stimuli; proto-typical forms of this were proximity fuses that used radio waves to detect the targets they were homing in on, and so detonate the shells which housed them. Equally influential was the Sperry ball turret, which placed the human gunner in the middle of a continuous feedback loop of incoming data and outgoing gunfire: with its hydraulic servomotors and machine guns, the cyclopean-looking turret was a primitive sort of cyborg, or cybernetic organism. So, like so many technological advances, the ones which typified cybernetics were born out of man's compelling desire to kill his fellow man – preferably at a distance. Rid locates Wiener and cybernetics on the intellectual map of the mid-twentieth century – positioning them somewhere between the architectural modernism of Le Corbusier, who saw the house as 'a machine for living', and the behaviourism of Pavlov and B. F. Skinner – psychologists who understood the human psyche in mechanical terms, as subject to a feedback loop which could be hijacked to reinforce certain sorts of behaviour. In fact, cybernetics, taken as a theory of the congruent behaviours of humans and sophisticated machines, seems entirely behaviouristic to me – while the enlargement of the idea to encompass man–machine interaction introduces troubling philosophic questions, such as whether any meaningful distinction can be drawn between inorganic and organic entities operating in the same way.

Rid himself writes that 'By 1970, cybernetics had already peaked as a serious scholarly undertaking, and it soon began to fade. Its scientific legacy is hard to evaluate.' He acknowledges that 'cybernetic ideas and terms were spectacularly successful and shaped other fields: control engineering, artificial intelligence, even game theory'. But ruefully concedes, 'cybernetics as a science entered a creeping demise, with therapists and sociologists increasingly filling the rolls at the American Society for Cybernetics'; which might seem about as damning as imaginable a judgement on a field of intellectual endeavour – if that were the correct way of understanding cybernetics, which I don't believe it is. Since the inception of wireless broadband in the early 2000s there's been an increasingly febrile climate surrounding our use and understanding of a suite of technologies I like to refer to as BDDM (Bi-Directional Digital Media). The proleptic insights of thinkers as diverse as Marshall McLuhan, Jean Baudrillard and Guy Debord into the ontological and epistemic impacts of mass mediatisation are now felt experientially by those masses; our bodies may still patrol the streets, but our minds, increasingly, are smeared across a glassy empyrean – and we feel this deep and existential queasiness as our emotions are pulled hither and thither by the ebb and flow of massive feedback loops: an acid reflux of imagery and data to which we're subject twenty-four hours a day, 365 days a year.

Which is presumably why there have been a rash of books, of varying quality, which attempt to explain what the hell's going on – although for once, the Devil really isn't in the detail, since nobody imagined signing a mobile phone contract was tantamount to becoming a cyborg. James Gleick's searching and thoughtful *The Information* (2011) limned the origins of the current Age of Data, and Nicholas Carr's *The Shallows* (2010) and *The Glass Cage* (2014) looked respectively at the cognitive impacts of the internet and automation. Last year saw the publication of Laurence Scott's *The Four-Dimensional Human*, which with lyrical cadences hymns the emergent phenomenology of the BDDM realm; and this year came Greg Milner's *Pinpoint*, a history of the US military global positioning satellite system, the technology of which, arguably, is most foundational of the cosmic cat's cradle humanity has woven together out of the virtual and the actual. Even veteran cineaste David Cronenberg got in on the act with *Consumed*, his first novel – an exploration of contemporary anthropophagy, which seems to suggest that the mediatised mind is indeed auto-cannibalistic. This is just a small selection of the books I've read on the broad subject – there have been, of course, many more; however, what struck me as I read Rid's contribution was how few references there are in these other works to cybernetics or any of the other cyber- prefixes. Indeed, it is quite possible to conceive of writing about the BDDM's impact – in the widest sense – without adverting the subject (or pseudo-subject) at all.

Rid's book reflects this redundancy: he begins in high theoretic style, and returns to these sunny uplands at the end and beginning of his chapters, but in between he gets bogged down in all sorts of practical details; notably the development of virtual reality technologies, cyborgs and computer encryption. All of these are interesting subjects, but they've been covered better elsewhere – Rid wants us to understand cybernetics as the *fons et origo* of all the shiny, happy things we see about us and hold in our hands, but to do so we needs must cleave to a very crude – and frankly implausible – view of human inventiveness. The story of computer encryption is indeed fascinating and bizarre: discovered by a technical officer at GCHQ in the early 1970s, the method of public key encryption depends on the impossibility of factoring very large prime numbers – it is, if you like, the modern era's equivalent of the golden mean or pi: mathematical axioms which mysteriously seem to underpin the very materiality of our world. The secret transmission of information is a vital aspect of waging war, and all the way from Bletchley Park to the NSA's massive data centres – vast server-farms, laid out on the high plains of the American west – computing has evolved in lock-step with superpower conflict.

Rid comes at all of this somewhat counter-intuitively through the *Whole Earth Catalog*, a biannual almanac of hippy survivalism published by Stewart Brand in the late 1960s and early 1970s. Rid proposes the Catalog, which was updated in response to its readers' input, as a proto-form of the sort of computer-augmented feedback loops which have come to typify social media – and it's true that counter-cultural types were early adopters of the internet, and formed the ranks of cyberpunks, and then so-called 'cypherpunks' who battled to wrest public key encryption from the spooks, so making the web safe for . . . well, safe for commerce, since without it you couldn't safely order Rid's book on Amazon. It is, as I say, a fascinating story – but one told rather more comprehensively by Gordon Corera in *Intercept: the Secret History of Computers and Spying* which came out last year. Corera, unlike Rid, brings the story right up to date – covering the impact of Edward Snowden and Wikileaks, and is far more authoritative on the nature and extent of current cyber-warfare. Rid, by contrast, remains hobbled by cybernetics itself – a snare that drags him back, again and again, to the early seventies, when the anthropologist Gregory Bateson saw in cybernetics a heuristic with which to interpret the phenomenon of consciousness itself.

Bateson's fundamental insight did indeed build directly on Wiener's work: for Bateson, not only were the man and the tool best considered as an integrated system, but the environment within which the man plied the tool should also be in the loop – a loop which, by extension, lassoes just about every sentient thing in the universe; 'what some call God', is how Bateson termed this collective consciousness, although you don't have to be a devotee of psychotropic drugs in order to see how uncannily his insight prefigures our web-based psycho-social smearing; after all, while we may hypothesise that consciousness originally arose as a by-product of language acquisition, at some point in humans' evolutionary past, in the future that's emerging it seems increasingly to be a by-product of media. I only wish Rid had pushed these rather more philosophic speculations further; his foundational observation is that cybernetics – in keeping with Wiener's own Manichean view – always generated imagined futures, whether utopic or dystopic. This gives him licence to investigate the imaginings of William Gibson et al., as they descried a world in which – to quote, as Rid does, the great hippy novelist Richard Brautigan – we are either 'all watched over by machines of loving grace'; or alternatively one that follows Randall Jarrell's monitory vision, in his poem 'The Death of the Ball Turret Gunner'. In five spare lines Jarrell evokes a darker version of Bateson's cosmic feedback loop, one populated by 'black flak and the nightmare fighters'. Jarrell suggests that in this automated realm of death the human subject will, soon enough, be surplus to requirements; the final line reads, 'When I died they washed me out of the turret with a hose.'

Believers in the 'singularity' – that supersession of biological by machine-intelligence which was first named by another cybernetics-influenced sci-fi writer, Vernor Vinge – can also be split into pro- and anti-, utopian and dystopian. Indeed, so marked is this response to the meld of man and machine, it leads me to believe that this is fundamentally what cybernetics was all about. Far from being some sort of 'top-down' theory, which carved out the conceptual space within which technological innovation might take place, it was rather a sort of cybernetic system itself, one which generated these visions, sent them out into the world, and then auto-corrected them in response to our feedback. Rid does understand this perfectly well, and he does his best to keep his narrative up there in the speculative clouds – his problem is that just like the rest of us, he can't help being distracted by all that shiny, ergonomically designed hardware. Distracted by that – and bamboozled also by the universal human tendency to scale up from our existential and very real apprehension of individual free will, to a hazy virtualisation within which all humanity is similarly endowed. It's this that makes most writers on technology plump for one or the other, and decide whether the rise of the machines is a Good or a Bad Thing – as if we really had any choice in the matter.

15 September 2016
Prospect Magazine

Literary Time

Lévi-Strauss (the anthropologist, not the jeans-originator), once observed that the original type of the visual artwork was the miniature – after all, even Michelangelo's frescos in the Sistine Chapel are miniatures, given they portray the creation of the entire universe. Well, just as any visual artwork is of necessity a compression or reduction of spatial dimensions, so all literary works do the same for temporal ones. The key thing to realise here is that any example of narrative literature contains within its papery confines the ticking of not just one, but several clocks: there's the period of time over which the story takes place; the different time periods allocated to the various characters (we may spend a day with one – several years with another), and the constantly shifting ratios between the time we take to read about any given sequence of events, and the narrative time the writer has dedicated to evoking them. Moreover, when a novel is written in the third person, and has an anonymous narrator, this numinous figure sits outside of time, and is able to time-travel at will.

Perhaps the greatest literary time traveller of all is the anonymous author of the Book of Genesis; he allocates (in the King James version) a scant 500 words to describing a process – the creation of the universe – we now believe to have taken some 13 billion years, and compresses the action into a mere six days, which obviously helps to keep up the narrative tension. Indeed, perhaps the best way to think of narrative at all is as a means of reducing almost infinitely long sequences of events into ones short enough to fit onto the page. As soon as literature gets going, writers begin to warp, twist and generally mess about with time – playing games that constantly recalibrate different timescales to dramatic effect. The novel form shivered into being out of other literary genres – most notably the epistolary. Setting down an exchange of letters on the page is tantamount to inviting the reader to consider the time they took to be posted back and forth: it compresses these longueurs, while leaving them latent in the text.

Early novels were also wildly experimental – consider Sterne's *Tristram Shandy*, in which its protagonist is the author of his own life story, yet refuses to present it in any chronological order, preferring to interpolate widely separated events. For my money Sterne's less well-known *A Sentimental Journey* is an even better example of time-warping: there's a walk of several paces from a carriage to an inn that takes up an entire chapter. But while time was often rendered elastically and ludically in 18th- and early 19th-century novels, it isn't until the measurement of time becomes properly – and, more important – publicly

accurate, in the mid-19th century, that the temporal dimension of fiction becomes seriously weird. In fact, it was
the train as much as the chronometer that standardised
time, and so brought its true incongruity into the collective
and creative imagination. Relatively high-speed rail links
meant that individual cities could no longer have their
own times – add in more affordable timepieces, and the
telegraph, and you have the conditions necessary for what
I term 'industrial time': whereby all conscious individuals
are insistently aware of occupying the same 'now'.

Really, this wasn't the case before – and fiction registers
the new dispensation with a whole rash of temporal experimentation: the second bestselling novel of the 19th century
(the first was *Uncle Tom's Cabin*) was Edward Bellamy's
Looking Backward, about a man from the Boston of the
1880s who sleeps for 113 years and wakes to discover
a sort of state-socialist utopia, complete with shopping
malls and credit cards – the novel was so influential that
a political party was founded in the States to further its
agenda. But it's in high-art experimentation rather than
the emergent genre of science fiction that we find the most
elegant and compelling of temporal arabesques: Proust's
Remembrance of Things Past is an attempt to turn the
novel itself into a time machine – although without the
whirring ivory, gold and crystal working parts employed
by H. G. Wells's more mechanically minded time traveller. Proust's protagonist, Marcel, uses memory – and
specifically sensual memory – as a means of accessing the
immediacy of events that have long gone. Influenced by

the philosopher Henri Bergson, Proust's objective was nothing less than to re-experience the past *and* convey the experience to his readers. No wonder the novel runs to thousands of pages.

Joyce's *Ulysses* also has the mass of an object that can warp the temporal field – and unsurprisingly, in its structure and his approach, the novelist was responding to Einstein's first paper on General Relativity, which was published in 1905, and theorised that space and time were in fact different aspects of the same phenomenon. For Joyce's protagonists, Leopold Bloom and Stephen Dedalus, Dublin is a universe, while their long day's tramping the 900-page novel describes (although 'novel' is probably an inaccurate term for Joyce's masterwork, the form of which defies any idea of crude linearity) is effectively the whole span of recorded time. Inasmuch as they are humans, Bloom and Dedalus are also planetary bodies, each with its own unique temporal field – the narrative, such as it is, plots the way they remotely affect one another.

Joyce was once asked what he'd done during the First World War, and he replied 'I wrote *Ulysses*' – other writers weren't so sequestrated: J. B. Priestley was seriously wounded in the trenches twice, and no doubt saw a great many of his comrades killed. In common with many of his traumatised generation, Priestley looked for a means to somehow cheat the way time's inexorable march had driven all these young men into the grave. Some looked to spiritualism to bring their loved ones back – Priestley found his elixir in the time-travelling theories of a philosopher called J. W. Dunne, who hypothesised that human consciousness itself had some of the capabilities of the novel; specifically, that within us there's a sort of narrator-figure, who has access to an atemporal viewpoint – and a sort of 'express' timeline, that allows it to move between different pages of the life story. Priestley applied Dunne's ideas most particularly in his play *Time and the Conways*, in which the crucial speech is a restatement of Einsteinian physics in emotional terms: if we can only fully realise that time isn't simply a linear progression of events, but that all time is accessible to us eternally, we can free ourselves from suffering and conflict.

This is just the briefest of surveys – as Einstein's theories percolated down further into popular culture, temporal experimentation in the narrative form became more and more extravagant; nowadays myriads of chrono-plots are hatched every second. I wish I had the space – and of course the time – to introduce you to some more of them.

2016
Port Magazine

The Printed Word in Peril

In February of this year, at an event at the 92nd Street Y's Unterberg Poetry Center in New York, while sharing the stage with my fellow English writer Martin Amis and discussing the impact of screen-based reading and bi-directional digital media on the republic of letters, I threw this query out to an audience I estimate was about 300-strong: "Have any of you been reading anything by Norman Mailer in the past year?" After a while, one hand went up, and then another tentatively semi-elevated. Frankly I was surprised it was that many. Of course, there are good reasons why Mailer in particular should suffer posthumous obscurity with such alacrity: his brand of male essentialist braggadocio is arguably very much surplus to requirements in the age of Trump, Weinstein, and fourth-wave feminism. Moreover, Mailer's brilliance, such as it was, seemed even at the time he wrote to be sparks struck by a steely intellect against the tortuous rocks of a particular age while he labored tirelessly to the very end, principally as the booster of his own reputation.

It's also true that, as J. G. Ballard sagely remarked, "For a writer, death is always a career move," and for most of us the move is a demotion, as we're simultaneously lowered into the grave and our works are remaindered. But, having noted all of the above, it remains the case that Mailer's death coincided with another far greater extinction: that of the literary milieu he'd come to prominence in, and that had sustained him for decades. It's a milieu that I hesitate to identify entirely with what's understood by the ringing phrase "the republic of letters" although the overlap between the two was once great indeed; and I cannot be alone in wondering what will remain of the latter, once the former, which not long ago seemed so very solid, has melted into air.

What I do feel isolated in – if not entirely alone – is my determination, as a novelist, essayist, and journalist, not to rage against the dying of literature's light, although it's surprising, in some ways, how little of this there is, but merely to examine the great technological discontinuity of our era as we pivot from the wave to the particle, the fractal to the fungible, and the mechanical to the computable. I referred above to "bi-directional digital media" – by which I mean the suite of technologies comprising the wireless-connected computer, handheld or otherwise, the worldwide web and the internet. Henceforth, I'll abbreviate this to BDDM. I first began consciously responding, as a literary practitioner, to the manifold impacts of BDDM in the early 2000s – although, being the age I am, its effects on me have been operating throughout my working life – and I first started to write and speak publicly about it around a decade ago. Initially I had the impression I was being heard out, if reluctantly – but as the years have passed, my attempts to limn the shape of this epochal transformation have been met increasingly with outrage, and even abuse, in particular from my fellow writers.

As for my attempts to express the impact of the screen on the page, on the actual pages of literary novels, I now understand that these are altogether extraneous to the requirements of the age for everything to be easier, faster, and slicker in order to compel the attention of screen viewers. It strikes me that we're now suffering collectively from a "tyranny of the virtual," since we find ourselves unable to look away from the screens that mediate not just print but, increasingly, reality itself.

I think there are several explanations for the anger directed against anyone who harps on the message of the new medias, but in England it feels like a strange inversion of what sociologists term "professional closure"; but instead of making the entry to literary production and consumption more difficult, embattled writers and readers, threatened by the new means of literary production, are committing strange acts of professional foreclosure: holding fire sales of whatever remains of their unique and non-transferrable skills – as hermeneuticists, as vessels of taste (and therefore, the canon), and, most notably, as transmitters and receivers of elegant virtualities that in many instances had endured for centuries. Surveying the great Götterdämmerung of the Gutenberg half-millennium, the hopeful finale to Ray

Bradbury's *Fahrenheit 451* often comes insistently to mind. When Montag, the onetime "fireman" or burner of books by appointment to a dystopic totalitarian state, falls in among the dissident hobo underclass, he finds them to be the saviors of those books, each one having memorized a lost and incalculably precious volume – one person *War and Peace;* another, the Bible.

In March of this year, I gave an interview to the *Guardian* in which I repeated my usual – and unwelcome – assertion that the literary novel had quit center stage of our culture and was in the process – via university creative-writing programs – of becoming a conservatory form, like the easel painting or the symphony. Furthermore, I fingered BDDM as responsible for this transformation – the literary novel being simply the canary forced to quit this particular mineshaft first. The response was a Twitter storm of predictable vehemence – and more than 700 comments on the *Guardian*'s website, which, reading over preparatory to writing this article, I found to display all the characteristics of the modern online debate: willful misunderstanding and misinterpretation of my original statements, together with criticism that is either ad hominem or else transparently animated by a superimposed ideological cleavage.

In among the relentless punning on my name – selfish, self-obsessed, self-regarding, etc, etc – there are a few cogent remarks: some critics comment that the literary novel has always been a marginal cultural form; others, that its torchbearers are now from outside the mainstream Western tradition – either by reason of ethnicity, heritage, sex, or sexual orientation – and both these and others aver that the novel form is alive and kicking, that paperback sales have actually risen in the past few years, and that readers are rediscovering the great virtues of the printed word as a media technology.

All of these viewpoints I'm more than willing to entertain. What I'm less prepared to consider is arguments that begin by quoting sales figures that show the sales of printed books increasing and those of e-books in decline. The printed books being sold are not the sort of so-called "difficult" reading that spearheads knowledge transfer but picture books, kidult novels like the Harry Potter series, and, in the case of my own UK publisher at least, a great tranche of spin-off books by so-called "vloggers" (a development Marshall McLuhan anticipated when he noted that new media always cannibalize the forms of the past). As for the decline in e-books, this is because the screen is indeed not a good vehicle for the delivery of longform prose; and anyway the printed literary novel (or otherwise challenging text) is competing not with its digital counterparts but with computer-generated games, videos, social media, and all the other entertainments the screen affords. Moreover, I'd wager that the upsurge in printed-book sales, such as it is, is due to greater exports and the continuation of, in the West at least, a strange demographic reversal, since for the first time in history we have societies where the old significantly outnumber the young.

*

England is a little-big country, simultaneously cosmopolitan and achingly parochial, which means there tends to be only one person assigned to each role. For years I was referred to as "the enfant terrible" of English letters – a title once bestowed on Martin Amis – but while with advancing years this ascription has obviously become ridiculous, I haven't been bootstrapped – like him – to the position of elder literary statesman but booted sideways. As a commentator on the *Daily Telegraph*'s website puts it: "When I see Will Self's name trending on social media, I feel . . . that the old boy has expressed some opinion that I will broadly agree with, but because he has become such a toxic figure his pronouncements manage to alienate his natural allies and strengthen the cause of his enemies."

Be all this as it may, in December of last year an authoritative report was delivered on behalf of the Arts Council of England. Undertaken by digital publisher Canelo, it compiled and analyzed sales data from Nielsen BookScan demonstrating that between 2007 and 2011 hardcover fiction sales in England slumped by £10m, while paperback fiction suffered still more, with year-on-year declines since 2008. In one year alone – 2011–2012 – paperback fiction sales fell by 26 per cent. Sarah Crown, the current head of literature for the ACE, commenting on the report to the *Guardian*, said, "It would have been obviously unnecessary in the early 90s for the Arts Council to consider making an intervention in the literary sector, but a lot has changed since then – the internet, Amazon, the demise of the net book agreement – ongoing changes which have had a massive effect." And so 2018 will be the first year since the abolition of the latter – a law against publishers discounting that supported small retailers and modest-selling authors alike – in which the British government has, effectively, subsidized the literary novel, which at least represents a willingness to buck the trend of the past quarter-century or so, a period that has seen the relentless conflation of cultural, social, and financial capital.

In the United States there's been a far more consistent and public critique of BDDM's impact on literature, on education, on culture and cognition generally. There is, of course, a great deal of empirical research concerning the impact of screen media on the mind/brain; but for this essay I concentrated on a couple of academic papers written following experiments conducted by a Norwegian education researcher, Professor Anne Mangen, of the Norwegian Reading Centre, based at Stavanger University. One paper is entitled "Lost in an iPad: Narrative engagement on paper and tablet"; the other "Reading linear texts on paper versus computer screen: Effects on reading comprehension." The papers covered two studies, one conducted with Norwegian university students in 2014, the other in 2013 with high-school students, in which screen reading and paper reading were compared. Mangen's work is cited by Nicholas Carr in *The Shallows*, as are an impressive number of other papers summarizing studies attempting to tease out the impacts on the human subject of screen – as opposed to page – interactions.

The references for Mangen's two papers alone give an impression of a rapidly burgeoning field, with studies being conducted all over the world, leading to papers with titles such as: 'Effect of light source, ambient illumination, character size and interline spacing on visual performance and visual fatigue with electronic paper displays' and 'The emerging, evolving reading brain in a digital culture: Implications for new readers, children with learning difficulties, and children without schools'. Of course, Carr makes the weaselly point in *The Shallows* that the digitization of academic papers, far from coinciding with a greater breadth of reference, has led to a sort of "clumping" effect, whereby unto the papers most cited will be given yet more citations. We might think of this as the Googlization of scholarship and academia generally, since it mirrors the way the search engine's algorithms favor ubiquity over intrinsic significance.

It's probably the case that interested parties lurk behind many of these studies, at least those that show the impact of screen as against page to be effectively negligible, or compensated for by improvements in other areas of human cognition. I certainly don't think Professor Mangen's work is at all compromised in this fashion; however, reading through the elaborate methodologies she and her collaborators devised for these comparisons – ones that attempt the creation of "laboratory conditions" and the imposition of a statistical analysis on data that is hopelessly fuzzy – I became more and more perplexed. Who, I thought, besides a multidisciplinary team in search of research funding, could possibly imagine that a *digital* account of the impact of reading digital print on human cognition would be effective? For such an account rests on the supremacy of the very thing it seeks to counteract, which can be summarized as a view of the human mind/ brain that is itself computational in form. Whereas for literature to be adequately defended, its champions must care, quixotically, not at all for the verdict of history, while uttering necessary and highly inconvenient truths – at least for the so-called "FANG" corporations: Facebook, Apple, Netflix and, of course, Google, whose own stated ambition to digitize *all* the world's printed books constitutes a de facto annihilation-by-transliteration of the entire Gutenberg era.

Mangen's statistical analysis of questionnaire responses filled in by cohorts of tablet or booklet readers does establish that under certain controlled circumstances reading on paper affords important advantages – allowing for greater retention of information and comprehension of narrative than digital reading. We can quibble about swiping versus scrolling, the length of the texts employed in the studies, the formulation of questionnaire items, and the significance – or insignificance – of the respondents' perception of these texts as factual or fictional. We can also point out that laboratory conditions simply cannot replicate the way our use of BDDM is now so completely embedded in our quotidian lives that to attempt to isolate a single mode – such as digital reading – and evaluate its cognitive effects is quite impossible.

Mangen's papers suggest that as our capacity for narrative engagement is compromised by new technology, we experience less "transportation" (the term for being "lost" in a piece of writing), and as a further consequence become less capable of experiencing empathy. Why? Because evidence from real-time brain scans tells us that when we become deeply engaged with reading about Anna Karenina's adultery, at a neural level it looks pretty much as if we were committing that adultery ourselves – such is the congruence in the areas of the brain activated. Of course, book lovers have claimed since long before the invention of brain scanning that identifying with characters in stories makes us better able to appreciate the feelings of real live humans, though this certainly seems to be a case of correlation being substituted for causation. People of sensibility have always been readers, which is by no means to say reading made them so – and who's to say my empathy centers don't light up when Anna throws herself to her death because I take a malevolent satisfaction in her ruin?

Carr's *The Shallows* reaches a baleful crescendo with this denunciation: the automation of our own mental processes will result in "a slow erosion of our humanness and our humanity" as our intelligence "flattens into artificial intelligence." Which seems to me a warning that the so-called singularity envisaged by techno-utopians such as Google's research director, Ray Kurzweil, may come about involuntarily, simply as a function of our using our smartphones too much. Because the neuroscientific evidence is now compelling and confirmed by hundreds, if not thousands, of studies: our ever-increasing engagement with BDDM is substantially reconfiguring our mind/ brains, while the new environments it creates – referred to now as code/space, since these are locations that are themselves mediated by software – may well be the crucible for epigenetic changes that are heritable. Behold! The age of Homo Virtualis is quite likely upon us, and while this may be offensive to those of us who believe humans to have been made in God's image, it's been received as a cause for rejoicing by those who believe God to be some sort of cosmic computer.

But what might it be like to limit or otherwise modulate our interaction with BDDM so as to retain some of the cognitive virtues of paper-based knowledge technology? Can we envisage computer–human interactions that are more multi-sensory so as to preserve our awareness and our memory? For whatever publishers may say now about the survival of print (and with it their expense accounts), the truth is that the economies of scale, production, and distribution render the spread of digital text ineluctable, even if longform narrative prose were to continue as one of humanity's dominant modes of knowledge transfer. But of course it won't. It was one of Marshall McLuhan's most celebrated insights that the mode of knowledge transfer is more significant than the knowledge itself: "the medium is the message."

For decades now, theorists from a variety of disciplines have been struggling to ascertain the message of BDDM considered as a medium, a task hampered by its multifarious character: Is it a television, a radio, an electronic newspaper, a videophone, or none of the above? McLuhan distinguished confusingly between "hot" and "cold" media – ones that complement human perception and ones that provoke human sensual imagination – but BDDM holds out the prospect of content that's terminally lukewarm: a refashioning of perception that will render imagination effectively obsolete. In place of the collective, inter-generational experience of reading *Moby-Dick*, centuries-long virtualities will be compressed to the bandwidth of real time and fed to us via headsets and all-body feely suits, "us" being the operative word. With a small volume in your pocket, you may well wander lonely as a cloud, stop, get it out, and read about another notionally autonomous wanderer. But The Prelude Experience, a Wordsworthian virtual-reality program I invented just this second, requires your own wearable tech, the armies of coders – human or machine – necessary to write it, and the legions of computers, interconnected by a convolvulus of fiber-optic cabling, needed to make it seem to happen.

What the critics of BDDM fear most is the loss of their own autonomous Gutenberg minds, minds that, like the books they're in symbiosis with, can be shut up and put away in a pocket, minds the operation of which can be hidden from Orwellian surveillance. But the message of BDDM is that the autonomous human mind was itself a contingent feature of a particular technological era. Carr – representative in this, as in so many other areas – wants there to be "wriggle room," yet his critique of BDDM rests firmly on technological determinism: humans don't devise technologies to solve particular problems, nor are those technologies "value neutral" in terms of their impact but rather "monkey see, monkey do." Technologies arise spontaneously and spread mimetically, in the process acting reciprocally upon the minds they're born of.

So what does this wriggling look like? Well, it looks like programs devised to stop computer users going online, it looks like stressed-out parents, worried by poor academic performance, trying to police their children's online behavior; it looks like the "slow" movements devised to render everything from transportation to cuisine more mindful. It looks, in short, like a cartoon I remember from *Mad Magazine* back in the early 1970s in which hairy proto-eco warriors are mounting a demonstration against the infernal combustion engine: "Right, let's get going!" shouts one of the organizers – and they all clamber into their gas-guzzlers and roar away in a cloud of lead particulates and carbon monoxide. Why? Because the very means we have of retreating from BDDM are themselves entirely choked by its electro-lianas. Sure, some wealthy parents will be able to create wriggle room, within which their conservatory-educated offspring can fashion old-style literary novels, but this will have all the cultural significance of hipsters with handlebar mustaches brewing old ales. The philosopher John Gray was, I suspect, being more perspicacious when he said that in the future – the very near future, it transpires – it's privacy itself that will become a luxury; and by privacy he means not simply the ability to avoid being surveilled – in the real world as well as the virtual one – but the wherewithal to maintain what Emily Dickinson termed "an equal and separate center of self." The self we perceive to be in a symbiotic relation with the printed word.

Which returns me, suitably enough, to the much punned-upon self that's my own. In conversation and debate with those who view the inception of BDDM as effectively value-neutral – and certainly not implicated in the wholesale extinction of literary culture – I run up time and again against that most irrefutable body of evidence: the empirical sample of one. Marx may have said that history is made by the great mass of individuals, but these individuals pride themselves on their ahistorical position: they (and/or their children) read a lot, and they still love books, and they prefer to read on paper – although they may love reading on their Kindle as well. The point is, they tell me angrily at whatever literary reading or lecture it is that I'm delivering, that rumors of the serious novel's death are, as ever, greatly exaggerated.

Well, I have considerable sympathy for their position – I, too, constitute an empirical sample of one. However, the study I've embarked on these past thirty-odd years, using my sole test subject, has led me to rather different conclusions. If I didn't find screen-based writing difficult to begin with, or a threat to my sense of the fictive art, it's simply because early computers and word processors weren't networked until the mid-1990s; and until the full roll-out of wireless broadband, around a decade later, the connection was only made with electro-banging and hissing difficulty. I didn't *return* to writing on a manual typewriter in 2004, because apart from a little juvenilia I'd never written anything long on one before. And I didn't even consciously follow this course; it just seemed instinctively right. If there are writers out there who have the determination – and concentration – to write on a networked computer without being distracted by the worlds that lie a mere keystroke away, then they're far steelier and more focussed than I. And if, further, they're able to be transported sufficiently by their own word-stream to avoid the temptation to research online *in media res*, then, once again, I'm impressed.

For me, what researchers into the impact of screen-reading term "haptic dissonance" (the disconnect between the text and the medium it is presented in) grew worse and worse throughout the 2000s. As did the problem of thinking of something I wished to write about – whether it be an object or something intangible – and then experiencing a compulsion to check its appearance or other aspects online. I began to lose faith in the power of my own imagination, and realized, further, that to look at objects on a screen and then describe them was, in a very important sense, to abandon literature, if by this is understood an artform whose substrate is words alone. For to look at an image and then describe it isn't thinking in words but mere literalism. As for social media, I was protected from them initially by my own notoriety: far from wanting more contact with the great mass of individuals, having been a cynosure of sorts since my early thirties, I desired *less*. At an intuitive level I sensed that the instantaneous feedback loops between the many and the few that social media afforded were inimical to the art of fiction, which to a large extent consists in the creation of one-to-one epiphanies: "Oh," we exclaim as readers, "I've always felt that way but never seen it expressed before . . ." And then we cleave to this new intimacy, one shorn of all the contingencies of sex, race, class, and nationality. By contrast with the anonymous and tacit intimacy to be found between hard covers, social media is all about stridently identifying ourselves – and not simply to one another, but to all. In the global village of social media it's precisely those contingent factors of our identities – our sex, our race, our class, our nationality – that loom largest; no wonder it's been the medium that's both formed and been formed by the new politics of identity.

But at the level of my person, and my identity, I've been striving for the past fourteen years to make the entire business of literary composition more apprehensible: the manual typewriter keeps me bound to sheets of paper that need to be ordinally arranged, for no matter how flimsy, they're still objects you can hold and touch and feel. Nowadays, I go still further: writing everything longhand first, then typing it up on the manual, and only then keying it into a computer file – a process that constitutes another draft. If readers need to know where they are in a text, and to use this information to aid their grasp on the narrative and their identification with the characters, then how much more important is this for a writer? Not much more. Because readers and writers are so tightly dependent on each other it's specious to make the distinction – indeed, I'd assert that there's a resonance between the act of writing and the act of reading such that the understanding of all is implicated in that of each. Yet to begin with I noticed nothing but benefits from my own screen-based reading – thousands of texts available instantaneously, the switching between them well nigh effortless, and the affordances of the substrate (to use the scientific terminology) including instant definitions, elucidations, and exegeses. Researchers hypothesize, and here I quote from Mangen's "Lost in an iPad," that "reading a novel on a tablet or e-reader doesn't feel like what reading a novel should feel like." Far from this bothering me, however, I embraced it, and soon found myself no longer reading texts of all kinds in quite the same way; moreover, my sense of them being discrete began to erode, as I seamlessly switched from fact to fiction, from the past to the present, from the concrete to the theoretical and back again. Reading on paper, I had a tendency to have maybe ten or twelve books "on the go" at once. Reading digitally, this has expanded to scores, hundreds even.

In the world of the compulsive e-reader, which I have been for some years now, on a bad day it feels as if you're suffering from a Zen meditational disease, and that all the texts ever written are ranged before your eyes, floating in space – ones you've read and know, ones you haven't read and yet also know, and ones you've never even imagined existed before – despite which you instantaneously comprehend them, as you feel sure you would any immaterial volume you pulled from the equally immaterial shelves of this infinite, Borgesian library of silent babel. But precisely what's lost in this realm – one that partakes of the permanent "now" that is intrinsic to the internet – is the coming into being of texts and their disappearance into true oblivion. As it is to humans, surely it is to the books that we make in our image: A book that lives forever has no real soul, for it cannot cry out in Ciceronian fashion "O tempora, o mores!" only tacitly and shiningly endure.

The canon itself requires redundancy as well as posterity, which returns us, neatly if not happily, to Norman Mailer. Of all the dead white men whose onetime notoriety is now seen as a function of time and custom, rather than intrinsic worth, Mailer is probably one of the worst offenders. His behavior was beyond reprehensible – and, let's face it, his books weren't even that good. Why did I light on him, when we've been witnessing the twilight of these idols for years now, as the postwar generation of male American writers shuffles towards their graves, their once proud shoulders now garlanded round with the fading laurels of their formerly big-dicked swagger? Possibly in order to galvanize my readers' critical faculties: many of you will object – along with the *Guardian* commenters – quite rightly, to the view that a literary culture is sliding into oblivion, on the grounds that another is arising, beautiful and phoenix-like, from its ashes.

For are we not witnessing a flowering of talent and a clamor of new voices? Is not women's writing, and writing by those coming from the margins, receiving the kind of attention it deserved for years but was denied by this heteronormative, patriarchal, paper-white hegemony? One of the strongest and most credible counters to the argument that in transitioning from page to screen we lost the artforms that arose in and were dependent upon that medium is that this is simply the nostalgia of a group who for too long occupied the apex of a pyramid, the base of which ground others into the dust. Younger and more diverse writers are now streaming into the public fora – whether virtual or actual – and populating them with their stories, their realities; and all this talk of death by iPad is simply the sound of old men (and a few women) shaking their fists at the cloud.

In this historical moment, it perhaps seems that the medium is irrelevant; the prevalence of creative-writing programs and the self-published online text taken together seem to me to represent a strange new formula arrived at by the elision of two aphoristic observations: this permanent Now is indeed the future in which everyone is famous for fifteen minutes – and famous for the novel that everyone was also assured they had in them. How can the expansion of the numbers writing novels – or at least attempting to write them – not be a good thing? Maybe it is, but it's not writing as we knew it; it's not the carving-out of new conceptual and imaginative space, it's not the boldly solo going but rather a sort of recursive quilting, in which the community of writers enacts solidarity through the reading of one another's texts.

For in a cultural arena such as this, the avant-garde ends mathematically, as the number of writers moves from being an arithmetic to a geometric coefficient of the number of readers. We know intuitively that we live in a world where you can say whatever you want – because no one's listening. A skeuomorph is the term for a once functional object that has, due to technological change, been repurposed to be purely decorative. A good example of this is the crude pictogram of an old-fashioned tele-phone that constitutes the "phone" icon on the screen of your handheld computer (also known, confusingly, as a smartphone).

Skeuomorphs tend, for obvious reasons, to proliferate precisely at the point where one technology gives ground to another. I put it to you that the contemporary novel is now a skeuomorphic form, and that its proliferation is indeed due to this being the moment of its transform-ation from the purposive to the decorative. Who is writing these novels, and what for, is beside the point. Moreover, the determination to effect cultural change – by the imposition of diversity quotas – is itself an indication of printed paper's looming redundancy. Unlike British novel-ist Howard Jacobson, who recently took it upon himself to "blame the reader" for the decline in sales of literary fiction, rather than the obsolescence of its means of repro-duction, I feel no inclination to blame anyone at all: this is beyond good and evil.

What's significant about MeToo and BlackLivesMatter is that they're movements that are designated by the *scriptio continua* of BDDM, with the addition of a hashtag. What will become of the unicameral mind, convinced of its own autonomy, that the novel and other longform prose mirrored? For I do believe this transformation is indeed about who we are as much as about what and how we read. The answer is, I've no idea – but the indications are that, as ever in the affairs of humankind, new technologies both exacerbate the madness of crowds and activate their wisdom. At one level I feel a sense of liberation as all these papery prisons, with their bars of printed type, crumple up, and I float up into the crystal sphere, there to join the angelic hosts of shiny and fluorescent pixels. That there's no more ego-driven and ego-imprisoned creature than the writer (and by extension the reader) is a truth that's been acknowledged for a very long time. Before he pronounces that "of the making of many books there is no end," the Preacher asserts that all is vanity – and he means writerly vanity. Apparently, there's now an algorithm that parses text for instances of the personal pronoun and can diagnose depression depending on their ubiquity – and isn't it notable that as the literary novel quits center stage of our culture, we hear a frenzied exclamation of "I! I! I!" What can this be, save for McLuhan's "Gutenberg Mind" indulging in its last gasp, as it morphs into a memoir or a work of so-called "creative non-fiction."

If the literary novel was both the crucible of a certain sort of self-conception – one of autonomy and individuality

– then it was equally the reinforcer of alienation and solipsism. I was taught to read by my mother, who, being American, knew all about phonics and flashcards – the trendy knowledge-transfer technologies of the early 1960s – with the result that I could read by the time I went to kindergarten. So, it's been a long life of the Logos for me – one, I'd estimate, that has placed me in solitary confinement for a quarter-century or more, when I add up all that reading and writing.

It was only when finishing this essay that I fully admitted to myself what I'd done: created yet another text that's an analysis of our emerging BDDM life, but which paradoxically requires the most sophisticated pre-BDDM reading skills to fully appreciate it. It's the same feeling – albeit in diminuendo – as the one I had when I completed the trilogy of novels I've been working on for the past eight years: books that attempt to put down on paper what it feels like for human minds to become technologically transformed. I felt like one of those Daffy Ducks who run full tilt over the edge of a precipice, then hover for a few seconds in mid-air (while their realization catches up with them), before plummeting to certain death: look down, and you may just see the hole I made when I hit the ground. Look a little more closely, and you may see the one you're making right now, with the great hydrocephalic cannon ball of a Gutenberg mind you've used to decipher this piece.

At the end of Bradbury's *Fahrenheit 451*, the exiled hobos return to the cities, which have been destroyed by the nuclear conflicts of the illiterate, bringing with them their head-borne texts, ready to restart civilization. And it's this that seems the most prescient part of Bradbury's menacing vision to me; for I see no future for the words printed on paper, or the artforms they enacted, if our civilization continues on this digital trajectory: there's no way back to the future – especially not through the portal of a printed text.

October 2018
Harper's

The Secret Agent

There is a passage in Siegfried Sassoon's wartime diaries, in which he recounts the experience of sheltering in a dugout on the Western Front during a particularly savage German bombardment, with a group of officers – and men – all of whom were reading the works of Joseph Conrad. Whether you consider this as reflecting well on the Britain of the early twentieth century, or negatively on that of the early twenty-first – when literacy rates are falling – the fact remains that at this time Conrad was one of a handful of writers capable of bridging the gap between paramount artistic ambition – repurposed for the machine age by Ezra Pound, with his slogan 'Make it New!' – and the quotidian enjoyment of a rattling good yarn. To this day, the inclusion of Conrad on the small pantheon of genuinely significant Modernists remains, if not moot, critically, at least dubious in a more obvious sense: for where are the real affinities between his crotchety project and Joyce's ever-expanding word-sea, or the crumbling Classical edifice of the early Eliot?

Michael Hofmann writes of that other lofty Modernist eminence, Kafka, that there are no 'foothills' for readers on their way to encounter his work – as there indubitably are with Joyce and Proust – but that instead you find yourself, all at once, tricked by his commonplace tone and simplicity of diction into being stranded in this minatory and unstable realm. As for Conrad, is it too neat to observe that as he was manoeuvring awkwardly into the drydock of the English language, so Samuel Beckett was casting off, and setting two courses: one towards the metrical and mellifluous French tongue that Conrad had spoken since childhood – the other into those deconstructive doldrums where the intimacy between meaning and language is finally sundered.

To read Conrad – and this is true in particular of *The Secret Agent* – is to find oneself, while apparently making clear headway, in fact, with all sails trimmed, beating hard against the wind. In his most celebrated work, the novella *Heart of Darkness*, Conrad fashioned a tale-within-a-tale, in which the genocidal hell of the Belgian Congo was nested cosily on the deck of a pleasure yacht moored in the Thames estuary. In the novel he wrote after this one – *Under Western Eyes* – which is its thematic sequel, if not a narrative continuation, Conrad created a sort of 'once-removed' first-person narrative, whereby the English translator of a Russian agent provocateur's diary mixes its content with his own contemporaneous accounts of the individuals featured in its pages. Conrad's own stated intention was that this device should impress upon his democracy- and clarity-loving English-language readers the obscurity of the Czarist despotism's doublethink.

At least superficially, while charged with the same sort of ambitions, *The Secret Agent* avoids such narratological stratagems: recounted from an impersonal third-person perspective, the story of Adolph Verloc's undoing as a secret agent has a beginning, a middle and very definitely an end; nevertheless, such is its narrator's tone – and such is the text's stylistic oddity – that the tale becomes credible despite, rather than because of its manner of being told. Conrad has a way with the idiomatic substratum of English – its vast storehouse of internal allusion – that's at once timorous and radical: he snatches up turns of phrase, holds them up to the light, then very slightly – yet wilfully – misapplies them. English is a syntactically elastic language that forgives the clumsiest rearrangement of its parts, and Conrad's prose seems to revel in this licence pushing sentences ever so slightly out of joint, so as to produce an uncanny overall impression: it looks like beautifully crafted English prose – and it reads as such (at least silently), yet somehow it just . . . *isn't*.

To this, in the matter of *The Secret Agent*, Conrad admixes a great deal of facetiousness. Again: it's said of Kafka that at private readings of 'Metamorphosis', he would be so overcome by the hilarity of his own tale that he'd corpse; but just as it's difficult to reassume the strictures of fin-de-siècle Prague, and so recapture the sheer anarchic defiance of Gregor Samsa's transmogrification, so it's equally hard to join in the hollow laughter of Conrad's narrator as he anatomises his repellent revolutionists: certainly they are ridiculous – and, as events will transpire, incompetent – but is it possible, at this remove, for us to revel in accounts of their physical deformity and social exclusion? Conrad, in his Author's Note on the novel, written some fifteen years after its publication, is at pains to defend its jocoseness – as he is the Grand Guignol of the novel's finale – and employs a curious dictum, 'taking care of my business', to express his unswerving commitment to what might be termed 'the rights' of the artistic imagination – if, by this, is meant its liberties.

Comfortable for many years with his sinecure as the secret agent of the Baron Stott-Wartenheim, the Russian embassy's spymaster, and his proceeds from his pornographer's shop in Soho, Mr Verloc is appalled when the Baron's successor, the far more Machiavellian Mr Vladimir, orders him – as Conrad might put it – to sing for his supper, by committing a terrorist outrage. 'What do you think of having a go at astronomy?' the Russian proposes, reasoning that in the post-Darwinian world of late-Victorian England, science is the only true religion. Such a plan: to bomb the Greenwich Observatory, as if it were somehow possible, conceptually, to destroy time – and along with it capitalist society – might seem to be the very essence of Conrad's facetious inventiveness, were it not that an outrage of this sort was apparently planned – and imperfectly executed – by a French anarchist, Martial Bourdin, in February 1894. There's this fact – acknowledged as a source by Conrad himself in his Author's Note on the novel – and there's also the inherently fanciful nature of terrorism itself, which depends for the most part on the imagination of its victims. This, in contradistinction to conventional warfare, which is utterly prosaic: unstoppable bullets striking immovable ranks.

While infinitely more devastating, the September 11th 2001 attacks by Al Qaeda 'franchisees' on the Twin Towers of the World Trade Center in New York, the Pentagon in Washington, and potentially a third target in the capital, were also examples of how terrorist logic fuses symbolism and reality. Both weaponry – jet airliners – and targets, were chosen for what they represented: under the aegis of its neoliberal boosters, the high-rise office block and the high-speed transit system are realised as part of what anthropologists term a 'symbol set': one which, when employed by a skilled practitioner – such as a shamanic tech entrepreneur – magics progress into being. In the aftermath of 9/11 much was made of the supposedly 'medieval' cast of the Islamist terrorists' mindset; who, it was supposed, were – in a chilling echo of Curtis LeMay's policy for North Vietnam – determined to bomb the West back to the Middle Ages. But the truth is that terrorism – like the delusions of schizophrenics – adapts its wild ideas from the most current machine dreams.

We know very little about Bourdin's motivations – or his political associations – but we know a great deal about the inexorable progress of Greenwich Mean Time in late-Victorian England – and in the world more generally. The symbol set of steam engines, steel rails, precision chronometers – and latterly, the telegraph – conjured over a span of three or four decades, the programming of the incremental division of time into the Western collective consciousness, and so democratised what had been formerly the preserve of elites; namely, the zeitgeist. When the blood dripping from the carving knife plunged into Adolph Verloc's chest strikes the parlour floor, it seems – in the ears of his murderess – to merge with the ticking of the clock on the mantelpiece. Some critics have seen this as Conrad's buried hint that had the poor idiot boy, Stevie, been successful in fulfilling Mr Vladimir's scheme, the first great age of globalisation would, indeed, magically have gone up in a puff of smoke. The Greenwich bomb would've been – if you like – a sort of Victorian steampunk version of the millennium bug that so troubled us in the dying days of the twentieth century.

Space, time and their odd interlinkages seem to lie at the very core of Conrad's thinking in this novel: Stevie's evening occupation in the dingy shop where he lives with his mother, sister and Mr Verloc is to sit at a table covering sheets of paper with strange and wild patterns of interlinked circles – ouroboroses and lemniscates: round and around, again and again. His moronic repetitiveness, Conrad seems to be suggesting, reflects an inexorable aspect of the world: there are no counterfactuals; what is – will be, forever and ever, world without end. There's this, and since this is a novel concerned fundamentally with physics – understood as the interactions of moving bodies within defined spaces – Conrad preoccupies himself a great deal with their minutiae, focusing, for example, on Mr Verloc's black bowler hat, not only because of its overt and deathly symbolism, but because its gyres and tumbles are also synecdochally attuned to those of other, larger and more significant bodies.

In our own era terrorism has been treated jocosely by satirists – sometimes, as in the case of the journalists at *Charlie Hebdo*, at the cost of their lives. Chris Morris's film *Four Lions* pretty much does for contemporary British-born Islamist wannabe terrorists what *The Secret Agent* aimed to do for its readership: make them see what repelled Conrad about all 'revolutionists': their absurd moral vanity – believing as they truly do, that they really do know what's best for everyone. And moreover, to expose the paradoxical cowardice in such an attitude; for just like the contemporary suicide bomber, the evil Professor, who walks the streets of London, ever prepared to blow himself – together with whoever might accost him – to pieces, is really a craven figure, unable to assume the very ordinary burden of survival.

Conrad, while eschewing narrative experimentation, manipulated the novel's timeframe so that many of the outrages associated with the Fenian bombing campaign of the 1870s could act as the models for anarchist outrages of the 1890s (when the action putatively transpires); and it's in the light of such blurring that we should view his ban-jaxed conception of these propagandists of the deed. In his Author's Note he claims that there were times during its writing when he was 'an extreme revolutionist' – and this may have been true, for there's no disputing his capacity for the Stanislavsky Method more or less *avant la lettre*. According to his wife Jessie's posthumous memoir, following completion of *Under Western Eyes*, Conrad fell into a feverish delirium in which he conducted long conversations with its characters. But then, when it comes to his characterisation of Michaelis the 'ticket-of-leave apostle', whose simplicity is just as repellent as the Professor's ever-ready murderousness, Conrad could also be accused of precocious fat-shaming.

The pathetic figure of Stevie being led to his inadvertent – yet inevitable – death by the bulky figure of Verloc, his deformed father figure, takes us back to the seedy revolutionary underworld frequented by Conrad's true father, the aristocratic Polish patriot, Apollo Korzeniowski. That Conrad could straddle these worlds: the demi- and the beau-, the workaday and the exalted, is attested to in every scene of *The Secret Agent*; yet, just as eras are blended in the novel to create a sort of time-that-never-was, looked back on from the early 1900s, so the Polish émigré writer's wonky sense of England's complex social stratigraphy creates a politics-that-never-was as well. What Conrad understood perfectly well, though, was that the English of his own era weren't so much utopians as uchronians: fervent believers in a Merrie England that may never have existed (one in which knights were bold and social relations happily organic), but which they nonetheless confidently expected a return to.

In a certain sense, as a fundamentally pessimistic – and let's not forget, aristocratic – conservative, out of Nietzsche by way of Dostoevsky (despite all his denials of such influences), Conrad had no interest in politics – if by that is understood a reasoned attempt to guide the affairs of humanity, either in whole or part. The current efforts by a demagogic – if not despotic – Russian regime to destabilise British politics would have been at once no surprise and a complete one for Conrad, whose essay 'Autocracy and War' set out his political thinking in the period he was writing *The Secret Agent*. In it, Conrad is both percipient about the impact of mass media on mass events, and uncharacteristically optimistic about the demise of Russia as a great power following what he assumes will be defeat at the hands of the Japanese, with whom they were then at war.

Rumours of Russia's death have continued to be greatly exaggerated – not least by liberal humanists of the kind Conrad so particularly despised; and the Skripal poisoning precipitated in leafy Salisbury last year by Russian military intelligence operatives has loud overtones of Mr Vladimir's whacky plot – anyone familiar with the novel you hold in your hand will have thought, immediately upon learning of the poisoned cosmetic products sprayed on door handles, of poor Stevie, carrying the old one-gallon copal varnish can, hideously adapted by that malignant and mad bomb-maker, the Professor, to be a lethal device. Discussing the bomb's premature explosion with the equally grotesque Ossipon, with whose ultimate fate Winnie Verloc's will be entwined, the Professor remarks, 'He either ran the thing too close, or simply let the thing fall.'

And it is here – at the level of physics – that the fates of all the characters in *The Secret Agent* are truly decided: for they all – the criminal and the legitimate – run things too close, or simply let them fall. Conrad, surely, in his depiction of Verloc's murder and its aftermath, surpassed all others – contemporary or otherwise – in his evocation of what it might be like to take a life, and the immediate psychic consequences for the killer: the complete and utter loneliness of Winnie Verloc after the murder is foreshadowed by this beautifully exact evocation of a psychic state, seen from within: 'Her personality seemed to have been torn into two pieces, whose mental operations did not adjust themselves very well to each other.' A deracinated Polish aristocrat who tried to reinvent himself as a tweedy English country gentlemen – the pseudonymous and multilingual Conrad knew all about being torn in pieces.

Some critics, while ascribing Flaubert's pitiless forensic vision to Conrad, have saddled him with this operating protocol as well: '*Madame Bovary, c'est moi!*' They look to Conrad's marriage – which they're convinced was unhappy – for *The Secret Agent*'s biographical models. But while the affinities between Jessie Conrad and Winnie Verloc's mother may be the obvious ones – both being obese, poorly educated, dark complexioned etc. – the truth is that Conrad revealed his genius here in the very breadth and depth of his sympathy: forced into the bondage and abuse of a loveless marriage simply in order to provide for her adored simpleton brother, it's Winnie Verloc's great existential act that does indeed destroy time – if by that is meant the abolition of any distance between character and reader, which is the true mark of great literature. And of course, there was a terrorist campaign actually underway at the time Conrad was writing the novel – although it's seldom mentioned in the critical literature. A campaign, moreover, which involved its adherents in the most fanciful and inventive acts – so, although it's not usual to view Conrad in this way, perhaps when he wrote of being an 'extreme revolutionist' it was the Suffragettes he had in mind.

2018

Introduction to the Folio Society edition of
The Secret Agent by Joseph Conrad

What to Read?

Even if – as per my last essay for *Lit Hub* – we know *how* to read, there remains the equally vexed question of *what* we should read. If the 21st century is notable for anything much at all when it comes to literature – and I use the term in its broadest sense, as will become clear – it's the spiking of formerly big literary guns, and the dismantling of what used to be understood as the canon. In truth, the canon was both a comparatively recent phenomenon – if by this is meant a collection of texts the reading of which was deemed essential if you were to consider yourself cultured – and never by any means the overbearing and fortified phenomenon its detractors love to hate and besiege.

This is not to suggest that prescriptivism isn't a perennial when it comes to our reading habits – or that such categorical judgements haven't been prejudiced by values and attitudes that many today find deeply unpalatable. Telling people what they should read is, very obviously, congruent with telling them where to go, and what seat they're allowed to occupy on the bus.

Nonetheless, for those who view the very notion of the canon as inherently elitist, it's worth noting that the phenomena mostly clearly implicated in its formation were the democratising processes of the late 19th and early 20th centuries: the massive extension of free education – not just to little white proto-patriarchs, but to girls, and children from diverse communities as well – together with the technological improvements in the replication and dissemination of literary texts. Following this, the canon arguably became most salient precisely at the point when its foundations were already beginning to crumble by reason of such tectonic movements and technological changes. Meanwhile, its ideological battlements were under assault by a curious alliance of feminists, structuralist and deconstructionist literary critics, together with the aggrieved intelligentsia of either minority groups, or newly independent nations that were formerly colonised by West Europeans.

Put bluntly: the canon only really existed – in my view – as a genuinely culturally conditioning phenomenon for a few decades before it began to fire blanks. Prior to that there was an evolving literary culture that, by definition, was restricted to the literate. Its influence may have shaped general culture and values – but just as natural religion allows for far greater latitude than preachers of the vulgate would allow, so this proto-canon scarcely affected the cultural mores of the unlettered. In some ways the analogy would be between the Protestant Reformation and the inception of web offset printing combined with universal literacy: Just as the aim of the former was to make Divine writ accessible to all – so the latter was hell-bent on making the writ of humanity similarly ubiquitous.

The Book of the Month Club, the vast readerships for newspapers, and magazines such as *Time* or the *Reader's Digest* – these contributed to canon formation in the early years of the last century quite as much as the novelising of Joseph Conrad or Virginia Woolf. The standardised teaching of literary criticism only comes into being in the 1900s with the schism within classical philology between the study of the meaning of literary texts, and that of their underlying linguistic structure. Yet in a few short decades people came – entirely paradoxically – to believe both in the undoubted existence of a literary canon, and its baleful effects on what we now call inclusiveness. Surely the only possible explanation for this was that many diverse people really were being told what to read by a group of people exhibiting considerably less diversity themselves.

The paradox here is that the canon – inasmuch as it existed at all – was trumpeted by those engaged in its formation, as simultaneously an expression of cultural values particular to Western societies, and those viewed as somehow universal. We can blame the Enlightenment for this: its luminaries believed first and foremost in civilisation's 'progress' – as they understood it – and this necessitated all the world's cultures being remade in their favoured image. This basic conflict between the West and the rest resonates down the centuries, and is recast in each successive generation: the current culture war between those who wish university literature departments to be far more diverse in the works and authors they teach, and those who cleave to what they view as an unshakeable tradition being only its latest iteration.

Let me be clear, and Shakespearean: a plague on both their houses – both sides are, in my view, equally wrong-headed. The traditionalists cannot circle their wagons around a prescribed/proscribed division that figures themselves as the all-wise Solomons without making the canon a synecdoche of the social and economic hierarchies as currently constituted; but neither can the revolutionists retrospectively alter the canon to correct the prejudicial, purblind perspective of the past – to do so would be to enact a sort of cultural counterfactual: rendering the readers of today somehow magically altered in terms of their own acculturation. No longer will they view Shakespeare as the fount of a host of commonplace tropes and idioms in contemporary English – but rather look to previously obscured writers for these linguistic modes, thereby establishing quite a different culture.

Besides, the revolutionists are quite as prescriptive about what we should read as the traditionalists: for them, a literary diet of writers previously excluded from the canon by reason of sex, ethnicity etc is a necessary concomitant to – if not cause of – a more egalitarian society. Good luck with that one. For my own part, I sincerely believe that the culture wars currently underway are the precursor of a more general collapse: like it or not, viable cultures, while voraciously consuming other influences, nonetheless remain true to their own espoused values – rendering a genuine multi-culture a contradiction in terms. This is by no means to say that I don't believe we should read as widely and as deeply as possible. Indeed, I'd argue that in the current parlous situation such eclecticism and absorption is our principal prophylactic, protecting us from the blights and pestilences that surround our cultivated little enclaves. My own experience teaching at university level for the past decade has been sobering, as I encounter more and more students whose reading – regardless of which authors or works they've encountered – is simply insufficient, in terms of overall bulk, to allow them to understand such concepts as the Bloomian anxiety of influence, whether or not they're able to figure the late critic as a reactionary defender of the canon.

To understand influence, or the relation of literary genres to one another, you need to have absorbed sufficient quantities of text to make intuitive comparisons – while in order to lose yourself in a given work, you need to be able to get far enough into it in the first place. The multiple mediatised distractions that now howl to us from our handheld computers militate against this level of engagement, as does the anxiety induced by events in the wider world, such as the Coronavirus pandemic. However, if my own arguments strike you as tendentious then let me share with you someone else's insight, that of the English novelist David Lodge. His campus satire, *Small World*, published in the mid-1980s, features a cast of wannabe celeb academics jetting around the Anglosphere in a slipstream of signifiers and apercus. Yes – it was an innocent era, when such antics constituted the very essence of 'culture'.

Anyway, early in the novel, the Morris Zapp character (based on the American literary critic, Stanley Fish) tells an anecdote concerning a party game played among the members of the English faculty at his university, in which they drunkenly admit to canonical texts that they haven't read. One colleague duly conceded that he had no acquaintance whatsoever with *Hamlet*, and then – since the head of the department was present, and presumably less amused than the rest of the company – woke up the following morning to discover he'd been fired. This neatly conveys the nature of the canonical under conditions of late capitalism: it elides with the forms of arcane knowledge and technical jargon that all professions rely on to effect closure in their given economic sphere. (Arguably, deconstruction as a literary-critical theory has gained traction more because of its impenetrable jargon than its philosophical debunking of the possibility of textual veracity.) There's this, and there's also the commoditisation of the canonical implicit in this episode – and indeed, in the entire marketisation and commodification of culture that's so marked a feature of the zeitgeist.

The newer mediums' power to sell books means that what's good for sales has to be figured as good for literature – no matter that they're simultaneously displacing the codex at the core of our culture. Nowadays, getting into the canon is like relocating to one of those nice, safe, plague-free and largely white enclaves – such as New Zealand – where a million bucks, cash down, can buy you citizenship. In part this has to be because of the sheer volume of stuff being put into circulation – as Stalin so wisely observed, 'Quantity has a quality of its own.' Back in 2003, just before the full inception of bi-directional digital media (the technological assemblage of the internet and the web wirelessly configured), the Mexican academic Gabriel Zaid published a witty book-length essay provocatively entitled *So Many Books: Reading and Publishing in an Age of Abundance*.

Beginning with the chilling calculation that, at the time he was writing, a book was being published somewhere in the world every thirty seconds, Zaid went on – somewhat counter-intuitively – to propose that such an avalanche of paper in fact represented the ability of the medium to continue to shape the culture. Arguing that within such abundance there necessarily existed great diversity; and that such diversity in turn entailed multiple foci around which debate could circulate, he suggested that we not feel that worried about an aesthetic and intellectual climate in which important works nonetheless failed to find in excess of a thousand readers. But of course, by 2003 the digital writing was already on the literal screen – if not behind the metaphoric paywall – and Zaid's further musings on the meaning of a literary culture in which far more people identified as, um, writers than readers, were in my view shadowed by the great perversion of publishing by means of a billion keystrokes that was already underway. For what are the social media if not the literary forms most central to the cultural life and collective social being of our age – a fact attested to more than slightly by the recent lifetime ban served on former US president, Donald Trump, by Twitter.

If we dismiss once and for all the absurd notion that the difficulty or simplicity of a given literary text represents an axis parallel to that which – supposedly – runs from dead white men to the contemporary and woke (a supposition that's insulting to all parties concerned), then we can liberate ourselves from the spurious notion that what we read will somehow – in Kafka's rather mocking formulation – constitute 'the decisive moment in human history'. Just as if we acknowledge the truth that what people actually read in practice are little gobbets of text pinging about in cyberspace – the lexical equivalents of sub-atomic particles with only liminal existence – we can stop believing that genre fiction (for example) is some kind of 'guilty pleasure'.

All of which is by way of saying: read what the hell you like. In a literary culture in which a Booker Prize winner (Bernardine Evaristo) can give an interview to the *Guardian* newspaper in which she states that 'life's too short' for her to read *Ulysses*, clearly the old idols have fallen. But then, they haven't been the old idols for very long. No, read what you want – but be conscious that, in this area of life as so many others, you are what you eat, and if your diet is solely pulp, you'll very likely become rather . . . pulpy. And if you read books that almost certainly won't last, you'll power on through life with a view of cultural history as radically foreshortened as the bonnet of a bubble car.

19 February 2021
Literary Hub

On Writing Memoir

I never wanted to write a memoir. No, really: I never wanted to write a memoir – or an autobiography for that matter – if such an exercise is understood to be a factual account of the events in my life, and the psychological states associated with them. Nietzsche writes in *On the Genealogy of Morals*: 'Memory says "I did that." Pride replies, "I could not have done that." Eventually, memory yields.' This is a general truth, I'm sure – as applicable to some virginal recusant, just as much as it is to those of us whose lives have been rather more . . . maculate. And it's for this reason, among others, that I never wanted to write a memoir: it would be, by my own lights, immoral to allow my yet vigorous pride to so overwhelm my enfeebled memory – a faculty weakened quite possibly as much by my own active turpitude as any blameless ageing.

But even if my memory were entirely reliable (and, where it was not, I were able to fill in the gaps with third-person testimony and textual or other evidence), there remains the sheer inventiveness of my pride, which, no doubt determined – in its own crazed way – to try and make me look good at all costs, would seek to paint up the most discreditable incidents and reprehensible behaviours as way-stations towards, if not enlightenment, at least some sort of . . . maturity. Yes, memory at its very best may be a competent researcher – but pride is always a brilliant novelist. And moreover, a novelist with a simple rubric to hand, one enjoyed by the many – an adaptation of the hero's journey to our era of weepy public catharsis and media-shriving.

Yes, I never wanted to write a memoir – and especially not one of those miserable affairs that describes its author's life as a progression along the road of excess; one that leaves him, Montaigne-like, immured in the tower of wisdom, and writing about it with a mixture of pornographic self-indulgence (what could be more deliciously transgressive than to revisit the sins of youth?) and bogus piety. Wittgenstein sagely remarked: 'If a person tells me he's been to the worst of places, I have no right to judge him. But if he tells me it was his superior intelligence that enabled him to go there, I know he is a fraud.'

Actually, I say my recollection is faulty, but I quoted these words – which I haven't read in decades – from memory, and correctly. Moreover, there is in fact a considerable amount of textual evidence concerning my own existence: a paper maven despite my peripatetic lifestyle, I've kept a lot of correspondence, journals, agendas and diaries. Moreover, I'm of an age that the witnesses to my life – at least most of my own generation – are for the most part still alive. Surely, given these resources, if the full force of Nietzsche's dictum were kept ever in mind, it might be possible to write a memoir both creditable and true? Possibly – but it certainly wouldn't be readable, given that the meaning of a life cannot ever be discovered in a mere recitation of facts: born, Braunau am Inn, Austria, 20 April 1889; died, Berlin, 30 April 1945.

Which is not by way of suggesting that I'm Hitlerian in my habits or proclivities, only that a biography can never be considered as commensurable with a mere itemisation of agreed facts: rather, the relation a lived life bears to the black marks on the page is more akin to the way musicians turn minims and crotchets into the sublime craziness, of, say, Beethoven's *Grosse Fugue*. Moreover, my life is still being played – and it's this that makes the 'I' of conventional memoir seem so very fictive to me. In thinking about my instinctive recoil from writing a memoir, it's this 'I' that seemed most salient: a sort of bollard of a pronoun, barring the way ahead. I was helped to circumvent it, in part, by a paper I read written by my old philosophy tutor, Galen Strawson, entitled 'Against Narrativity'.

Strawson has long been a fierce critic of our naïve and unreflective understanding of our 'selves', but in this paper he takes aim at two contemporary shibboleths, which relate equally to psychology and literature. The first of these is that in a determinate sense, what we're engaged in as reflective self-consciousnesses is the construction of some sort of narrative. Strawson sets up his target with a quote from another of my mentors, the neurologist and writer

Oliver Sacks: 'each of us constructs and lives a "narrative" . . . this narrative *is* us, our identities.' His target set up, he then swiftly demolishes it with an appeal to common sense; how can we be synonymous with the little boy or girl who grazed their knee in the playground ten, twenty, thirty – possibly even a half-century ago? You don't need to appreciate the paradoxical nature of Theseus's ship in order to intuit you and that child cannot be in any meaningful sense synonymous – and that moreover, the thinking 'I' that has been identified with both of them, cannot be that much more than a sort of temporary persona. Strawson elsewhere suggests that we come into being anew after each period of unconsciousness – mayfly entities, ephemeral and buzzing; while in 'Against Narrativity' he skewers the prideful pomposity of those who not only fall victim to the idea that our selves are stories, but that the writing of them is some sort of moral obligation.

After all, who can he or she be, this person who confidently asserts that they know all about their earlier – and arguably multitudinous – incarnations? In order to assert this or that about Will-of-the-past, I must assume this 'I' to be no mere Will-o'-the-wisp, but some sort of godlike creature – omniscient, omnipotent and, most importantly, standing outside of time, so that he may assert such things, confident in the knowledge that nothing that will happen to him subsequent to the writing of the memoir will retroactively invalidate it. (And may I make a small further whinny of contempt here for all those who not only memorialise their multitudinous selves, but do indeed also write further revisions, as if they were Stalinist dictatorships of one.)

This is why I have little time for the exhaustive and overtly autobiographical fiction of Karl Ove Knausgård – it's not that I don't want to hear about the minutiae of this brooding, self-lacerating Norwegian's life, it's just that the more he confidently asserts that it was he who did this or felt that, the less I'm inclined to believe him: in his case the problem is surely the raw accretion of detail – at best, psychologically inclined fiction can produce some sort of schematisation of our psychic life: its strange gallimaufry of half-formed language, synaesthetic imagery and perceptual intrusions – light as a feather's brush, or heavy as a vehicle's impact.

When I was working on my *Umbrella* trilogy of novels I tried to do just this; and when it came to considering how I could portray the mental life of my protagonist, Audrey Death, born in the 1890s, it seemed obvious to me that most of what she thought and felt during, say, the First World War, would be completely alien to me. At the most prosaic level, the very scraps of advertising slogans, snatches of popular song, and phatic expressions overheard scores of times daily, would be incomprehensible – once out of context – to me and my potential readers. And it's not just these distant pasts or perspectives that are another country to us – surely even our own being becomes alien to us, once it has passed over into the void of even the recent past? I find it surpassing strange to try and recall, in true detail, what I was thinking and feeling any given day last week, let alone last month, year, or – gulp! – decade.

But Knausgård Senior (the writing I) confronts Knausgård Junior (his younger self) with complete lucidity; each speaks unto the other with a total comprehension that seems, at least to me, resoundingly fraudulent the more exquisite the detail with which it's limned. I wonder if, in a way, the popularity of Knausgård's exhaustively quotidian 'struggle' doesn't reflect the inception of social media during the same period. All those selfies posted on Instagram – all those tweets proclaiming ephemeral (yet passionate) likes and dislikes; all those meals that live forever on Facebook, despite long since having been evacuated – what are all these, if not the multitude conforming resolutely to the dictum that they all have a novel in them? To be specific: an autobiographical novel prolapsing with the Hitlerian bombast of its own trivia.

I have more time for Rachel Cusk's elegant reinventions of her own life – not least because they avoid the devilish details that Knausgård delights in. I find Cusk's polyunsaturated persona, which she's smeared across three volumes now, more credible, precisely because I know that the 'I' in the books cannot be in any sense synonymous with the thinking 'I' that wrote them – there's too much patent invention in the texts, not least the long and elegant conversations that, were they real, would've been absolutely impossible to recall in tranquillity and verbatim. Cusk nevertheless obtains her fictional frisson by the assumption of real underpinning: our passage is eased into the fantasy of her life by our assumption of its underlying facticity. One way of looking at this is that we've become rather lazy when it comes to the heavy imaginative lifting required to read novels of the purest invention – there's this, and (at least among liberals), a preoccupation with the idea of supposed authenticity of voice, the psychological correlate to the moral duty of giving a good (and prideful) account of yourself.

Hence, in part, the rise of so-called narrative non-fiction: among which books are often ones attempting to tell the story of their author's life without recourse to invention. Olivia Laing's are a case in point: shards of herself speared into the contemporary world, so that she can register – through her own quivering – the perturbations of the zeitgeist. By embarking on particular modes of experience – the impact of loneliness, or a journey down a river – Laing avoids the totalising requirement of formal biography, to somehow present the whole of the person, and make it synonymous with the thinking, writing I. Laing is following in a long line of such writers, who've used their own psyche as exploratory tools with which to investigate the world, rather than engaging in literary navel-gazing: in my own narrow sub-genre, the memoir of addiction, Thomas De Quincey's *Confessions of an English Opium-Eater* did just this.

Of course, the exhortation to 'write about what you know' is as old as the tablets upon which Moses inscribed Yahweh's moral listicle, but nowadays this has become a flat-out injunction: *only* write about what you know – in particular, only adopt a fictional persona that conforms to your own salient characteristics, such as skin colour, or genital type. Nowadays, I might well be told to 'stay in my lane', rather than write from the perspective of, say, a first-wave feminist like my Audrey Death. The logical endpoint of this is that there will be no fiction but what the French term 'autofiction': texts that are novel-like – containing invented scenes, and for the most part third-person impersonal narrations – but which closely conform to the facts of the writer's life.

Autofiction is so big in France that they have an exponent such as Annie Ernaux who uses the genre to anatomise the experience of everywoman in the late 20th and early 21st centuries – or like Édouard Louis, who adapts it to rage against the late industrial machine that mangled his parents' lives. Perhaps it's the particular fondness for the so-called 'hermeneutic circle' you find in French intellectual life that makes autofiction quite so appealing – after all, if a text can only be understood in terms of itself, then it makes it an ideal vehicle for a culture that believes the only understanding is self-knowledge.

Which brings me back to my own miserable lucubration – I quoted Nietzsche at the outset, and, as some of the more ethically perspicacious of you will have realised, thereby precipitately raised the bar when it comes to claims of accurate self-examination. It doesn't matter if I hide behind philosophical drapes, thrusting a character called 'Will' on stage in my place, the reader will still be free to make as negative a judgement of me, the writing, living, 58-year-old, father-of-four-adult-children me, as they do of my jejune doppelganger, on the grounds that my stratagem simply hasn't worked. I wanted to write not a memoir, or an autobiography, or indeed a work of autofiction in which I somehow managed to resolve the contradictions of 'my' own past – let alone one in which I tidied that past up, and gift-wrapped it with a ribbon of fancy prose. No, I wanted to depict as accurately as I possibly could what it was like to be a 17-year-old middle-class boy, succumbing to heroin addiction in the North London suburbs, in the era of punk and Thatcher.

That was all I set out to do, and I discovered that when I not only created 'Will', but set him running – like some amphetamine-fuelled clockwork bunny – in real time, that he acquired a definite reality of his own. In being thus exteriorised – I could enquire into his interior mental states. As I say: there was actually quite a lot of written material I could've consulted – not only my own diaries and letters, but corroborative material from my long-deceased parents, both of them writers in their own right. For the most part I eschewed the documentary in favour of the emotive: inhabiting Will's persona, just as I have in the past those of my fictional protagonists, I propelled him into the unfunny slapstick of hard drug addiction, and registered his emotional and physical responses. So sharp and enduring were these feelings that I believe they gave me a massive factual shot in the arm: the first person to read the text when it was completed was my girlfriend throughout the period the memoir describes: 17–25. Far more lucid and less debauched than I, except for one or two corrections, she considered I had done full justice to the *actualité*, which includes a portrait of my younger self that is not so much warts and all, as all warts. Is this the pride that bases itself on moral laceration, and gratifies itself with creepy self-abasement? I don't think so – I certainly feel distanced from the Will of 'Will' – and believe that distance enabled a certain pitiless objectivity; with it I hope also comes some objectivity about the heroin pandemic that swept Britain in the late 1970s, and which I believe was one of the vectors that has carried a certain nihilism into the core of our collective being.

However, along with the pitilessness I also have considerable compassion for a young man who was clearly suffering from mental illness, and whose background was at best neglectful – at worst abusive. Oh, and I quite like Will's jokes – I hope you will, too.

13 December 2019
Guardian

Apocalypse Then

Henri Bergson anticipated our current predicament, writing in 1907: 'If it is a question of movement, all the intelligence retains is a series of positions: first one point reached, then another, then still another. But should something happen between these points, immediately the understanding intercalates new positions, and so on . . . indefinitely.' The ellipsis is my own – and, rather than indicating the absence of a word or words, it stands for just that act of intercalation, together with the fermata or rest, during which such notionally discrete 'moments' may proliferate.

I've been using the ellipsis, in this way, in my own writing now for a long time – I first encountered it in the novels of Louis-Ferdinand Céline, where, for that poet of political delirium, ellipses goad the reader on: evidence of there being too much to be said . . . and too little time to say it in – the motion of Céline's prose is thus impulsive: an onrushing flight from the horrors of the First World War . . . into all those subsequent and devolved horrors. Yet even for Céline the possibility exists to intercalate – time remains putatively divisible. It was Bergson's primary insight to understand that the Western Logos decks itself out in time as if it were a garment to be adjusted: not enough time? I'll just let this seam out a bit – or perhaps introduce a temporal pleat . . . For Bergson: 'Metaphysics dates from the day Zeno of Elea pointed out the inherent contradictions of movement and change, as our intellect represents them.'

Psychologically, we experience duration all the time – yet so wedded are we to naïve realism that we conceptualise temporality by analogy with spatiality: time is a container into which we put events. So it is that we travel half the way towards environmental apocalypse, and half the remaining half, and half the half which yet endures, and so on ad infinitum, conveniently never arriving at the complete failure of crops, the crash of the internet, the inundation of low-lying land, and the collapse of our mega-structures – our parametrically designed equivalents of Shelley's 'vast and trunkless legs of stone . . .' So, I wonder, having spent the best part of the last decade writing a trilogy of novels – ones mapping the overlays of technology, war and human psychopathology throughout the last century – whether my promiscuous dotting was evidence of my own furious heel-digging effort to resist the ineluctable character of time itself . . . ?

In 'Deep Adaptation: A Map for Navigating Climate Tragedy', a paper published on the internet in July of last year that has subsequently been widely disseminated, Professor Jem Bendell argues recent studies and real-time data indicate that so-called 'runaway climate change' is already underway. According to Bendell, feedback loops are now operating which intensify warming in a way non-correlative with anthropic CO_2 emissions; rendering both control of these emissions, and the so-called 'sustainability agenda' linked to this, wholly redundant. Instead, Bendell calls upon us to acknowledge 'that climate-induced societal collapse is now inevitable in the near term . . . and therefore to invite scholars to consider the implications.'

As to why it is that we have been unable to acknowledge this imminent collapse – Bendell's paper points to our – and Max Weber's – old friend, professional closure: it simply hasn't been in the interests of all those climate change scientists and sustainability advisors to acknowledge a truth far more inconvenient than the raw fact of global heating itself: namely, that even if there was some point in time (!) at which it *would* have been amenable to anthropic influence, that point has long gone. It would be a consummate and hubristic irony indeed, were it to transpire that humanity's demise had been paradoxically occasioned by the very experts we looked to for a way through this deadly impasse – but as I say, I doubt this is the case.

Rather, the particular affective orientations of the human being, severally and alone, are more than enough to account for our collective paralysis: highly sociable and necessarily political apes that we are, you don't need to be an evolutionary psychologist – or, indeed, reductionist of any stripe – in order to grasp that no rational calculus of our self-interest will ever be meaningfully commensurable with that of all humanity, then, now, and in the future. I say 'humanity', but as with any species-entity, I'm not sure this is a meaningful designator at all – and perhaps that's where yet more of the problem lies: to say what is necessarily good for this assumed group, we must further assume the very properties we wish it to have: a coherent character, efficacious autonomy of action (commonly understood as free will), and – most implausibly of all – some sort of destiny.

This latter, born of diallelus, is the most persistent delusion enshrined in human ideologies – contemporary ultra-liberalism being only the most egregious of them. That great minds, no less than small, are incapable of ridding themselves of this was evidenced by the late Stephen Hawking's response to a question asked following his final Reith Lecture in 2016. Tasked with commenting on 'humanity's future', the great theoretical physicist – whose life had been spent in search of that elusive 'theory of everything' (an epistemic snafu, if ever there was) – responded to the effect that, while current environmental problems represented a parlous pinch point, once we've passed through this, we'll be free to fulfil our destiny by colonising other solar systems.

Yes – he used the D-word, I kid you not: a D-word that is itself constitutive of another hugely operable D-word: denial. The fulcrum upon which Bendell's paper pivots represents a sort of argument-from-denial; although, to the philosophically minded it can also be figured as a leap from purely quantitative data to a whole range of theoretical predictions. Bendell's analysis of the academic literature of climate change, in all its multifariousness, trawled up only two mentions of possible societal collapse, and while professional closure may supply the manifest explanation, the latent one surely relates to our inability, individually and collectively, to cope with what might be termed 'creeping normalcy' – Bergson's duration, recast for the era of mass senescence. Yes, just as no one ever looks forward to senility, followed by death, and only takes each day as it comes – so everybody is nodding away on the great over-heated sun porch of our planet, unable any longer to apprehend the speed of change, as our cloudy minds continue to intercalate.

Why should this be? Bergson's theoretical agonist, Albert Einstein, ushered in an era in which relativistic space/time replaced spatialised temporality – or at least should have. It's said of this scientific revolution that its effects were felt less widely because of the incomprehensibility of the Einsteinian universe, as against the commonsensical aspect of the Newtonian one. To which I can only reply: Balls!* Freudianism, Modernism, Surrealism – and in a rather more concrete arena, psychogeography: all are responses to the relativism of space/time. In his *The Production of Space*, Henri Lefebvre writes, seemingly glossing Virginia Woolf's remarks on the arts: 'The fact is that around 1900 a certain space was

---

* The sort dangling from a Newton's cradle rather than a human scrotum.

shattered. It was the space of common sense, of knowledge (*savoir*), of social practice, of political power, a space thitherto enshrined in everyday discourse, just as in abstract thought, as the environment of and channel for communications; the space, too, of classical perspective and geometry, developed from the Renaissance onwards on the basis of the Greek tradition (Euclid, logic) and bodied forth in Western art and philosophy, as in the form of the city and the town . . .'

The cultural logic of postmodernism is itself a regression to pure relativism – but too late have we apprehended this; or, rather, those thinkers who have proposed alternative ways of being, now that there's a filthy great atomic bomb propped up – like some anamorphic skull – in the pictorial space of Western Humanism, have themselves got lost in the woods, where they've blundered into the darkest of thickets. As it happens, the British built environment, with its massively ageing housing stock, is an instantiation of this, the terminal moraine at the end of history: we need look no further than the Tudorbethan, as a style that takes its content from deep-seated notions of the uchronic, to appreciate what's going on. The English have, of course, always indulged in reveries of an imaginary era when everything was harmonious: people were happy in their work, whatever their estate, while social relations were serendipitously organic. These 'times that never were' include Pickwickian London and its epithetic poverty, quite as much as Merrie rural England; moreover, right and left partake of the same uchronic fantasy

– set down as much in Morris's *News from Nowhere* as Chesterton's *The Napoleon of Notting Hill.*

British cities' stratigraphy is notable for recursive layers of uchronic styling: Tudorbethan semis were succeeded by the botched Modernisms of the post-war house-building boom, which were followed, in turn, by their right-to-buy bowdlerisation. The auto-cannibalisation of our own urbanity, is, I'd venture, irreducible to any one schema of causality – economic, political, systemic – but rather, is constitutive of our collective being, as, terrified by what lies over the event horizon, we shit bricks incontinently in our own flowerbeds. Now, you can look up to the open decks of the high-rise blocks in my area, and see row after row of fake Georgian doors, each with its mingy fanlight, implanted in the glaucous hide of flammable cladding. Perhaps this is the best way of thinking about it – this is the epoché demanded of us: try and bracket the phenomena we see around us, and imagine that they're all about to end.

The capacity of bi-directional digital media (the assemblage of the internet and the web), to create a planar and atemporal culture – a permanent 'now' within which to indulge uchronic fantasising – is only the latest and most egregious of these, the vectors that, rather than carrying our culture forward, are parabolic waveforms collapsing on the beach of the present. By analogy with Bendell's argument: it's the absence of both tradition and willed futurity from the culture of omni-Now that tells us something's afoot. We can't call it decadence – that would be too . . . decadent: and only in the dark recesses of the web itself lurk true millenarianism and other apocalyptic thinking. Yet who can deny that – if we perform the epoché – we can see this is very much what you would expect a culture on the verge of complete collapse to look like.

Most days I cycle past Selfridges, the upmarket department store on London's Oxford Street. As the Mayor, Sadiq Khan, brutes about his new sustainability agenda, and egregious signs trumpet the city's Ultra Low Emission Zone, the limos lined up outside continue to belch out a mephitic mixture of lead particulates and greenhouse gases as they burn up the fuel – the extraction, refining and sale of which has afforded the limo drivers' clients the income necessary to keep them waiting while they spree-shop inside. I need say no more.

There is, I think, a further reason why we've been quite so unable to apprehend the scale and rapidity of the environmental crisis: Marx's celebrated dictum apropos the 1848 revolutions needs to be reversed – this current imbroglio is the tragic recapitulation of farcical disasters. Writing in the late 1950s, Marshal McLuhan dated the inception of what he termed the 'unified electrical field' to the late 1920s, when the assemblage of communications and transportation systems achieved a bi-directional network of seeming simultaneity. Guy Debord, writing in the 1980s, dated his own 'spectacle' to the same decade – while Baudrillard's simulacrum partakes of this lineage as well. I agree that humanity's collective ontology – inasmuch as the real is always an augmentation – began detaching from its material substrate at around this time, but it's only with the inception of the web and the internet that the virtual tail became truly capable of wagging the actual dog.

Just as we thought we had the measure of pseudo-events, and their capacity to effect real ones, so we also believed that no horrors could trump those of the twentieth century, which began with the hideous ironic reversals of the First World War, and culminated in the devastating combination punches of the Holocaust and Hiroshima. If, as the literary theorist Paul Fussell proposed, August 1914 was a sort of feint – the grand armies marching off to war, drums beating, flutes piping, followed by the sucker punch: the trenches, where the machine guns traversed this assembly line of death – then we must apply the same rubric to events since 1945.

The Holocaust, together with our background faith in species-destiny, gave birth to the cosmic solecism of human rights, while all of humanity, following 6 August 1945, was reborn into a terrifying double-bind: the very institutions we looked to as guarantors of these notional rights were themselves possessed of vast stockpiles of weapons capable of destroying each and every one of us. Some people like to speak of our current era as AA rather than AD – by which is meant 'after Arkhipov' rather than after the death of Jesus Christ, Arkhipov being the Soviet nuclear submarine commander who refused Khrushchev's pre-emptive strike standing order during the Cuban missile crisis, and thereby prevented nuclear Armageddon. The post-Arkhipov era has been characterised – for obvious reasons – by this sublimated, yet effective, mass delusion: that the destruction of our species can be averted by the decisive action of a single individual.

This is doubtless why many continue to believe that myriad individual choices – to not take that plane flight, or purchase those carbon credits, or refuse that plastic bag – will save the planet and us along with it. But as I think I've effectively argued above, anthropic climate change is not a heater than can be switched off. The unified electrical field softened us up for the impact of the internet and the web – just as the Holocaust and Hiroshima rendered us curiously complacent about our ability to act collectively to avert disaster. The entire world has become leery of being the boy who cried wolf: so unwilling to trumpet the bad news, lest we open ourselves to the mutual accusation of . . . scaremongering.

Yes, this is how the world ends: with nine billion-odd souls trying to avoid a social solecism . . .

Spring 2020
Real Review

The Technology of Journalism

At the superheated climax of *The Day the Earth Caught Fire* (1961), as the world sweats and waits to see if the apocalypse will be averted by the simultaneous detonation of a series of nuclear bombs that will, it's hoped, correct the tilt in the earth's axis caused by, um, the simultaneous detonation of a series of nuclear bombs, the chief subeditor of the *Daily Express* pins two possible front pages to the noticeboard in the composing room. One reads: 'World Saved', the other 'World Doomed'. As nice a rendition as can be imagined of the British press's perennial conviction that it makes the news rather than merely reporting it – yet what renders this science-fiction disaster movie more dated than it should be (given it treats of modish *rechauffage*) is surely this selfsame concentration on the material production of newspapers.

Shot in the *Daily Express*'s own purpose-built Streamline Moderne office block on Fleet Street, and featuring Arthur Christiansen as its editor – a position he had occupied in what we must, perforce, call 'the real world' – *The Day the*

Earth Caught Fire premiered at the Odeon Marble Arch two months after I was born, a mile and a half away in Charing Cross Hospital. The intersections between fiction and reality are heavily underscored in the film by use of footage showing every aspect of putting out a daily news-paper, from the morning conference, through research (a matter of clippings libraries and bracing boffins on the phone), to page plans, layouts, the actual making-up of the galleys by the compositors, their incorporation with photographs into reprographic film, and the final offset printing of the web of newsprint being run through the rollers and treadles of the press.

Needless to say, there are also plenty of sequences in which folded and bundled newspapers are deposited at the stands, there to be torn open and flogged to the teeming, broiling masses – such could only be accounted the great-est of realism in a society in which newspaper reading was a sort of endemic virus, causing such disparate symptoms such as sooty fingertips and fervid opinions. But there are, of course, no counterfactuals – and the world saved in *The Day the Earth Caught Fire* is the world in which print media was, if not exactly doomed, at any rate enter-ing a period of decline. Some twenty years later, in the early 1980s, when I first began hanging around newspaper offices, the basic processes remained the same. Describing for one of my sons the climacteric of British unionism in the late 1970s, I animadverted on how it was at once surpassing strange – and altogether fitting – that it was in the newspaper and coal-mining industries that the most flagrant abuses of the closed shop and flexible rostering were to be found. This isn't right-left, ding-dong argument at all, once you recognise that in this – as in so many of the great historical divisions – both sides were in the wrong.

The miners were digging up ancient trees that had been rendered carboniferous – while the members of the National Graphical Association were busy turning the Western Logos into great logs of newsprint. The awed voices in which journalists spoke of 'the stone' (which was in fact metal) reflected a working environment in which job demarcations were so rigid journalists were obliged to remain one side of the fundamentalist object, and the members of the compositors' chapel on the other; reflected this – and also the flickering of hot metal's last gleaming: Mene! Mene! Tekel Upharsin! in 62-point Helvetica Black Condensed ranged across three columns. Then, as now, I was only a bystander to all of this – a mere freelance, whose visits to Fleet Street offices were only to drop off cartoons or a few pars of copy. Nonetheless, I picked up some of the arcana of pre-computerised print production – and by 1988, when I began running a small contract publishing business in Southwark, I knew enough to mark copy and graphics up for the typesetters along the way in Tabard House.

If I descant on these matters it's not because of some nostalgia for the days of leading and nicking lead, but because I believe what made me an effective jobbing hack was, in part, engaging with these processes – and then seeing them transformed by the arrival of computerised page-making systems. For the little contract magazines I published, I sometimes did all the interviews and other research, wrote the copy, took the photographs – then, using the new Aldus PageMaker software on a Mac Classic computer, made up the pages; and in lieu of the old marked-up copy and graphics, took the discs back along the road to the setters, who were still generating the final film to print from. In a way, the truncation of the print process that came with the arrival of computer-aided designing anticipated the truncation of the journalistic process that's come with the computerised distribution of media. Just as all those men – and they were, almost universally, men – solely responsible for one or other aspect of print manufacture, were amalgamated into a single figure tapping a keyboard, so all those leg-men and leg-women, those fact-checkers and researchers, those snappers and subs, have been similarly corralled. Now, any hack worth their salt has another reason for echoing the Gerasene Demoniac and saying: 'My name is legion; for we are many.'

There are, of course, no technical solutions to creative problems – but journalism is as much a craft as an art, and as the years passed the technology of freelancing altered to reflect the shiny new screen-based reality. I had a little shorthand when I began interviewing people – but this was already only the reprographic braces to accompany the revolving belt of the cassette tape. The first time I covered an election in the early 1990s, I was still phoning my copy in at the end of the day, having scribbled it out on the campaign bus. The measured cadences required to enable the copytaker at the other end to do their job, retroacted, I believe, into its composition: you certainly gave what you were writing a great deal of thought when you knew you'd have to read it aloud more or less immediately.

But then came the moment – following, as I recall, a snappy exchange with William Hague, who was on the campaign trail with the newly acquired (and spellchecker averse) FFion – when I equivocated: should I compete with the other hacks in the sprint to the phones in the impromptu press centre set up in a primary school class-room, or should I run for the printers instead, generate a hard copy of my piece and fax this through to the subs' desk? Alternatively, did I have time to risk the novel pro-cedures involved in connecting my laptop, via a modem, to the phone, and sending my peerless prose down the line in the form of a series of electronic pulses? The adage has it that all genuinely revolutionary technologies are perceived by their first users as magical – but remembering this dank afternoon in rural Devon, I think not of some moment of mystical wonder, but the sort of fiddly manipulation of bones, hairballs and other fetish objects that constitutes more workaday witch-doctoring.

Following an unprecedented cyclone making its dev-astating way across Western Europe, Pete Stenning, the one-time star writer at the *Express* whose slide into alco-holism is the subplot of *The Day the Earth Caught Fire*, makes his way into the office along a devastated and soft-boiled Fleet Street. In the vestibule he encounters a sweaty printer who tells him that short-staffed, he and his colleagues had to work so late getting the first edition 'it'll cost them a packet in overtime'. Stenning is dismissive: 'You're getting paid, aren't you.' He heads upstairs, and in the newsroom his one remaining friend, the veteran reporter Bill Maguire, puts him to work collating facts and figures – while at another desk a sub blocks out a cross-heading by hand: 'IS THE WORLD'S CLIMATE CHANGING?' Piqued by this demotion to mere researcher, Stenning asks Maguire: 'Why don't I do five hundred steaming words about how mankind is so full of wind it's about to out-blow nature?' To which Maguire replies: 'Yeah, fine, but after you've done me those figures.' There we have it again: the wholesale transformation underway from steaming words printed by hot metal, to dry facts conveyed by computer coding. As I say: there are no counterfactuals – and while the world of newspapers may have been temporarily SAVED, mankind remains full of wind and about to out-blow nature.

24 July 2020
Times Literary Supplement

St George for the French

Six years ago I delivered a talk for BBC radio in which I labelled the writer, George Orwell, 'a talented mediocrity' – not, I hasten to add, because I really think either his work, or the life that produced it really is, or was, mediocre, but purely because of the misplaced reverence bestowed upon him by the English. The phrase 'talented mediocrity' I took from an observation made by another English writer – G. K. Chesterton – who himself revelled in the title 'the prince of paradox'. One of the paradoxes Chesterton identified in their national character is that 'the English love a talented mediocrity', by which he meant that while by no means immune to brilliance in all its forms, nevertheless, it's a certain image of themselves, collectively, that they want to find incarnated in their great men and women.

This image, while not in a strict sense being one of 'mediocrity', is unflashy, modest and possessed of sang-froid. Of necessity – being raging Philistines themselves – the English detest the showmanship of public intellectuals (the glamorous position occupied by philosophers and other serious thinkers in France is quite unthinkable here), while continuing to worship the so-called 'gentleman amateur'. Indeed, one such currently occupies the highest office of state – and gained that position off the back of a Brexit referendum which was fought, and won, partly on a pledge to 'get rid of the experts'. What Boris Johnson and George Orwell have in common, however, is not their prose style – Johnson's is woeful, Orwell's, at its best, can be masterful – but their status as Old Etonians.

Eton, the vastly expensive school that has provided Britain with its ruling class for centuries now, is at the epicentre of this cult of the amateur – and by extension, the talented mediocrity. And while Orwell's fans on the left may wish to claim him for socialist egalitarianism, the fact is that it's his air of patrician disengagement that really attracts them: the dog-whistling of a masterful authority deriving from class and class alone. It's this, and his determination to present himself as a laconic but straight-talking character, immune to the foppery and flippancy of the hated foreigner, that have resulted in Orwell being perceived by the English as quite other than he really was.

There's this – and there's also *Nineteen Eighty-Four* and *Animal Farm*, the two books he wrote towards the end of his life that caught the wave of the zeitgeist, and propelled Orwell into a kind of eternal association with the totalitarianisms of the twentieth century, their downfall, and their never-to-be-countenanced resurrection. I'm not going to write at length about either of these books; suffice to say that with the former, Orwell's career decisively intersected with politics in such a way as to make him one of those writers – other examples are Salman Rushdie and Alexander Solzhenitsyn – who can no longer be given purely literary consideration. The publication of *Animal Farm* was delayed because British publishers were anxious about being seen to undermine the alliance between the US and the USSR, and originally Orwell penned a preface that complained about the supine character of those publishers who required no government censorship, being perfectly prepared to do the job for them.

Animal Farm thus represented one of the first major cultural works produced by a socialist in the West who had grown profoundly disillusioned with the Soviet regime – Orwell followed it up in 1949 with *Nineteen Eighty-Four*, his adaptation (the word really isn't too strong, such are the similarities) of Yevgeny Zamyatin's extraordinarily prescient satire of the Bolshevik regime, *We* (1921). Together, the two books burnished Orwell's image as a prophetic figure – and it's partly in this guise that he remains revered to this day. The panoptic state that keeps its citizenry under constant surveillance, and which aims to control their very thoughts, came to be described – in English – as 'Orwellian'; and this adjective even displaced 'Kafkaesque' as a general marker of the bureaucratically ordained conformity of contemporary life.

Both *Animal Farm* and *Nineteen Eighty-Four* have their good points – the latter is particularly strong in its evocation of war-exhausted London in the 1940s, which was the material Orwell used to construct his grim vision of

Airstrip One, the province of Oceania in which his protagonist, Winston Smith, is doomed to live and die. While
Animal Farm has an uncanny quality: a children's story
that can only be fully understood by adults who retain
an inner child. But as I say: once they ascend to being a
political figure, a writer's prose can be seen to suffer: we all
experience terrible longueurs when what we're searching
for is to be told how to live and what to think. Orwell then
went and died relatively young – 'always a career move for
a writer', but for a political figure such as he'd become, it
was arguably disastrous – not least because his final act
before expiration was to send a list of cultural figures he
considered Soviet 'fellow travellers' to Britain's internal
secret service, MI5. It was this that forever defined him as
the politically Janus-faced 'St George': a personification
not of the writer's restless and relentless desire to create,
but the English's own desire to have it both ways.

So, let us celebrate this Pléiade edition of Orwell's works
by getting back behind this image, whether of a talented
mediocrity or a two-faced saint, and consider instead the
novels, stories and reportage that made him the writer he
was. Significantly, his first published article was in French,
and published in France. After leaving Eton, Orwell went
not to university, but entered the British Imperial Civil
Service as a policeman. Posted to Burma (Myanmar), he
experienced British colonial rule precisely at the point
at which its grip was weakening. Orwell's first novel,
Burmese Days, is a swingeing attack on the imperialists,
which opens out from experiences he detailed elsewhere

in essays such as 'A Hanging' and 'Shooting an Elephant', which exhibited the British 'civilising mission' in all its wrongheadedness and hypocrisy.

Orwell's first published book was two such long-form essays sandwiched together. *Down and Out in Paris and London* remains my personal favourite of his works. Following four minatory years in the east, Orwell returned to Europe, and fell into a destitute and bohemian existence in Paris. Perhaps the key to understanding Orwell – rather than the image the English have of him – is his class position: he described himself as hailing from 'the lower upper middle class'; a more slang expression for this, in English, is 'shabby genteel'. The Blairs ('Orwell' is the *nom de plume* he gave himself to disguise authorship of his first book, because its contents would have shamed his status-obsessed parents) had a sense of elevated position, but no money to back it up. Hence Eric's – Orwell's given name – sense of being deracinated and his antagonism towards his own origins. Many *déclassé* bourgeois English writers seek solace by sucking up to the aristocracy (one such was his friend, the critic and literary editor Cyril Connolly), but Orwell's entire momentum as a writer came from being downwardly mobile.

Down and Out is a masterful examination of life on the margins, with painfully memorable characters – the madly bigoted White Russian former cavalry officer, Boris, deserved a book of his own – and marvellous set pieces, such as the description of a *plongeur*'s daily work at the Babylonian 'Hotel X'. The English section of the book displays a pitiless eye for the downright shabbiness and – bizarre to say – bad taste involved in English poverty, as against its more colourful continental cousin. Throughout the 1930s, Orwell built on this foundation fictionally – writing three more novels that effectively satirised English class mores, while also limning the sepia situations within which such scenes – typified by dramatic irony – are played out. But *Keep the Aspidistra Flying*, *A Clergyman's Daughter* and *Coming up for Air* are only one side of the Orwellian equation.

Beginning with a commission from the left-wing publisher, Victor Gollancz, to research the Depression-era conditions of the working class in the north of England, Orwell ended up producing another long work of narrative non-fiction in two parts: first his examination of the lives of the poor in such places as the eponymous Wigan Pier, and a second section in which he analysed his own conversion – as a middle-class Englishman – to socialism, and examined the prejudices of his class towards such egalitarianism. *The Road to Wigan Pier* aroused much controversy – Orwell was, of course, viewed on the right as a 'class traitor' – but also sold many copies, and provoked much of the discussion and indignation its author might have hoped for from his earlier examination of poverty.

But anyway, by the time this book was a cause célèbre, Orwell was already gathering the material for his next: *Homage to Catalonia*. In this work, which deals with his disillusioning experiences fighting for the POUM anarcho-syndicalist militia in Catalonia and Aragon, from December

1936 to June of the following year, Orwell follows his normal dyadic rubric: initially full of hope and idealism, the infiltration and perversion of the popular front by Soviet communists and their fellow travellers coincided with the collapse of the Republican cause. If anything led Orwell directly to his obsession with the threat of Soviet totalitarianism it was this experience – which ended with him being shot through the neck and almost killed.

An experience which at least had the virtue of fore-grounding Orwell's own literary-political methodology: which was to interpolate his own body – as well as mind – into the events he wished to analyse. In this, he was a sort of gonzo journalist *avant la lettre*; and indeed, a great deal of his literary output consisted of the sort of jour-neyman writing – reviews, columns, latterly radio talks – that the English literary world classes as 'Grub Street' (after the novel *New Grub Street* by George Gissing, about the literary milieu of 1880s London). In England, Orwell is erroneously revered as the author of an essay 'Politics and the English Language', in which he lauds his own un-adorned and homespun style as the acme of English prose. Orwell's message: that the most complex ideas and sub-tlest velleities can be expressed in the simplest of language is clearly (!) nonsense – however, he himself *was* a writer who could do this a great deal more than most; and in this resided his peculiar genius.

A sufferer from lung infections from an early age – as well as a prodigious smoker – it's unclear when exactly Orwell contracted the tuberculosis that eventually killed him in 1950; however, the bullet wound he received fighting in Spain certainly exacerbated his condition. He lived the remainder of his life first in London, working for the BBC as a producer of talks, then retreating to the remote island of Jura in the Scottish Hebrides, where he wrote *Nineteen Eighty-Four*. I've visited the house, Barn Hill, where he wrote the novel – and have had the eerie experience of talking to the grandson of the man who rented it to him. He referred – quite casually – to 'Blair', as the writer was known to the family, as we sat drinking the predictable tea, in the even more predictably chilly and austere kitchen: a tiny distant part of Scotland that felt – by reason of this strange association with one of its most revered writers – to be . . . forever English.

October 2020
Les Inrockuptibles

Will Self-Driving Cars Take My Job?

For many of us who had reached our majority long before the inception of the bi-directional digital medium consisting of the internet and the worldwide web, exploring this new realm has always been problematic. Indeed, so enduringly so is it for me that I still find it difficult to write the term "surfing" without recourse to James Joyce's perverted commas. When I think of surfing, I remember floating in the surprisingly chilly waters off the coast of southeast Australia, loosely cradling the board with one arm while scanning the horizon for a wave that looked as if it would rise high and break cleanly. Being an inexperienced surfer in heavy seas, I made the wrong judgement and got badly dumped as the wave I picked to ride collapsed in on itself. Smashed headfirst onto the ocean floor, I was knocked unconscious for thirty seconds and nearly drowned. That was thirty-six years ago. I haven't surfed since.

So it may be a problem of homonymy leading to an irrational phobia as much as anything else. I do, of course, make use of the web – what contemporary working writer doesn't? But my searches are targeted: the aim being to get onto the site, extract the information and leave as quickly as possible. I feel permanent possibilities of sensation pullulating beneath the smooth and shiny screen – and fear following links, or initiating further searches, lest I be smashed headfirst onto the seabed of the collective consciousness, where I'll be rendered brain-dead by advertisements for novelty oven gloves, and wonky videos of men having sex with donkeys.

There is this generational revulsion from the web's polymorphous perversity – but also a more personal one. Obviously, I didn't reach the age of forty-three – in 2004, when, with the inception of wireless broadband, the true Age of the Web began – without any consciousness of the oddity of my given name. I studied philosophy at university, where both my fore- and surname were key terms in any number of texts – while the disjunction between what I was called, and what these terms meant gave me an intuitive understanding of Saussure's arbitrary signs ("What's in a rose?" and all that blank-verse jazz). Then, in treatment for drug addiction in my mid-twenties, I was introduced to a doubly apposite characterization of this malaise as "self-will run riot".

If someone tells you that they never Google themselves they're outright lying, and exhibiting that greater vanity which is the vanity of vanities identified by Ecclesiastes – who also, if I remember rightly (a specious expression nowadays when we all know the facts are at one's fingertips), said that of the making of many websites there is no end. Arguably, the entire phenomenon of social media is simply the creation of webs within webs, in which the searchers cannot but find themselves ensnared. Just as I was old enough to know the oddity of my name in 2004 – so I was also notorious enough not to want to be suddenly personally accessible to all and sundry. I already had difficulty dealing with the volume of correspondence I received – whether electronically or in letter form. I'd already had a lot more than the fifteen minutes of fame allotted by Andy Warhol – while also falling victim to a phenomenon Guy Debord dubbed "spectacular celebrity".

Debord – hymning with Warhol – foretold a future in which "a financier can be a singer, a lawyer a police spy, a baker can parade his literary tastes, an actor can be president, a chef can philosophize on cookery techniques as if they were landmarks in universal history". The great Situationist believed this was coming about because of "a parodic end to the division of labour", but he didn't quite anticipate the way the web would enact this bottom-up quite as much as top-down. I'd already offered the public quite enough of my cookery techniques and awful singing by the time Facebook came along, and I recoiled from taking selfies for obvious reasons. As for Twitter, I averred around the time of its inception that the only circumstances under which I'd "tweet" would be if a live songbird flew into my mouth. It's a commitment I've stuck to, while observing that some of my peers have not been so tight-lipped.

Perhaps they'd argue that the requirement, as journalists and novelists, to remain breasting the zeitgeist rather than floundering in its wake has rendered such scruples otiose. But from where I'm treading water, Marshall McLuhan's dictum holds good: and the message of the new media is, of course, that the only thing that matters is novelty and concision. 280 characters would be pushing it – and only 1 per cent actually hit this limit – but a single image (which, as any editor knows, speaks about five thousand characters) is better. This is why we reached "peak photo" in 2015, when it was estimated that more photographs were taken that year than in the entire previous history of photography. Nowadays you can confirm – via a few keystrokes, and Messrs Page and Brin's marvellous search engine – that yes, that image you have just snapped has already been snapped by a multitude; for there's nothing new to see under the sun, and the sands of time are trickling away between our senescent fingers.

As for long-form writers, the very idea that emotion confected in instantaneity – which is the raison d'être of Twitter – could somehow replace its recollection in tranquillity is prima facie absurd. (All this being noted, my experience of watching this, the second Century of Self develop [to follow the calendar initiated by Adam Curtis in his documentary film on the incestuous relationship between psychoanalysis and public relations] has been bizarre.) What's the point in gaining so very little of someone else's attention – but such a lot of their intemperance? And by the same token, what's the point in acquiring notoriety, but no regard?

If you're famous, on a good day it's as if you're the much-loved resident of a cosy village: you walk down the main street and people shout "Hello Will!" from their front gardens. But on a bad day, you go out into the world crackling with anxiety – after all, since you might well be known – in a certain prejudicial sense – to anyone you meet, there's also a good chance they've been talking among themselves, such that your intimacies have become common currency. It's this state of virtually enhanced paranoia that I've witnessed numerous young friends – and my own children – become victim to. Fame, yes – but without any of the ostensible benefits. Debord claimed for himself the status of the last non-spectacularly famous person, by virtue of his desire to destroy the entire shiny edifice of consumer capitalism – after him there would only be a deluge of celebrities: those merely tautologically well known.

Yes, Elvis has quit the cultural building – leaving behind only the warbling winners of *Britain's Got Talent* and *The Voice*. Under such circumstances, those of us who bartered our own talents for a mess of pixellated pottage probably have no right to feel aggrieved; instead, we should retire to the margins, or join Debord way off grid. I would've done that, really – if it were not for the surprising benison afforded me by an instance of sheer nominative contingency, rather than determinism. I refer, of course, to "Will Self-Driving Cars Take My Job?" Around eight or nine years ago, just as the twittering and image-splattering of the socially mediated began to be so egregious and so ubiquitous that I feared for my mental health, I realized that a simple web search for my name took the key-stroker not to some neglected and painful portion of my existence, but to any number of posts on this pressing matter.

That an autonomous computer-operated car would represent a major breakthrough in the quest for artificial intelligence is a given. As a driver for many years, who, for the past ten has eschewed owning a private car, or using one with any regularity, I was a little fazed by my sideways incorporation into the emergent neural network. On the rare occasions I did drive, I found myself when crossing bridges, pondering whether, if a group of children strayed into the roadway, I would sacrifice their lives or those of my notional passengers. As for taking people's jobs, when Rishi Sunak's furlough scheme comes to an end, and thousands lose theirs, I hardly want to be standing in the same line-up with AlphaGo, Deep Blue and millions of lesser computers jockeying for supremacy in the labour market.

I realize that Will Self answering the question "Will self-driving cars take my job?" has the bewildering quality of a *mise en abyme*, like the curious sensation one has, sitting in a restaurant booth with mirrors on either side, and watching one's infinite selves recede ad infinitum. After all, there is also the distinct possibility that self-driving cars, by reason of their close kinship with deep-learning programs capable of generating readable text, will take [ital] *my* [ital] job. Indeed, given this piece's fantastical facetiousness, and its trademark melange of the Mandarin and the demotic, you'd be perfectly entitled to suspect it's been written by a computer which has digested a lot of my old copy.

(But before I find myself singing "Daisy, Daisy, give me your answer do . . ." in a progressively deeper and more somnolent voice –)

I need to get a grip: the fact of the matter is that just as the financial crash of 2007–8 put the climate emergency on the back burner for several years, so I suspect the Coronavirus pandemic will do the same for AI research. Coming from very different philosophic positions, both James Lovelock and Ray Kurzweil, Google's chief scryer, have foretold a supersession of our cranially coddled wetware by hardware; but from where I'm sitting – still in considerable reclusion, due to an underlying health condition for which I have to take immuno-suppressant meds – it's less a case of the singularity being nigh than a sense of being singled out enduring. Because when I search for my name on the web nowadays, it's no longer a case of Will Self-Driving Cars Take My Job? But instead: When Will Self-Isolation End?

2 October 2020
Times Literary Supplement

Reading for Writers

It's torture to me – no, really: torture, and I'd sooner undergo considerable physical pain rather than have to endure this psychic one. To what do I refer? Why, reading contemporary fiction, of course. For this, the last of my essays on reading for *Lit Hub*, I'd like to discuss reading as a writer. I am a writer – and I do read; but whether or not you know my work, or feel it lends any weight to my opinions is probably less important than those opinions themselves. I want to say something like 'When it comes to their reading habits there are two kinds of writers . . .' because a nice binary opposition often stimulates us to . . . Well, to what? Surely only to confirm ourselves as being on the right side of the divide, and that's not very interesting at all – or even credible. No, when it comes to their reading habits there are probably as many different ones as there are individual writers – but that being noted, and following the above, I never cease to be amazed by those of my peers who spend a great deal of their leisure time reading works written by others of our peers. (Or at least:

so they claim – the ever-present pressures of commoditisation rear their hydra-heads here; for if you don't puff your
peers' works, you can't complain when yours remain . . .
uninflated.)

But the analogy which explains my own semi-recumbent
position would be this: doing the work required to get
readers to suspend disbelief – which is surely the very first
requirement of the fiction writer – is exhausting. One way
of thinking about it is that the writer has to divide themselves psychically into reader and writer while sustaining
a strange commerce between the two: writing as if you
didn't know who that reader was, and reading in the same
spirit. What's entailed then is a sort of vital alienation from
your own self – and it's out of this, I'd argue, that the necessary criticality emerges required to make the judgement
calls implicit in the production of quality prose.

Another way of conceptualising this diplopic state is
that it is itself a form of suspension of disbelief – you know
fine well reader and writer are the same individual: you.
But in common with Lewis Carroll's Red Queen you've
strengthened your fabulating muscles to the point where
you can believe as many as six impossible things before
breakfast – including that you have two separate beings
confined within your mind, both passionately engaged
with literature. But it's exhausting – this suspension, quite
as exhausting as suspending something physical in the air
above you. I always think of seals – not that you see them
performing in circuses anymore, but I have memories of the
poor creatures, corralled in the ring and fishily induced to

mount daises upon which they'd squat, balancing brightly coloured beach balls on their moist and pointy noses.

Well, just suppose you were a seal. (And hopefully your fabulating muscles are strong enough to keep your knowledge to the contrary aloft.) Surely the last thing you'd want to do after a hard day at the circus is watch another poor seal doing precisely the same thing. That's what it feels like to me when I read someone else's fiction after a session spent trying to craft my own: a deep sympathy born of the same muscles tensing in the same places induces a dull ache, interspersed with piercing pains when I see my fellow amphibians try something fancy. There's this, and there's also further suffering to be gained from adopting the reader's (or circus-goer's) view, but without the balm of any disbelief. What do I mean by this? Well, anyone who's ever stood in the wings of a theatre during a performance will know: the audience's deeply credulous faces can be seen turned to the footlights, as they sop up scenery you know is merely a painted flat, and emotions you can tell are being faked, since the performers' expressions become sicklied o'er so very suddenly as they exit.

It's as if we were pursued by bears, such is our desire to stay in the fantasy rather than collapse back into the reality of the situation, but the writer – I'd argue – is compelled to abide precisely in this divided state: at once effortfully suspending disbelief, and collapsing under its weight. Is it only contemporary fiction that induces this specular nightmare in me? Well, yes – and I certainly don't discount the possibility that my own ego may be bound up in it as well.

Because if reading my peers' works pains me – while that pain is compounded by two countervailing pressures – there are also two equally upsetting emotional reactions. On the one flipper, if the seal in question is making an appalling mess of it – dropping the ball, yelping hysterically while slipping saltily off the dais – I can't suspend any disbelief at all, and am simply suffused with pity: for them, for me, for the entire bob of literary artificers. But on the other, if they're balancing that ball brilliantly – spinning it, flipping it, catching it with artful aplomb – I'm visited with the most terrible sense of envy.

At least that's not as bad as the futility one can feel, as a contemporary writing reader, on returning to classics read before – or, worse still, tackling one of the acknowledged greats for the first time. With these works the very fact of their survival can make them seem top-heavy: a great encrustation of regard attaches to them, such that they might collapse on top of you, crushing you to death with their marmoreal prose. I can't help thinking that it's this – besides the obvious and understandable political objections – that's created much of the animus against the canon: a sort of febrile *ressentiment* aimed by writers who feel their own potential claims on posterity being eroded against the giants who have preceded them, and whose immortality is ensured. Because let's face it, even the best of today's works face an uphill struggle when it comes to attaining classic status. In sheer quantitative terms there are so very many books published nowadays, it stands to reason that the proportion of them that can reasonably be expected to be still being read a decade hence – let alone a century – must be proportionately smaller.

In this regard, I had a sobering episode a couple of years ago when my adult children and I had to clear out the old family home. When my late wife and I bought the house in the mid-1990s, as working journalists we bought several newspapers every day; as regular book reviewers we were sent – unsolicited – several publishers' bound proofs of new books every week; and then there were both volumes that had been inherited – the rump of parental and grand-parental collections – and those that were being bought. As a confirmed bibliophile (albeit a gourmand rather than a gourmet), once I began to do reasonably well as a writer I decided to allow myself this ongoing treat: if I wanted a book – any book – I would buy it.

For a long time I refused to discard anything – and by *anything* I do mean that copy of *The Ford Fiesta Workshop Manual* missing both covers and chewed by the puppy. My argument was – as per my previous essay for *Lit Hub* on what we should read – that our four children needed to grow up alongside the same sort of melange of literature that I had. We would exert no pressure on them to read, nor otherwise turn up the pedagogic thermostat – rather, they would absorb text by means of the sheer physical presence of it in their lives, for every way they turned they'd run up against a groaning shelf. Eventually, running out of wall space, my wife prevailed on me to at least get rid of actual duplicates of works – and from there it wasn't too much of a stretch, I thought, to begin deaccessioning in earnest; for by then the writing was no longer on the wall, but the screen – and it was perfectly clear that if the next generation were to become serious readers, propinquity was insufficient to stimulate them.

The criterion for keeping or rejecting any given thing was this: did it have lasting value? (In other words: had it already lasted – or did we confidently believe it would.) Or: did any of us have a reasonable expectation of reading it within the next five years? Sentiment was no good reason for making the cut – especially given that all those 1980s and even 90s paperbacks were already suffering from perished glue and its sequel: falling leaves. As I say: I thought we'd applied this rubric pretty exhaustively – but when we came to sort through the books again, there were scores – nay, hundreds – that didn't meet these criteria. Time, as many lit-critically minded people have observed over the years, is the best judge – and I was shocked how poorly, in particular, my contemporaries fared when it came to making this new selection. Did I want to read this sensitive novel about growing up in rural Wales again? Well, no – since I could scarcely recall having parsed it the first time. Those figurative trees, felled to make paper pulp, were chopped down once more as novel after novel got the axe. The only category of books that suffered even greater winnowing were the plethora of works concerned with the zeitgeist: clever analyses of this subculture or that trend, collections of cutting-edge journalism long since blunted by time – and memoirs of politicians who'd rusted away on the scrapheap of history.

If I recount this mournful deaccessioning at some length (a sort of bathetic counterpart to Walter Benjamin's celebrated essay, 'Unpacking My Library'), it's because it made me realise two things: firstly, that my idea of what it was to be *un homme ou une femme de lettres* had been weirdly bound up (if you'll forgive the pun) in the codex. I might pour scorn on the fusty, tweedy image of the literary type, immured by leather-bound volumes in their room of their own, but the truth was I did think there was some sort of osmotic relationship between possessing all those tomes, and writing more of them – almost as if an essence thereby extracted was suffusing my own word-stream. I believe modish academic critics call this 'inter-textuality'. And secondly, that just as the Roman emperors receiving triumphal accolades were accompanied by slaves tasked with whispering in their ears: 'Remember, Caesar, you are mortal . . .' so every writer, no matter how fixated they may be on that desideratum, posterity, must acknowledge their works' limited shelf-life as well their own mortality.

And not just this – but still more worryingly, their interchangeability with exactly those works by their peers that they've just boxed up and humped to the charity-run thrift shop. I have to say, while this state of mind has some timeless aspects, I nonetheless feel that it's a growth area of uneasiness. With so many more books and writers – while there seem to be appreciably fewer serious readers, surely there's going to be a lot less posterity to go round. I already note that my own generation of writers seem, as we enter our sixties, significantly less imposing than those even a half-generation above us. In part this has to be a function of ideological shifts that are by no means unwelcome: the need to make pedestals available to those formerly denied them – but it remains, as well, a reflection of a culture in which literature is no longer centre stage (or screen).

I don't need no Yaddo, bro – over the years and now decades, I've created numerous little writers' colonies of my own: isolated cottages rented or borrowed, hotel rooms and serviced apartments in distant cities in which I would immure myself to write in solitude. I used to travel frequently to Manchester in the north of England, where I found the atmosphere – not that I experienced it much – particularly congenial for this enterprise. One afternoon I took a break from typing to have a smoke on the balcony, and while I was out there I was joined on an adjoining one by a man about ten years younger than me. Recognising me as we mutually inhaled – he inflated my ego by saying: 'Do you know, I'm absolutely amazed to meet you in person, because I read a novel by you when I was a young man and it had a really profound effect on me.'

I'm English enough (I'm half-American) to have experienced some embarrassment during the ensuing minutes, as my disciple struggled to remember any of the following: the title of the novel, what it was about, and what precisely the epiphany it had engendered had been. I offered up a few suggestions – but they didn't help much either – so I delivered him from his misery: 'Really,' I said, 'it doesn't matter – the important thing is that you read and responded to literature, not that I wrote it.' I didn't mean it when I said it – but on reflection, I do believe this: what we're engaged in, as writers and readers, is the creation of a collective work: a great quilt to which we both add original patches, and alter those already sewn. If it hadn't have been my novel that had provoked this man's epiphany, it might well have been someone else's – quite possibly one of those I so expeditiously despatched to the thrift shop.

All of which is by way of saying: there are no 'guilty pleasures' when it comes to reading; even if it's your metier, read what the hell you like – everyone else is. And moreover, as I think the above makes clear: all of us tend to forget much of what we read anyway. Homer Simpson puts it with characteristic eloquence: 'Every time I learn something new it pushes old stuff out of my brain.' I would say, though, that for the writer of fictions, quality definitely has a quantity of its own: creative-writing teachers may try and instil in their students the rudiments of plotting, and try to convey the great gearing into it of character development, but for those who have read hundreds – nay, thousands – of novels, such formalist analysis has become entirely intuitive. I pretty much spent the entirety of my twenties lying in bed reading the novels of the Western canon (as it was then defined), and I don't regret this in the slightest.

Of course, it could be that when you began this essay you weren't looking for an established novelist's musings on his complicated relationship with his peers, and his anxieties concerning his influences – but rather, for a rule-of-thumb guide to how to read specifically for research.

I've answered part of that question: no amount of absorbing others' metaphors will teach you how to make your own. (Or indeed help you to avoid them, Kafka-style, altogether.) As to reading purely for research, beyond the bold generalities, easily obtained from the obvious reference works, in my experience the key to producing works that seem, while invented, to have the whiff of *actualité* about them, is to seek out an obscure first-person account of the situation or the events you wish to depict – and thoroughly plagiarise it. The poet W. H. Auden used to write in the margins of books 'GETS', which stood for Good Enough to Steal.

2 July 2021
Literary Hub